Wilson Wall

THE ORCHID HUNTERS

THE CROWOOD PRESS

First published in 2025 by
The Crowood Press Ltd
Ramsbury, Marlborough
Wiltshire SN8 2HR

enquiries@crowood.com
www.crowood.com

British Library Cataloguing-in-Publication Data
A catalogue record for this book is available from the British Library.

For product safety-related questions please contact: productsafety@crowood.com.

ISBN 978 0 7198 4563 5

Typeset by Simon and Sons
Cover design by Sergey Tsvetkov
Printed and bound in India by Parksons Graphics

CONTENTS

Introduction

In the UK we have just over 50 species of orchid that are regarded as native, out of a worldwide total of about 28,000. These have all appeared in recent geological times after the climate changed and the last glaciation of Great Britain was rapidly declining, about 12,000 years ago. All our native orchids are terrestrial and by tropical standards relatively small, although just as charming and immediately recognisable as orchids. The fascination with tropical orchids in Europe developed over a very long period as global trade increased through the years from the sixteenth century until now.

In many other cultures around the world there was a far longer cultural association with orchids than in Europe, largely due to the wild and showy species being native of those lands. For example, in Japan orchids were a symbol of both respect and admiration, and growing orchids was a defining part of being highly cultured. One of the native species of Japan, which has been grown for many hundreds of years, is *Dendrobium moniliforme*, called *sekkoku* in Japanese; this is a species with a range of hues from white to pink and with fragrant flowers. In China the range of native species was much greater than in Japan, as would be expected with such a vast landmass ranging in temperature from the hot and humid to the cold and dry. One of the most significant genera in Chinese orchid culture is *Cymbidium*, made up of approximately 470 species from South-East Asia and China. At the time that Aristotle was active in Greece, the Chinese poet Qu Yuan (*c.* 340–278BCE) is credited with starting Chinese orchid culture. It was, however, much earlier when Confucius (*c.* 551–479BCE) made the observation that the orchid produces its fragrance regardless of the paucity of admirers. While this is true, if we believe ourselves to be the only audience, it does not take into account the need of the orchid to attract pollinators, which has been one of the great forces driving the evolution of these strange and exotic flowers.

In the West, orchid culture was slow to develop, as there are no wild epiphytic orchids with showy flowers, so developing interest was entirely dependent upon travellers and collectors who brought home orchids from far distant places as beautiful curiosities. It was at the end of the seventeenth century that the first record of orchids in cultivation in Europe appeared. These were two different species from the New World, but were regarded as significant enough to appear as illustrations in book form. The writer and, as far as we know, illustrator of the book was Paul Hermann, who travelled widely in Africa, India and Sri Lanka (Ceylon in his day). He was a collector himself and Director of Hortus Botanicus at the University of Leiden, where his influence gained him access to many private collections of newly imported plants. His work, *Paradisus Batavas*, was written in Latin and published posthumously in 1698.

From this small start European interest in tropical orchids grew, but it was not until 1732 that we have a record of a plant being grown in Britain; this specimen was *Bletia purpurea* from the Bahamas. This is not to indicate that no other orchid plants had been grown or imported before, it is simply that these are the only ones we know of with certainty. It is quite likely that over the years there had been sailors who had brought back exotic flowers from around the world and some of them could quite possibly have survived the journey home. What is also quite likely is that these plants would have been killed as soon as winter temperatures started to fall, if they had not succumbed to inappropriate planting before then. While epiphytes are now well known, in the early years of exploration it was something of a novelty to find such staggering flowers growing attached to trees and rocks. So when they arrived on our shores, the soils would have been too heavy and the atmosphere too dry and cold. We know that conditions were not perfect for these plants, as it is recorded that in 1768 the Chelsea Physic Garden had several orchid species that survived for a short while. This included species with which we are now very familiar, such as *Epidendrum* and *Vanilla*, the only orchid to produce a commercial product. In 1778, Dr John Fothergill (1712–80) introduced two terrestrial orchids into his own collection, one of which was *Cymbidium ensifolium* from China. His success in this was at least in part by utilising the new technology of glasshouses. Fothergill himself was a physician and created a considerable collection of plants at what is now West Ham Park, which is in east London. It is of note that, although Fothergill was instrumental in introducing the orchids to the UK, it was not he who collected them, but was one of the growing groups of traders and explorers who worked either directly or indirectly for wealthy collectors like Fothergill.

It was in 1787 that Kew Gardens had their first success in getting imported orchids to flower with two American species of *Encyclia*. This was of particular significance as the following year HMS *Bounty* started a trip to Tahiti with two staff from Kew, where they collected 1,000 breadfruit plants, as well as other sundry species, among which were several orchids. Unfortunately, this was the ill-fated trip where the crew mutinied against Captain Bligh in 1789. Regardless of this disruption, Kew Gardens became a significant supplier of plants to collectors and botanical gardens, orchids included, throughout the eighteenth and nineteenth centuries.

Joseph Banks sent seeds to Kew while travelling with Captain Cook and, in 1772, the first plant collector for Kew, Francis Masson, travelled to South Africa. Sponsored collectors became a regular feature of exploratory expeditions and orchids a very lucrative part of the cargo home. With an increasingly formal record of plants being received and grown at Kew Gardens we know that in 1789 there were fifteen species of orchids imported and grown at Kew, and by 1830 over 70 species were in cultivation.

For all of the collections and casual importations that arrived in Britain during this period, we can say with some certainty that the interest in tropical orchids started its exponential rise with the accidental arrival of *Cattleya labiata*. This was accidental for many reasons. The first reason was that it arrived in the UK, not as a plant, but as packaging around other plants. The second reason was that it was spotted as interesting foliage when it did arrive, and the third reason was that it flowered after it had been cultivated. This particular orchid was indeed a surprise and caused quite a sensation upon flowering. It was named by Lindley, a famous botanist of the time, in honour of William Cattley, the grower. The collector, William Swainson, was largely forgotten, but this was not unusual. Many fabulous orchids were discovered and sent home by collectors who became footnotes, rather than central players, in the story of orchid cultivation. This was the frequent lot of collectors and was as much as a result of the way they worked as anything else.

When it became obvious that collecting plants overseas, and the further away the better, was of great financial potential, it also became apparent that leaving the collecting of plants to amateurs and casual collectors could not guarantee a supply sufficient for demand. Indeed, some plants might be missed, or ignored, as in the case of *Cattleya*. To this there was an obvious solution. Large growers and dealers in exotic plants were making sufficient profit to directly fund collectors in the field. Such collectors may have worked for several nurseries, each one with their own specialism, so while collecting in a general way any plants that piqued their interest, these would be sorted into groups that would appeal to specific growers of that sort of plant back in the UK. Swainson was this type of collector. He would collect to order, or collect material that he thought would make a return, and send his entire bounty home to be disposed of for the best price.

Swainson collected widely and had such a diverse knowledge of the needs of his plants and the processes used to preserve specimens that in 1822 he wrote *The Naturalists Guide for Collecting and Preserving Subjects of Natural History and Botany*. We can infer that his collecting was of a relatively straightforward botanical type, since in the whole of the 60+ pages of his book, only three pages dealt with the collecting and transport of plants. The rest dealt with preserving such diverse animal remains as shells and bird skins. On the subject of sending plants to the UK, he suggested that transporting live plants should be a last resort and that sending seeds home would be a much better idea.

It was this perception of collectors being professional that had what we would regard in the 21st century as a prejudiced outcome. The nineteenth century was a quite different time in many ways: Britain held sway over the largest empire the world has ever known and it was proudly controlled by a small elite of civil servants. Well into the nineteenth century it was regarded as normal for the monarch to influence foreign policy, and in 1860 the Foreign Office still only had 60 permanent staff and would routinely approach *The Times* for intelligence reports.

This situation was reflected in many other aspects of Victorian life. For example, it was this century in which we find the origin of Gentlemen versus Players as a game of cricket. Gentlemen were amateurs who could only claim expenses, while Players were professional players paid by their county cricket board. Into this highly structured social hierarchy emerged the professional collector, paid for by gentlemen; therefore, the collector was just doing a job and consequently, by dubious logical extension, not materially part of the scientific endeavour of exploration and description. This was a direct reflection of the class system that engendered a sense of entitlement in those who were better off. The line of reasoning was that gentlemen do it for themselves, as they did not need the money; therefore, they were somehow better than those who had to do it for the money.

A change in this attitude towards field collectors started with another major change in the social climate – the rise of the professional scientist. Until the nineteenth century, science was carried out by the wealthy and self-funded, or by individuals, such as the microscope pioneer Antonie van Leeuwenhoek (1632–1723), who was a successful Dutch draper with his own business. Science was a leisure pursuit for those with both money and leisure. It was not so much that people did not want to be scientists, but that there was no formal method by which they could make it a profession; there was simply no method of formally applying for a post of scientist. We can understand how this was seen as normal with a quotation from *Memoirs of the Life of Sir Humphry Davy*, published in 1836. This was written by his brother, and uses the notebooks of Sir Humphry quite extensively.

> Amongst the middle and higher classes, there was little taste for literature, and still less for science, and there [*sic*] pursuits were rarely of a dignified or intellectual kind.

This was quite likely the prevailing thought of the middle classes at the time; after all, life for the previous thousands of years had predominantly been agrarian, and any knowledge of a scientific nature that could not be directly applied to life was deemed of little value. The change to an industrial base changed attitudes, as the builders of steam engines and railways had to have an understanding of what they were doing beyond a simple mechanical interpretation of the machinery they were making. So by the time professional scientists appeared, so too, had interest developed in plants and animals to be found beyond the garden gate. What remained, however, for a long time was the traditional gap between collectors and scientific interpreters of plants sent from overseas.

It is hardly surprising that the first orchids would arrive in the UK, collected by excited travellers and explorers, and sent home with little or no supporting information. It would be later that these same casual collectors would start to record their findings and the sites from which orchids were taken. More than this, the people sending them home would have contacts with horticulturalists, whether at Kew Gardens, the Chelsea Physic Garden or botanical gardens arising in port cities such as Bristol and Liverpool. Some would also be acquainted with the larger horticultural companies, of which there were an increasing number, that were specialising in plants from overseas, either for growing outside in gardens, or inside in orangeries and conservatories.

These early collectors would rarely confine themselves to such a specialist group as orchids. These were curious individuals let loose in a world full of wonders. There were many who would spend time shooting livestock and despatching dried skins of everything from reptiles and mammals to birds, along with plants, to stock the museums, as well as the botanical gardens of Britain. Although the nineteenth century was the time that science and engineering were becoming the great wealth-generators at home, it was still a time when overseas administration was carried out by the well-educated but ignorant. This may sound like a contradiction in terms but it was a commonplace finding that a classical education ill-befitted a job as a colonial administrator, which simultaneously was the education many administrators had received. In this sense a classical education would be largely Latin, Greek and history. One of the other groups that were widely distributed throughout the world was the military; again, the officers were often well-educated and with time on their hands. Under such circumstances, curiosity and a natural propensity to collect the rare and unusual resulted in a lot of orchids being collected and sent home, in this case not by professional collectors, but by civil servants and army officers. A good example of this is Colonel Robson, who introduced several species to the UK in the nineteenth century.

Many professional plant and animal collectors, whether they specialised in orchid hunting or were general collectors for a commercial market, left little by way of information about themselves. Others were larger than life and wrote memoirs and travellers' tales for a public that was hungry for adventure, but unable to travel to these far-off exotic locations themselves. In the 21st century this thirst for travel and adventure is sated by natural history, travel and holiday programmes on television. In the not so distant past this was not so and, even further back, books of travel writing were commonplace and very popular. Robert Louis Stevenson published *Travels with a Donkey in the Cevennes* in 1879 when he was in his twenties and this established him as a writer. Similarly, though ten years earlier, Mark Twain had written *The Innocents Abroad*, which has remained a very popular piece of travel writing, and during his lifetime it was said to be his bestselling work.

With this legacy of written travel stories, it is hardly surprising that some of those intrepid collectors, who had spent years in the field, would also tell of their trials and tribulations, successes and failures while collecting plants for the genteel markets of Western Europe and the USA. Frank Kingdon Ward described his travels in India and Myanmar, or Burma as it was called then, in *Plant Hunting on The Edge of The World*. Ernest Wilson published his book *Plant Hunting* in two volumes, the first later being given a more enigmatic title for his stories of plant hunting in Africa and Australasia with *Smoke That Thunders*, the local name for the Victoria Falls in Zambia.

As time went on and the thirst for new plants grew, new ways were looked at to try to keep the plants alive in transit; for example, structures such as Wardian cases, which had originally been used for the growth and transport of ferns. These small conservatories superseded previous techniques of plant transport, which were often no more sophisticated than packing plants into barrels. Originally devised in the 1830s, these were used to ship plants around the world with great success and, although they are best known for moving rubber plants to Sri Lanka and tea plants to India, they were also significant in transporting orchids to new homes in Great Britain. Although many orchid plants did not survive in the enclosed space, enough did to make it a worthwhile method of transport. Other techniques involved hanging plants in baskets or sending dormant tubers that would, hopefully, sprout when they arrived at their destination.

It cannot be over-emphasised just what a problem it was to transport tropical plants from their homes to northern climes on the other side of the world. It is now taken for granted that we can send cut flowers in refrigerated containers by air and live plants in any way we consider suitable. In the eighteenth and nineteenth centuries such facilities were just not available. So anything sent in the first half of the nineteenth century in vessels under sail from, say, India might take four to six months for the voyage. When the Suez Canal was opened in 1869, steam vessels, either pure steam or auxiliary steam, could save 23 or more days on the journey; better still the journey could be scheduled, as the ships were no longer travelling at the whim of the weather. There was also a problem that as the vessels were at sea for such a long period, and temperature control was non-existent, plants that would start to sprout could be badly damaged by days of continuous low temperatures. The importation of orchids via this new service of reliable shipping through the Suez Canal was touched on in the Chairman's Address to the Orchid Conference of 1885. It was here that the Chairman, Sir Trevor Lawrence MP, explained that it was now unwise to be carried away at auction so that an orchid is purchased for £10 or £50, as a collector may send over a ship-load the next day, so that the plants 'would be worth only as many shillings tomorrow'. We have further information regarding orchid prices in the nineteenth century from James O'Brien (1842–1930). He worked as a gardener and orchid hybridiser, becoming a member of the RHS Orchid Committee. He wrote that at the time of the Orchid Conference of 1885, many showy orchids were available at convenient prices, though beauty and rarity would inevitably command higher values. He compared this with sale-room records of Stevens' Auctioneers in Covent Garden from 1845 and 1846. In 1845, *Aerides maculosum* made £20 and *Dendrobium formosum* 15gn. Against this, in 1846 Stevens sold *Coelia machrostachya* from £10 to £12 10s, *Barkeria spectabilis* from £5 to £17 and *Epidendrum stamforidianum* at 5gn. In all, 168 lots at this sale realised £600. There were great fortunes to be made by the importation of orchids, on a par with importing fine silk or spices. In comparison, at this time a labourer would earn approximately four shillings a week. Before decimalization of the UK currency in 1971, a pound was made up of twenty shillings, each shilling being twelve pence. As this was an illogical system it was necessary to define a price in three columns, for example, £5 12s 6p was five pounds, twelve shillings and sixpence. As a rounding-up exercise, pounds were sometimes turned into guineas, each of which was 21 shillings.

As times have moved on, so has interest in orchids. After World War I there was definitely a drop in interest. Maintaining glasshouses was expensive, prohibitively so in some cases, and so large collections declined outside publicly owned botanic gardens. The fortunes of the orchid collectors revived around the middle of the twentieth century, so that now the worldwide trade in orchids is estimated to be about $10 billion or more. Some countries, such as Thailand and Singapore, gain a huge export revenue from the export of orchids to collectors of plants, but also, with the advent of fast, chilled transport, cut flowers.

In this arena of scientific endeavour and commercial pressure, collectors explored and discovered new orchids all around the world. Many of these collectors and explorers remain generally unknown, while others have plants named in their favour and books still in print regaling us with their travels. Here we will hope to show you why orchids were so prized and what motivated these intrepid individuals to risk life and limb in pursuit of horticultural rarities. There will be information about the biology and propagation of orchids scattered throughout, but this is only to help in understanding the story of the outstanding people who brought these extraordinary flowers to our notice.

> The legends of orchidology will be gathered one day, perhaps; and if the editor be competent, his volume should be almost as interesting to the public as to the cognoscenti.
>
> *About Orchids*, Frederick Boyle

To you the reader, I hope this is as interesting for you to read as it was for me to write.

Chapter 1

THE TROUBLE WITH ORCHIDS: WHY THEY ARE RARE AND HOW THEY GROW

There is something exotic in the appearance of orchid flowers, neither radially symmetrical like a daisy nor short-lived like a bilaterally symmetrical day lily, they are long-lasting and strangely symmetrical right to left. It is this bilateral symmetry that, although not a unique feature of orchids, certainly helps us to identify them. In more botanical terms, orchids have fused stamens and carpels and, generally, 'upside down' flowers. These flowers, described as resurpinate, form one way up and then rotate on their stem before opening. Sometimes, if the stem is ribbed, the twist can be seen when the flower is open, but for many orchids that have plain stems this is not so obvious. The different styles of growth of orchids can also puzzle. In the northern hemisphere, outside the tropics, orchids are like most garden plants growing in the soil; there are no true epiphytes to be found clinging to trees, nor lithophytes attached to rocky outcrops. Once in the tropics, however, the number of epiphytic and lithophytic orchid species climbs dramatically. These are plants that grow in difficult conditions and are consequently dependent upon a reliable rainfall and good humidity to survive.

Growth is slow and life is long for orchid plants and they also come in a huge range of shapes, sizes, colours and scents. In fact, there are about 28,000 species in 850 genera altogether, not to mention the many tens of thousands of varieties that have been bred over the years. All the orchids are found in the botanical family Orchidaceae, which is divided into six subfamilies. From there the divisions get smaller and smaller, progressing all the way to genus, species and variety. Notwithstanding this massive and complicated taxonomic system within which orchids live, they all share basic biological requirements: to get their seeds germinated and plants growing.

Right from the very beginning of domestic cultivation of orchids, two things were well known. The first was that orchid seed is the smallest of all plant seeds, being more like dust than anything else. Being so small it is extremely difficult to handle and it would seem to be almost inconceivable that a seed, the overall length of which may be less than a millimetre, could possibly be the generator of the magnificent flowering plants that were coming into Europe. Until the advent of magnifying lenses, the seed was often thought of as dust and the plants sterile. The second fact that was recognised was that orchid seeds were incredibly difficult to germinate, so much so that in the eighteenth and nineteenth centuries words like 'impossible' were frequently to be found juxtaposed with descriptions of orchids. Of course, simple observation tells us that it is not impossible, if it were they would have become extinct long ago. What wasn't expected was just how bizarre the life cycle turned out to be when it was finally discovered and described.

Orchid seed is so small that the energy contained within the seed is only enough to maintain the slow metabolism of a dormant life just ticking over, it is certainly not enough to promote germination. This is the big difference between most seeds and orchid seeds. If you consider an acorn or the seed of a grape, these are massive when compared with orchid seed, but most of the size difference is due to the amount of stored food available for germination. This is why these comparatively large seeds can germinate in the dark and send out roots and shoots: they have lots of stored energy, which is specifically for this purpose. Orchid seeds have none of this, but they still need to germinate, so where does the energy come from? Well, unknown until 1899, orchid seeds have to make an association with a fungus just to start growing. This is generally referred to as a symbiotic relationship, that is, both parties gaining from the association, but it is not always apparent what the fungus gains from the link. By the end of the twentieth century, it was quite well known that many plants, from all sorts of taxonomic groups, make symbiotic associations with various species of fungi. A hundred years earlier such things were completely unknown – it was assumed that a plant gained everything it required from soil and air, no interactions with other species being necessary.

This idea of plants in isolation from each other changed with an article published by Noël Bernard in 1899 describing orchid seed germination. The original article was written in French, but can now be read in English, translated by Selosse, Minasiewicz and Boullard in 2017. Noël Bernard lived from 1874 to 1911 and although born and educated in Paris, he died in north-west France at Saint-Benoit. The cause of death was tuberculosis at the age of 36. When he was 33 he married Marie Martin a mathematics teacher and a year later they were expecting a child who had a very colourful entry into French life. The pregnant Marie was out cycling and had a fall that resulted in the premature birth of their son.

Bernard made sure that the baby Francis survived by keeping him in an incubator and feeding him on a strange mixture of his own devising. Noël Bernard was regarded as clever, even as a child, so it was no surprise when he graduated with a bachelor's degree in a range of science subjects and was able to back his own decision regarding his premature child. The newly lettered Bernard took teaching jobs simply as a means of making money to help pay off his mother's debts. Even at this early stage in his career, by his own declaration he was a political anarchist. While we may regard anarchism as dangerous in modern times, it had a long philosophical, as well as political, history in the nineteenth century, so finding free-thinkers aligning themselves with these ideas was not unusual.

Bernard was looking at the bird's nest orchid (*Neottia nidus-avis*), a species that is unusual for many reasons, not least of all because this is a plant that has no chlorophyll, so it is entirely dependent throughout its life upon its symbiotic fungus to provide it with nutrients for growth. It is not from the tropics, but a northern terrestrial species that, even when in full bloom, is only ever a sort of shade of dirty yellowish-brown. He describes his initial experimental attempts to germinate seed, in the same way as any other seed, as failing to produce any plants. He then goes on to explain the way in which his fortuitous discovery of a fungal association was made. In 1899 Bernard started a year's military service and found himself stationed south of Paris at Melun. He had already been working on orchid seed germination when he was called up, so it is no surprise that when not directly involved in military activities he would be out in Fontainebleau Forest, which was close by. On one of these occasions while he was out, he had come across a bird's nest orchid, which had set seed but had been unable to shed the seed before being submerged under leaf litter. As he says, this probably happened the previous autumn, as by spring the seeds, which were still visibly in their seed pods, had started to germinate in large numbers. Examining the seedlings as they developed, he came to the conclusion that it was necessary for the mycorrhizal growths from a fungus to be present before germination could take place. Earlier observers of germination had often remarked on the presence of fungal hyphae, but had never made the link with the germination process itself. It seemed rather improbable that two independent species should be required for germination of plant seed. Ecology was a poorly understood area of science, so complete dependence of one species upon another was not often considered a very likely situation, except in the case of parasites. The logical comparison with lichens, in which the complete plant is a composite between fungi and algae, would have seemed reasonable, but although initially described as such in 1868, it remained broadly controversial for many years. Again, it was the assumption that all species are independent and autonomous that hindered the belief in lichens as dual organisms, just as it did with the idea of fungal symbionts being essential for orchid germination. Such was Bernard's conviction that this was the reason that orchid seeds germinate and why treating them like any other seeds would result in failure, that he immediately published his ideas and observations, even managing to persuade his commanding officer to let him have leave to present his results in person at the Académie des Sciences in Paris. Bernard continued his studies after he left the military and concluded that, although the fungus can live independently without the orchid, the orchid needs the fungus as an essential component for germination and, in some species, throughout its life. This was a far cry from previous ideas of orchid culture and seed germination, which had been haphazard at best.

Throughout the nineteenth century, when the desire for new and unique tropical orchids had developed, large sums of money were changing hands for wild plants imported into the country. So it was almost a natural progression for commercial growers to try to germinate seed to maximise the commercial success of their plants. This was going to be a broadly fruitless exercise that resulted in many ideas about these plants, which would eventually turn out to be wrong. In the eighteenth century it was considered possible that orchids did not reproduce by seed at all. This idea was probably reinforced by the dust-like nature of the seed making it very difficult to assess with the naked eye. Until magnifying glasses became widespread and capable of resolving details without chromatic or spherical aberrations, it was not possible to see the internal details of orchid seed, which would have been the only way to recognise that the seeds were genuinely that. Doubts as to the general fecundity of orchids to produce seeds was put to rest in 1804 when a larger than life character, Richard Anthony Salisbury (1761–1829), came on the scene.

Salisbury had been christened as Richard Anthony Markham, but apparently changed his name when he went to medical school in Edinburgh. This change was not done on a whim; it was a calculated commercial ploy. He changed his name in favour of a distant relative, only related by marriage, who said that on the basis of the name change, she would finance his life at medical school. As was common at the time among the well-heeled and independently wealthy, Salisbury left Edinburgh without graduating. While he was there he became friends with James Smith, who in years to come would found the Linnean Society in London. There is no doubt that Salisbury, as he was by then, was an exceptional botanist, but he was also a rather contentious character with a dubious reputation in legal and financial matters. An example of this looseness with the financial truth was that when he married, he was claiming to have, or at least have access to, a large fortune, but he was in fact in debt. It was this debt that resulted in the end of the marriage and him declaring himself bankrupt. Nonetheless, he was a very good botanist and in 1804 Salisbury was present at the first meeting of the Horticultural Society, which was later to become the

Royal Horticultural Society. In 1809 Salisbury became the first secretary of the newly formed Horticultural Society, but unfortunately when he relinquished the position his successor found a chaotic set of accounts that took some time to sort out.

During this period, at the beginning of the nineteenth century, Salisbury seemed determined to annoy as many people as possible. Included in the list of individuals that Salisbury managed to irritate was Robert Brown, a botanist now best known for his discovery of Brownian motion while he was studying pollen suspended in liquid by microscopy. Salisbury managed to do this by writing an anonymous article that criticised the expedition to the Congo in which Brown had been involved. As the anonymity was thinly veiled, it was quickly realised who had written it and this led to much ill feeling in the scientific community, especially amongst botanists. The result of this fracas of his own making was that Salisbury was scientifically shunned. Later on, in 1810, Salisbury was accused of plagiarism, which resulted in him being almost completely ostracised by the scientists of the day. It was long before the events that had caused his career to spiral out of control, that he made his most important contributions to botany; he was, after all, an extremely good botanist. One of these contributions involved laying to rest the idea that orchid seeds could not be germinated, long before Bernard's work showed how they germinated in the wild. It was at a meeting of the newly formed Linnean Society in 1802 that Salisbury reported germinating seeds of green winged orchids. This was reported in the Transactions of the Society two years later, in 1804. It is interesting that this is a northern terrestrial species, rather than an exotic tropical species, which would have been of more instantaneous interest to horticulturalists. The process seemed to have been one involving a lot of luck, but it worked and started the ball rolling for commercial growers to ponder the possibilities of growing new varieties from artificially pollinated flowers.

This knowledge that seed germination was a real event, observable if unpredictable, did not solve any of the problems associated with raising orchids from seed; that would take another hundred years to resolve with the work of Bernard. In the meantime the only way that seeds from tropical orchids could be germinated was by sowing them in close proximity to the adult plant. With hindsight we can say that this is because the symbiotic fungus is present in or on whatever the growing substrate is that the adult plant is in. Since at that time the fungus association remained unknown, it was even suggested that the presence of the adult plants in some way processed the soil to make it suitable for seed germination. Charles Darwin himself was perplexed by the question of why, if seed can be germinated, the plants are so rare. He recognised in his 1862 work on orchid pollination, *The Various Contrivances by which Orchids are Fertilised by Insects*, that with the enormous amount of seed that is produced by each plant through years of growth and flowering, we should find orchids everywhere and growing shoulder to shoulder. Just to put this into context, while we might consider many plants as producing a lot of seed, some orchids will produce upwards of 200,000 seeds every year for a century or more.

With the long gap between the work of Salisbury demonstrating that seeds could be germinated, and the work of Bernard demonstrating that seeds need a symbiotic association with a fungus to germinate, there was an intervening century. During this period, although cultivating from seed remained both unreliable and skilled, the world of orchid cultivation had not stood still. Commercial growers were trying their best to produce hybrids by any means possible. This was put quite clearly by Benjamin Williams in 1862 in *The Orchid Grower's Manual* where he said, 'Some time ago a gentleman said to me he should like to be in a country where the orchids grew in a wild state, in order that he might have a chance of hybridising them'. This reflected the observation among growers and collectors in the field, that different plants of the same species could be highly variable. While Williams does not suggest that raising plants from seeds would be a viable commercial proposition, he does say that orchids will produce large amounts of seed and admits that they are not easy to grow, needing a lot of care as they are not like other plants and can take up to twelve months before they germinate. As he goes on to say, they can be germinated either in the same compost or, if they are epiphytes, on the blocks of wood on which the parent plants are growing.

Even though there were some formidable difficulties in creating orchid hybrids, not least of which was the immense patience required to see a plant from seed to flower, some nineteenth-century growers were well known for their ability in this area. They developed skills in hand pollination and, even if the outcome was unpredictable, these horticulturalists would know which two plants were the parents of the seed. One of these highly skilled plantsmen was John Dominy (1816–91). In *The Orchid Grower's Manual*, Benjamin Williams mentions the skill and variety of orchids in several genera that Dominy had produced. This was in many ways a magnanimous compliment based on a mutual pleasure in the subject and acknowledgement of skill by one commercial grower for another. Dominy was not himself a collector but a skilled grower. He was born in the West Country, where early in life he decided on a gardening career. His apprenticeship was completed as a private gardener before joining a small commercial nursery in the West Country, where he stayed for only a few months. Immediately after this, at the age of eighteen, he joined the company of Messrs Veitch at their establishment in Exeter. He worked there until 1841, when he once again went to work in a private garden, this time the garden of J.P. Magor in Redruth, Cornwall. This was obviously a happy period, as he stayed for almost five years before being lured back to the Veitch Company in Exeter. Although based in Devon, the Veitch nursery was developing all the time, both commercially and in reputation, so in 1853 Veitch bought a nursery on the Kings Road, London and Dominy went to work there. It was only failing health in 1880 that compelled Dominy to stop working and retire. Dominy had originally been shown the complexity of the orchid flower and how it could be pollinated by hand by John Harris, a surgeon living in Exeter. This simple introduction to orchids led Dominy to become the first person to artificially hybridise two different species of orchid. The two parent plants were both of the tropical genus *Calanthe*, the seed producer being *C. masuca* and the pollen donor being *C. furcata*. The original hybrid flowered in 1856 after two years of growth and was instantly hailed as a great success by gardeners and horticulturalists. The botanists of the day, however, were not so enamoured and John Lindley, an academic botanist of great renown, was said to have opined that, 'You will drive the botanists mad'. This attitude amongst the academic community was reflected in the use of the term 'mules' for these hybrids and can still be seen today among some botanists. When John Dominy retired, the Council of the Royal Horticultural Society presented him with the Gold Flora Medal, part of the citation of which read '... for his successful labours as a raiser of hybrid orchids...'.

A significant development in orchid science and cultivation, though not at this stage in growing them from seed, took place five years after John Dominy had retired. In 1885, the first RHS orchid show was staged. Strictly speaking it was titled an orchid conference, but there were so many plants to be seen by visitors to the conference that it was a *de facto* show. The report of the conference was published a year later in the *Journal of the Royal Horticultural Society* of 1886. In his opening speech, Sir Trevor Lawrence even remarked that the conference was mainly about the cultivation of orchids, reflecting the intense interest in trying to develop techniques that were reliable and repeatable, rather than the hit-and-miss techniques of seed germination that was still being practised. It is also interesting that he commented on the paucity of funds limiting the development of orchid collections at Kew. This was a time when botanical gardens would gain some of the most interesting plants for their collections from private collectors who would leave them plants or whole collections in their will. It would certainly be true to say that some of the greatest collections were private rather than in public botanical gardens. Some of these large private collections were in places that would not have been expected. One such was the reputedly greatest collection of the genus *Odontoglossum*, which was at Trentham Hall in Staffordshire, the seat of the Duke of Sutherland. So although Sir Trevor may have lamented the lack of public collections, he was able to confirm that of the 5,000 species of orchid known at the time, 2,000 were being cultivated. Notwithstanding the developing techniques of hybridisation and routine cloning by creating divisions, most plants were still imported. Even the commoner species had sufficient commercial value to make it worthwhile to import them. In the same address to the RHS Orchid Conference, Sir Trevor also suggested that, while in the past collections had been amassed by private individuals of wealth who had sent out collectors to foreign parts on their behalf, this had changed and collectors were now financed by commercial companies.

The tone of the 1885 conference proceedings is particularly interesting as, while the overall conference was concerned with cultivation, it was the frustration that came through in the published proceedings. This was the frustration of failed seed germination and lost plants. Success was rare but when it was evident, it was lauded, which in itself indicates just how unusual such success was. This situation was going to continue through to the end of the century and the work of Bernard. What was changing for the horticultural community was the survival and flowering of plants that were imported – brought to the UK either by chance or as a deliberate commercial transaction. One of the major steps forward was systematically looking at how the survival of plants in transit from the tropics by sea could be improved. This was of considerable commercial value and the grower who could increase the survival rate of plants brought from overseas could make a great deal of money. As times changed, so too did Sir Trevor's – by 1899 he was the Chair at the Royal Horticultural Society conference on hybridisation. Although this is sometimes considered to be the first conference on genetics, it would be better to describe it as a conference on plant inheritance. The distinction is because, although Gregor Mendel had published his results on plant hybridisation many years before, they would not find a wider audience until it was translated in 1901.

In 1822, William Swainson had written a book, *The Naturalists Guide for Collecting and Preserving Subjects of Natural History and Botany.* This was a book that was the very essence of the nineteenth-century practice by colonial civil servants and administrators of sending plants and animals home from the colonies. Generally speaking, Swainson's book involved a lot of detail about preserving skins and shells, with a very short section on getting plants home while still alive. Having little to say on such a subject can only reflect Swainson's own interests, as by the time it was published, importation of exotic plants from overseas was already becoming a commercial business. The whole question of getting plants home from the far-flung corners of empire was simply created by the time it took for sailing vessels to make the journey.

As Swainson suggested, transporting plants should only be undertaken as a last resort, if seeds or roots could not be found. In the case of orchids, seeds were disregarded and rootstock alone would be of little use for most species. This left the only option of sending home entire plants. In previous years this would have been attempted, sometimes quite successfully, with plants in flower or, at the very least, having been seen in flower. Swainson was more interested in large-scale importation and so his solution was to suggest that holes should be made in the barrels or boxes that contain them. These boxes of plants should be placed in the middle of the sailing vessel in a way that enabled them to be covered in times of rough seas. Most of the small section of *The Naturalists Guide for Collecting and Preserving Subjects of Natural History and Botany* on sending plants home revolved around the drying and preparation of herbarium specimens, which could easily be transported just like any other dry goods.

It was some years later when an observation led to an invention that innovated the transport of delicate live plants around the world. This innovation was the Wardian case, an invention that had a considerable longevity in plant transport. Kew Gardens was still using them in a modified form until about 1962 to move delicate and actively growing plants around the world. The Wardian case was the invention of the eponymous Nathaniel Bagshaw Ward (1791–1868). Ward was a doctor in practice with a long interest in botany, which he developed over the years and resulted in him having a very large collection of herbarium specimens. With many nineteenth-century scientists, their interest and curiosity ranged quite widely, and it was this that led to the development of the Wardian case. Ward had put the pupae of a sphinx moth into a closed glass jar. Having described it as a sphinx moth we know it was some species of hawk moth, although he never states which species it was, even after it had emerged. While the moth pupae were in the bottle Ward noticed that a grass seed had started to sprout and a fern emerged, the latter presumably from a long dormant spore. After the moth had been removed Ward kept the container and allowed the plant's growth to continue. This gave him the idea for what was to become the Wardian case: a more or less sealed atmosphere for the benefit of the enclosed plants.

It was his contention that the industrial atmosphere of nineteenth-century England had a detrimental influence on plant growth, which, with hindsight, we can say with certainty was correct. He was quite well known as a keen student of cryptograms, that is, mosses and ferns, two groups that are particularly sensitive to industrial pollution. He was sufficiently well known in this field of study that in 1836 a new genus of moss was named in his honour as *Wardia*. It was his observations regarding pollution that motivated him to write a short piece in the form of a letter to Joseph Hooker, which contained the sentence, 'The depressing influence of the air of large towns upon vegetation had, for many years, engaged my attention'. Ward set about remedying this with the construction of a small, fully glazed case. These cases look in every detail like small conservatories and, although not hermetically sealed, they do restrict the flow of air and moisture. While the original intent was to exclude the polluted air from plants in culture, Ward quickly realised the value of his invention for the transport of plants on board ship and worked his invention into the subject of a book that he published in 1842.

Until his invention became available Ward claimed that plants would be overwatered or dehydrated on board the ships bringing them to Great Britain from far distant outposts of Empire. It was certainly true that survival of many plants not only improved by being transported in Wardian cases, but some species survived that would have perished on long journeys by sea. It became possible, for example, for ferns to be sent back from New Zealand to the nursery of Loddiges, one of the pre-eminent nurseries of the eighteenth and nineteenth centuries. This was a journey that would routinely take up to eight months. Ward claimed that for journeys across the oceans of between eight and nine months, a survival rate of 95% for transported orchids was possible and should be expected, with no care required other than to keep them in the light. This was not an idle guess on Ward's part as to what survival rate could be expected, as he had made some practical experiments on this very subject, although not with orchids.

In June 1833 he filled two of his cases with ferns and 'grapes', by which we assume he means vines. These were sent to Sydney in Australia and not only survived, but when planted they thrived. To check this was not just a chance piece of good luck, the Wardian cases were refilled in February 1834 and returned to the UK. The journey home was via Rio de Janeiro and took eight months. No water was given to the plants during the voyage and survival, once again, was almost complete. For this journey the case was effectively sealed, although as Ward himself acknowledged, Wardian cases were not hermetically closed and some movement of air in and out was not only inevitable, but desirable for the long-term survival of the contents.

Williams had a section in *The Orchid Grower's Manual* of 1862 where he wrote in some detail of the methods that should be used with what he describes simply as 'cases'. He also notes that the cases should be made with good stout glass that is not easily broken, with strong iron wire over the top to protect it. The other practical observation he made was that the cases should not be too near hot surfaces or fires in the vessel, as this will dry out the plants. Williams was certainly an advocate of the transport of orchids using Wardian cases, but these were really only suitable for small-scale importation of very special plants; for bulk imports, such cases were not able to contain all the plants in healthy conditions.

Even though the Wardian case was a great step forward in the survival of imported individual orchid plants, commercial tropical species were still generally imported as bundled plants with a poor rate of survival. Continued importation of plants was at least in part driven by seed germination being so unpredictable. Although germinating orchid seed was the only way that varieties and interspecific or intergeneric plants could be raised, it remained a hit-or-miss activity, so large-scale production of orchids for sale revolved around imported plants and creating divisions from already established plants that would most likely have been imported themselves. With all these commercial pressures, and the limiting possibilities of expansion amongst orchid growers reliant on division of existing plants, the search for a reliable method of growing orchids from seed was actively being investigated. The work of Noël Bernard in 1899 had demonstrated the complexity of the problem, but it was not clear exactly how to go about paring it down so that the information could be used in any sort of practical way by nurserymen.

It is here that the story of the orchid hunters diverges away from the usual concept of the intrepid explorer and into a different aspect of orchid hunting – looking for methods of artificial propagation of seed. This is an interesting aspect of the biology of these extraordinary plants and is worth describing for that reason alone. Even though this tale moves more towards science and the laboratory, rather than horticulture, there are characters and explorations, but perhaps on a smaller scale than across continents.

It is often said that growing tropical orchids from seed started with a reference to it made by David Moore (1808–79) in *The Gardeners' Chronicle* of 1849. As he reports, there had been no records of hybrids having been produced at this time, but the potential for doing so was considerable. This is a statement that shows a deep understanding of the potential of orchids to cross-fertilise, while at the same time recognising that germinating hybrid seeds, in fact any orchid seeds, was going to be a major hurdle. So while recognising the possibilities of orchid breeding, Moore also comments on the paucity of seed from tropical plants. Unknown to him, this was probably a reflection of the frequent need for specialised insect pollinators of tropical orchids, which would not normally be transported with the orchids from their tropical homes to domestic glasshouses. It was a suggestion made by Moore that sowing seeds on the roots and compost of already growing plants would prove successful, with germination being visible after about nine or ten days. Moore was born in Dundee, where he started as an apprentice gardener before moving to Dublin in 1828. After a varied career in different botanical gardens in Ireland he became Director of the Botanical Gardens at Glasnevin, Dublin, where he stayed in this post until his death. During his lifetime he was married three times, his first two wives dying through infectious disease, probably typhus. He was father to several children, one of whom, Frederick, he had with his third wife and he went on to become a very well-known orchid expert in his own right. In his later years, David Moore became polarised in his opinion of evolution, claiming that he could prove his concept of what we would now call intelligent design in the structure of plants. He also developed a difficult relationship with his superiors, specifically Professor McNab, who he believed was after his job.

For the next hundred years, Moore's ideas on methods of germinating seed would remain more or less the only way that seed could successfully be raised into plants. Although rarely in print, this idea of local germination had been voiced throughout the nineteenth century, often as a trick of the trade. What this method did not do was to make germinating orchid seed reliable and repeatable. The hit-and-miss nature of the process of sowing seeds on and around roots of parent plants, makes it all the more remarkable that so many varieties were being produced. We can only assume that this reflects the large amount of seed being produced by each flower after artificial pollination. The idea that artificial pollination was important as a method of producing seed in tropical orchids was widespread, but it also helped in the understanding of how it happens in the wild. Orchids don't have loose pollen like most plants; they have it in capsules called pollina. When a pollinating insect enters the orchid flower, the pollina are attached in a very specific position on the insect. When the pollina-carrying insect then visits another flower, the pollen is in exactly the right position to be deposited for pollination.

The first record of hand pollination of an orchid was around 1800. This was of the lesser butterfly orchid, at the time this was called *Habenaria bifolia*, but is now *Platanthera bifolia*. Being a northern temperate species, it was not regarded as a very exciting development at the time, what was more significant for the commercial growers was when the first tropical orchid was hand pollinated, which was *Vanilla*. As far as we can tell this was first successfully carried out in 1852, by Charles François Antoine Morren (1807–58). Morren was a medical practitioner with an impressive record of work and publications in the field of medicine, but in history he is best known for the simple hand-pollination of an orchid. It is true that *Vanilla planifolia* is the only commercially grown plantation orchid that produces a crop, other than flowers of course, and is, therefore, of considerable value to producing countries such as Madagascar. With vanilla producing such a valuable product, the French authorities at the time were keen to start a vanilla industry on their island of Réunion in the Indian Ocean. The reason for the excitement surrounding hand pollination of *Vanilla* plants is that it is a native species of Mexico down to the northern part of South America, so transplanting it to the Indian Ocean without its natural pollinators meant yields were very low until hand pollination became available. There were rival claims for the artificial pollination of vanilla, most notably by Joseph Neumann, but his claim is no longer accepted, as Neumann has become known for having claimed precedence for several other botanical advances after others had published their findings. Neumann also claimed to have hand pollinated the orchid *Calanthe*, which produced seeds from which he raised seedlings that flowered the following year, an impossibly short growing time. From early in the nineteenth century, various people claimed success in germinating orchid seeds, usually on the parents' compost, but increasingly with hit-and-miss recipes for enhancing success.

These announcements, either at meetings or in print, were so frequent that it was almost routine, except that the reason that successes were so often announced was that they were rare events, the norm being a very low germination rate and very high failure rate. One grower stated that of an entire seed pod of several thousand seeds, only one germinated. The problem was the lack of biological understanding of what the plants required, with the growers all using the same techniques that had been developed at the beginning of the nineteenth century. These had a very poor success rate when they were first used and this was a situation that had not significantly changed. The basic techniques relied to a greater or lesser extent upon the skill of the horticulturalist, learnt over many years regarding the best place to put the seeds, how the surface of the compost should be prepared and how often watering the seeds should be done.

It was during the twentieth century that both artificial pollination and *in vitro* germination came into their own, which started the industry of cut orchid flowers and production of named varieties available in garden centres all over the country. The first exponent of trying true symbiotic culture was Edmund Nikola Burgeff (1833–1976). He became Director of the Botanic Institute at Wurzburg in Germany and stayed there until his retirement in 1952. Although as a botanist his work had ranged quite widely, he did spend a considerable time looking at the germination of seeds from terrestrial orchids. Part of this work was putting the whole question of symbiosis and the relationship between orchid and fungus on a sound scientific basis. As part of this he developed methods for the isolation and culture of symbiotic fungi. These were very successful techniques and encouraged him to develop new ideas about the relationship between the orchid and its symbiont. Taking the next step, he created a whole new taxonomy for the fungi associated with orchids in symbiotic relationships.

The fungal taxonomy that Burgeff tried unsuccessfully to introduce was based on putting the symbiotic fungi into a separate fungal group that he called Orcheomyces. This turns out to be quite confusing taxonomically, as fungal symbionts are found in a wide range of different fungal groups, with many coming from the fungal family Basidiomyces. This system resulted in many symbiotic fungi being more closely related to symbiotic species from other families than to their naturally associated non-symbionts, hence the confusion. He then went on to develop a functional but unwieldy system where the symbiotic fungus was named *Mycelium radicis* followed by the name of the orchid from which it was isolated. This system, which never became widely used, was going to fail over time anyway, as further research clarified the relationships between fungus and orchid. The additional investigations undermined the two primary assumptions that Burgeff made. The first one was that any species of orchid only had one symbiont. The second was that the symbiont was unique to that species of orchid. While both of these are usually incorrect, the work surrounding symbiosis that Burgeff carried out was invaluable in our understanding of the way that orchids live and grow. It was Burgeff who introduced the Director of Singapore Botanic Gardens to the use of what was to become a pivotal orchid medium that had been created by Lewis Knudson and resulted in the first artificial hybrid in Singapore being raised in the 1920s. This was named *Spathoglottis* 'Primrose'.

While symbiotic germination techniques are useful, at the start of the twentieth century there was the sense that this somehow lacked the control of the living world that was expected of science. This attitude came about because during the nineteenth century, physics and chemistry had come of age; they seemed capable at the time of explaining everything and every phenomenon of the physical world. On the other hand, the late-comer to the science party, biology, was still very much in the throes of a descriptive science. It was this descriptive process that Darwin had used at great length in *On the Origin of Species*. It gave a functional explanation of observations, which did not explain why or how they came about. The reason for this, of course, was that genetics was in its very infancy with no notion of exactly how traits were passed down the generations. The change came with the work of Gregor Mendel, but this was some way ahead of its time and hidden from general view by being published in a very obscure journal. Originally in German and published in the journal of the Brünn Natural History Society in 1866, it was only after it had been translated by Bateson in 1901 that it reached a wider audience. Such was the nascent science of biology that terms such as 'genetics' were unknown until Bateson coined the word to describe the subject. So with scientific advances on all fronts, not just biology, it seemed reasonable to expect that it should be possible to create a completely defined growth medium for orchid seeds.

Noël Bernard tried to germinate orchid seeds asymbiotically from *Bletilla hyacinthina*, a terrestrial species native to South-East Asia with purple/lilac flowers. What Bernard used for his growth medium was based upon the ground-up tubers of orchids. This product is sometimes called salep, which traditionally is the ground-up tubers of species such as the early purple orchid, *Orchis mascula*. This failed to stimulate germination, but was a reasonable way to get started and led him towards the idea of incorporating more sugars into the medium. Unfortunately, before he could continue with this line of reasoning he died. Burgeff also tried asymbiotic seed germination using a defined medium, but his first attempts were also unproductive. He blamed this failure upon his glassware making the media alkaline. This is very unlikely as material tends not to leach out of glass in significant quantities, and when it does leach out, it is in very small amounts. It is more likely that the propagation medium was incorrect. From personal experience I can say that starting from scratch, it takes a lot of working out to try to produce a complete growth medium for orchids. This is for three main reasons: the first is that you have to produce a growth medium that can be sterilised; second, it has to provide everything that the seeds will need to germinate; and third, the seeds have no intrinsic food material to start them off. The breakthrough came when a plant physiologist from Cornell University, Lewis Knudson, approached the problem.

Lewis Knudson (1884–1958) first graduated in agricultural sciences from the University of Missouri, after which he went to Cornell University where he stayed for his entire career. He worked systematically on the problem of germination, originally with seeds from different species of *Cattleya.* These were sometimes from crosses between different species and later seed from two different genera, *Cattleya* crossed with *Laellia.* These are crosses that would not normally occur in the wild and so we can be sure that they had been created artificially. Knudson devised a recipe that was the starting point for asymbiotic cultivation of orchids. As Knudson pointed out, even with the correct symbiotic fungus, the germination rate of orchid seed is quite low, so a reliable and completely defined germination medium would be a massive step forward from the nineteenth-century technique of sowing seed in the vicinity of growing plants or on compost from around such plants. This was a practice of trying to germinate orchid seeds that by the time of Knudson already had a long history, but was as soundly based on understanding as alchemy.

There is no doubt that part of the mystique of tropical orchids stems from their steadfast reluctance to be pollinated and then produce seed that can be easily planted to raise more plants. Even when orchids were being imported in large quantities, there were still those of a scientific turn of mind, as well as those with more directly commercial requirements, who wanted to get to the bottom of what it was that influenced the germination of orchid seeds. Even after the conundrum had been solved, it was still commercially important that plants were imported. This had considerable repercussions for the wild populations of some species, as their distribution is often very limited. At the same time it would be necessary to hand pollinate these orchids to produce seed as the natural pollinators were often unknown for many years after discovery of the orchid.

The other side to this is that we have a conundrum that is worth considering. It is now possible to propagate all orchids from seed, so why are there still collectors of wild plants? This is not a straightforward question to answer because there are several different solutions, each one depending on the nuances within the question. Primarily orchid hunters are looking for the rare and exotic, while the more botanically than fanatically motivated are also carrying on the long tradition of searching out new species. Sometimes a locally common species may have such a small and compromised range of habitat that exploration seems the only way of finding possible new sites previously overlooked. This latter reason also has an interesting flip side to it. Instead of searching for new orchid sites, the explorer just wants time and space to roam, and should anything of interest come into their sphere of view, then it will be noted and carried as a certificate of justification. All of these things are credible, but what until recently has proved to be a lasting motivation was authenticity. A beautiful tropical orchid from far different shores carries with it a sense of authenticity. It was not reared in a sterile glass flask on a laboratory shelf, this orchid fought for its own survival and became the pinnacle of success. So when this plant is taken from the wild, it has with it the romance of wild places that the collector may never see, but the orchid hunter has.

Chapter 2

THE FIRST RECORDS OF TROPICAL ORCHIDS IN CULTIVATION AND CASUAL INTRODUCTIONS BY TRAVELLERS

The first European reference to orchids comes with the recognition of plants as being more than just part of the scenery. This may sound rather odd, but consider this, for most of the time until the last three centuries, all botanical knowledge was in the form of herbals under the control of apothecaries. For the rest of the population, plants, if they were noticed at all, came under one of three headings: poisonous, inedible and edible. In agrarian cultures that were dominated by the seasons, plants that were not edible raised little interest as life was marginal and most time was spent on the important activities associated with food production. Once the economy of these areas changed and there was time for leisure, and consequently non-survival-based education, it was natural that attention would be drawn to the world beyond the simple utility requirements of life.

It was into this arena, in about 372BCE, that Theophrastus was born, living an active life until his death in about 287BCE. He was born on the Greek island of Lesbos and was a prolific writer. In 323BCE when Aristotle fled from Athens, it was Theophrastus who took over the Peripatetic school of philosophy at the Lyceum. Of all his writings, most are lost, but two, which were botanical, we still have and it is quite possible that these survived because they were about plants and were seen as relevant by succeeding generations. These two are *Historia Plantarum* [Enquiry into Plants] and *De Causis Plantarum* [On the Causes of Plants]. In these works he was writing about Mediterranean species, and certainly not tropical ones. He did have a clear idea about what made an orchid and regarded the orchids as a unified group, so much so that he reputedly coined the word 'orchid' to describe this particular botanical collection of plants. Theophrastus was studying orchids from the Mediterranean, rather than tropical species, of course, and for several hundred years after his time there seems to have been few references to them. This changed when Pedanius Discorides (*c.* 40–90BCE) produced his work on medicinal plants *De Materia Medica*. This left a legacy that an education system of low-intellectual rigour but slavish adherence to classical works would not question; so it was that *De Materia Medica* remained unchallenged for 1,600 years.

Part of the mystique of orchids for early collectors and horticulturalists was the size of the seed. The vanishingly small seeds of orchids, which individually look little more than dust, were historically disregarded as being seeds at all. More than that, as orchid seed is so small it was not considered that orchids produced seed, so the obvious follow-on thought was that orchids did not reproduce via seeds. Since among those who considered such things this was assumed to be true, an alternative method of reproduction had to be found. Although the exact origin of the suggestion seems lost, Hieronymus Bock (1489–1554), known as Tragus, promulgated the idea that as these were mysterious plants, what better explanation could there be than that they sprang from material falling from mating animals? Perhaps a little strangely this myth was apparently confirmed in 1665 by a Jesuit by the name of Athanasius Kircher. While this myth of reproduction might seem odd, the idea of orchids not producing seed is quite understandable. With most species from the Mediterranean northwards having seeds that would be less than 1mm long, and most of that being air trapped in a fine net-like structure, the testa, any obvious comparison with wheat seed or olive stone would be impossible. The tropical orchid *Anoectochilus imitans*, from New Caledonia, is said to have seeds that are only 0.05mm long. It is here that we have to put this into an historical context of what can be seen with the naked eye.

It was only in the late sixteenth century that lenses became useable as magnifying glasses, and it was about this time when Antonie van Leeuwenhoek was producing lenses for his single-lens microscopes. These were capable of magnifying 200 times, but required considerable skill to use. In 1665 Robert Hooke published *Micrographia*, which quite literally revolutionised the way in which the microscopic world, until then invisible, was perceived. So we can see that it was only after the invention of the microscope that it would have been possible to recognise the detail that exists in the structure of an orchid seed. Even so, it would be some considerable time before the truth of orchid seeds as real, live and progenitors of orchids would be recognised. So while Kircher was giving his support for weird reproduction without any evidence, there were glimmers of acceptance that seed was produced by orchids and that it performed just like any other seed. The prime suggestion of this came almost as an aside in the work of Conrad Gessner (1516–65), like the work of Theophrastus this was also called *Historia Plantarum*, where he casually mentions orchid seeds in the text accompanying his illustrations. This particular volume was written between 1555 and 1556 but not published until 1750. Time passed after the publication of Gessner's work and by the middle of the nineteenth century orchid seeds were so well known that they formed the central part of the work published by Johann Georg Beer in 1863 as *Beiträge zur Morphologie und Biologie der Familie der Orchideen*, sadly not translated into English, where the colourful illustrations gave a clear indication of the range of sizes and shapes, but also the consistencies, across all the orchid species that had been looked at. All of these early investigations and assumptions were based on northern terrestrial species; tropical species, though biologically very similar, were different in scale and mode of growth, which increased the mystique of the family. The real change in interest and attitude towards orchids and their seeds came with the importation of tropical orchids. But of course, this was not a European monopoly as some areas were blessed with a natural flora that included large and exotic orchids.

We can see that the story of tropical orchids in cultivation has a long history, starting far away from the cold and damp northern climes of Europe, as trade and growth of empire developed across the globe. One of the aspects of domestic orchid cultivation, wherever in the world it is found or at whatever period of history, is that it is associated with a wealthy and stable culture, where time and money are available to indulge a hobby that by its very nature involves considerable resources. This is because they are decorative, rather than commercial. If there had been a crop to be grown, the orchids concerned would have been put into cultivation for centuries. There is such a crop, not one for mass consumption like wheat or barley, but one for delicate use as a flavouring like any herb or spice. This exotic flavour, unknown in Europe before the exploration of South America by the Spanish, is vanilla.

The genus *Vanilla* contains about 110 species that can be found in tropical and subtropical regions all around the globe. Although we think largely of vanilla, the flavouring, as coming from Madagascar, the plant from which it originates comes from South and Central America. Consequently, the bulk of commercial vanilla comes from *Vanilla planifolia*, grown in Madagascar, although with the genus being worldwide, there are several other species that produce commercial quantities of vanilla. In Pacific French Polynesia vanilla is made from *Vanilla tahitensis*, while *Vanilla pompona* produces Caribbean vanilla, being grown on the islands of the Caribbean and in Central America as well. The earliest references to vanilla come from the invading Spanish in the sixteenth century. Interestingly, although not well regarded as a culture by the Spanish, the Aztecs had a long history in which vanilla was a significant component. It was used in many ways, but not least as a flavouring in cocoa, this being a derived word from Spanish that was a corruption of the Nahuatl word *cacahuatl*. By contrast, while the Nahuatl for vanilla is *tlilxóchitl*, the generally used 'vanilla' is of Spanish descent via Latin. The oldest known herbal from the Aztecs is called *Libellus de Medicinalibus Indorum Herbis* from 1552, which was originally written in Nahuatl. This was translated into Latin by Badiano, from whom the shortened alternative title of *Badianus Manuscript* was derived. It was here that the earliest reference to vanilla is found but, of course, this does not mean that this was the earliest use of vanilla. It is more than likely that it had been used extensively as a flavouring for many years before this. It was also a commonplace product among other South American cultures, not least the Mayans of the Yucatan peninsula. There is some evidence of *Vanilla* cultivation on the peninsula in southern Belize, where there are areas with an unusually large density of *Vanilla* plants growing wild as if they had been under cultivation and had simply been left. As they are long-lived plants and also in their natural habitat, it would be reasonable to assume that left to their own devices they would grow and prosper to leave a sign of the past for us to interpret.

A very slightly later document, also originally in Nahuatl, is the *Florentine Codex*. This was originally *La Historia General de las Cosas de Nueve España* [The Universal History of the Things of New Spain], and it takes its shortened name of *Florentine Codex* from the copy in the Laurentian Library of Florence. One of the stranger aspects to come out of the naming of vanilla is that while the Nahuatl word was *tlilxóchitl*, it became distorted in translation into 'black flower', which has an irony in that the vanilla flower is actually white. The name comes from the black seed pods that ultimately produce the vanilla flavour. In contrast to this, our word vanilla seems to have come from the Latin *vagina*, which means sheath. It was still being referred to as *flore nigro* in some later texts, but this was normally accompanying woodcuts of the seed pods, as in the case of the *Florentine Codex*. Although the recognition of vanilla as a valuable commodity arose quickly once the method of production was known, it was the introduction into Madagascar and the large-scale cultivation of the plants that saw the rise of vanilla to the status of the world's favourite flavouring. The plant itself grows as a vine and, as such, was difficult to cultivate in European glasshouses, where support for the plant was often lacking, even though it grows quite easily. The plants need to be quite mature and, consequently, large before they flower, which is a reason that they have rarely been popular domestic orchids. The original, South American, use of vanilla was as an additive to cocoa, which would normally be taken unsweetened; it only became a popular flavour in Europe when it was realised that adding sugar increased potential uses. Although the minor confusion regarding the original naming of vanilla in the sixteenth century can be seen as of no consequence, it does mirror many other examples of incorrect representation of orchids as such things as parasites and carnivores.

Just as vanilla had an entirely separate existence with a cultural component all of its own, so too did orchids from further afield. Unlike *Vanilla* these did not have the benefit of large-scale cultivation to bond them to society; what they did have, though, was an air of mystery. So it was with orchids as cultivated plants in the Far East as well. Both China and Japan have a long tradition of orchid cultivation, which mirrors their long period of a strict social class system. This system, like all hierarchical societies and clubs, was set up for the progressive benefit of its members alone, and the higher in the hierarchy, the greater the benefit. In a feudal system this results in a small minority having control of resources giving them time to invest in such practices as the cultivation of plants, in this case orchids, of no practical value to wider society.

Unlike the floundering horticulturalists of the northern temperate areas of Europe, who could only guess at the conditions needed for correct cultivation of imported species, the Far Eastern growers started with a clear idea of the nature of the plants that they were growing. Many of them would have travelled around their country and been aware of the huge range of climatic conditions associated with the local flora and fauna. In Chinese culture, orchids were not seen as having any medicinal uses, which probably added to their assumed intrinsic value as purely decorative. As a consequence they were grown just for their beauty and their fragrance. Interestingly, in Chinese culture orchids were also seen as a primary subject for artwork; the earliest painting of a Chinese orchid that is still in existence was painted by Zhao Megjian (1199–1264). This particular ink painting, the *Spring Orchid Scroll*, is now in the Palace Museum in Beijing and is probably the oldest surviving illustration of an orchid anywhere. Some centuries later a multi-volume book was published between 1679 and 1701 that took the enigmatic title of the *Manual of the Mustard Seed Garden* or *Jieziyuan Huapu.* It is described as enigmatic because, while we see it as a collection of illustrations, it is actually a very influential manual of techniques for painting. The first volume deals with landscapes, but it is volume two that is of particular interest to us. In this volume there are detailed techniques for painting orchids, bamboo, plum blossom and chrysanthemums. It is in the section on orchids that the author writes that it is important to start with the leaves when painting an orchid, in order to enhance the grace of shape and form. The use of this artist's instruction book has carried on through the centuries, and across the sea from China to Japan, where it continued to be of considerable importance.

It is quite likely that Katsushika Hokusai (1760–1849) would have been aware of the *Manual of the Mustard Seed Garden*, even if he was not directly influenced by it, although the movement encapsulated in his illustrations of plants does show some parallels, if not direct influence. While in the imagination of the Western public Hokusai, like many Japanese illustrators, is considered a master of bamboo and cherry blossom, there is, needless to say, a lot more to his art than that. One of the reasons for this limited outlook is the popularity of contemporary prints of artworks by Hokusai. One of his series of painting was called *Large Flowers* amongst which was *Orange Orchids*. This particular illustration is relatively unknown because the prints made from the series were not very popular at the time of their publication of around 1832. We know this because the relatively small variation in the print quality between those that remain indicates that they were rarely, if ever, reprinted at the time of their original production. In 1772, another Japanese artist Jo-An Matsuoka, wrote *Igansai-Ranhin*. This is significant as in it he described *Cymbidium*, *Aerides*, *Dendrobium* and *Bletilla*, which are genera of orchids that would have been virtually, or in some cases actually, unknown in the West at the time. Enthusiasm for orchids in Japan became a significant aspect of court life, to such a degree that the Emperor became involved in trying to curtail the large sums of money that were being spent on plants.

So it was in the Far East that intense interest in orchids started a long time before it started in earnest in the West. Nonetheless, European interest in orchids did start almost as soon as the first tropical orchids appeared aboard trading vessels returning from distant ports. These were brought back by the captain and crew as exotic plants to be marvelled at, although as we shall see, few survived the trip aboard sailing vessels with little protection for them from cold and salt water. During the seventeenth and eighteenth centuries, the alternative way to investigate orchids, of Western scientists and explorers working in far distant lands and then sending their conclusions home, did happen, though rarely. One such explorer-scientist was Georg Eberhard Rumphius (1682–1702) who had a very eventful life, although many of the events were not very pleasant.

Rumphius joined what was effectively the military part of the Dutch East India Company shortly after the death of his mother in 1652. As a member of staff he travelled to Batavia, now Jakarta, the local headquarters of the Company and capital of the Dutch East Indies. It was here that he transferred to the civilian arm of the company becoming what was described as a Second Merchant. Although apparently not military, the hierarchy remained and as part of this, in 1662, he would move into the position of Merchant. It was at about this time, while he was visiting the Hitu villages on the north coast of Ambon, that Rumphius started to study and make notes and drawings of the flora and, to a lesser extent, the fauna of the Maluku Islands, east of Indonesia in the Banda Sea. By 1666, the year that saw the decline in the number of deaths due to plague and the Great Fire of London, Rumphius had moved to Ambon and was in a senior post from which he gained official sanction for him to work on his flora of the islands. It was in 1674, while he was in Ambon, that personal tragedy struck in the form of an earthquake. We have Rumphius's own account of what happened, which ties the date and time down quite precisely to Saturday 17 February at 7.30pm.

The earthquake of 1674 occurred offshore and, according to Rumphius, the locals were celebrating the Chinese New Year. The shock was sufficiently severe to make the church bells ring and to cause the collapse of many of the stone buildings in the town. It was predominantly the collapse of these buildings that caused the initial deaths of 79 individuals, 31 of which were Westerners, including the wife and two daughters of Rumphius himself. This was not the end of the catastrophe for the island. It seems that a submarine landslide was caused by the earthquake creating a tsunami, which had a run-up height of 100m (328ft). The end result, although difficult to be certain, was the deaths of about 2,000 individuals. By the time of the earthquake Rumphius had already become blind, apparently due to glaucoma, but with able assistants he continued his work on his magnum opus, *Herbarium Amboinense*, which was a huge work that would be recognised for its intrinsic value to systematic botany. Work was interrupted again for Rumphius in 1687 when a fire in the town of Ambon destroyed a proportion of the manuscript of *Herbarium Amboinense*, both the written component and the illustrations were lost. Nonetheless, regardless of the setbacks, work on the project continued until it was completed in 1690. At this point, with the manuscript completed, the modern writer imagines all will be well, but in this case it was not to be. The vicissitudes of Rumphius continued. His original manuscript was sent to Holland on board a ship that was attacked *en route* by the French and sunk. However, with great foresight and fortitude, probably borne out of past experience, Rumphius had retained a copy in Ambon, so he started the process of producing another version intended for publication and this one made it home. Unfortunately, upon receipt of the manuscript the East India Company stopped it from being published, as it was said to contain sensitive information. This ban on publication continued until it was lifted in 1704, two years after his death, but it then became difficult to find a publisher. When it was finally published in 1741 it was in six large folio volumes, written in Dutch but with a Latin translation alongside it. In it we have a very early text with illustrations of orchids from the Far East. It may seem odd that it was translated from Dutch into Latin, but this was the language that all European teaching systems regarded as key to becoming an educated person. This was no doubt fuelled by the Church, which still used Latin; the Church being, for many centuries, the primary educator. However, it would be wrong to use the dismissive term of 'dead language' when describing Latin, as it is much more of a language without borders, there is no jingoism associated with it. All those who would have used it on a day-to-day basis on farms and in markets have long since disappeared, but as a written language it continued as a method by which a single translation would cover all territories.

While illustrations of orchids were being seen more often as printed material generally became more readily available, it was still unusual.

As much as anything, the reason for this was that tropical orchids did not generally flourish after their sea voyage to Europe. So it was not until 1778 that Dr John Fothergill (1712–80) flowered two orchid species, *Phaius grandifolius* and *Cymbidium ensifolium*, this latter species has been referred to as *Jensoa ensata* and also *Epidenrum ensifolium*. Although it was on the premises of Fothergill that they flowered, he was not the collector; they had been collected and despatched by someone working in the Far East. Part of the reason that we know the name of John Fothergill, but not his collectors and suppliers, is that he was a very highly accomplished medic and natural historian. Although we are primarily interested in his work with orchids, he was very much more than a simple keeper of a greenhouse.

John Fothergill was born at Wensleydale in Yorkshire into a Quaker family, a tradition that he maintained throughout his life. After studying medicine at Edinburgh University, he moved to London where he very successfully set up a practice. Once established he bought his permanent home of Upton House in Stratford, Essex, the grounds of which are now West Ham Park, the house having been demolished long ago. Fothergill originally bought the house and 30 acres in 1762 from Admiral Elliot, after which he extended the land to about 80 acres, which is almost the same size as the current park. During his lifetime he had a collection of about 6,000 plants, both in the grounds and in his various greenhouses, making it a plant collection second only to Kew Gardens in size. It is said that part of the reason he was able to amass such a large collection was that he would accept a rare plant in lieu of a fee for his medical help.

After the death of John Fothergill, a friend and colleague, also a plant collector, Dr John Coakley Lettsom of Camberwell, published *Hortus Uptonensis*, which was the catalogue of plants that were in Fothergill's greenhouses at the time of his death. In 1783 it was Lettsom who published an account of Fothergill in which he reproduced the correspondences of Fothergill. In *Hortus Uptonensis* it is noteworthy that neither *Phaius grandifolius* nor *Cymbidium ensifolium* were listed as being present in his collection, even though it was only two years earlier that Fothergill had reportedly managed to get them to flower. This indicates that since we know that these are potentially very long-lived plants, conditions were probably not right for their long-term survival. In a publication of 1906, *Hortus Veitchii*, James Veitch produced a list of available species from the Veitch nursery that did not include *Cymbidium ensifolium* but did have *Phaius grandifolius* under the synonym of *P. blumei*, this latter being so separated by time from John Fothergill that he received no acknowledgement for his achievement of getting it to flower more than a century earlier.

In his various writings it is possible to discern an element of assumed knowledge, rather than practical experience, on the part of Fothergill. His extensive descriptions of methods for transporting plants from China and other eastern countries would require a great deal of determination on the part of the collector. This is because Fothergill does not seem to take into account the local availability of some of the materials and products that would be necessary to complete the task of packing and despatch to his formula. His natural assumption of authority is also evident in his suggestion to the individual loading the boat with plants, which, of course, will be in his travelling boxes, that they should request the captain to give up part of his cabin to look after the plants and make sure they stay away from salt spray and that they receive regular watering. In many ways this reflected the aspirational times of assumed power associated with a burgeoning economy and growing empire. Anything was possible, including asking a captain to look after your plants on the long journey home from the Far East. It is true that such things were done, but it was only a few years later that just such a situation resulted in disaster.

In 1787, Sir Joseph Banks proposed an expedition to take breadfruit from the Pacific Island of Tahiti to the West Indies for trial as a plantation crop to provide cheap and easily grown food. For this purpose a boat was refitted and renamed HMAV (His Majesty's Armed Vessel) *Bounty*. Because the refit had been made specifically for the project, giving more space for the plants, there was a resultant loss of accommodation for the crew. The idea was to sail to Tahiti, collect breadfruit plants and transport them halfway round the world to the West Indies, which would require a ship fitted out specifically for the purpose. HMAV *Bounty* was not a large ship, which is why the refit also involved reassigning crew accommodation. *Bounty* was 27.7m (91ft) long and 7.4m (24ft) at the widest. The great cabin, which would traditionally have been the living quarters for the exclusive use of the captain, was extended to a third the length of the ship and equipped with racking made up of planks with holes to secure the pots in which the plants were kept. The deck of the cabin was covered in lead sheet. This had the dual purpose of protecting the wood from rot caused by water running through the pots, as they would be watered daily, and collecting the condensation and run-off so that the water could be re-used. As well as this the cabin was fitted with a coal-fired boiler for heat to protect the plants in case of cold weather.

The cabin would have been the captain's quarters, and although William Bligh was a lieutenant in the Royal Navy at the time, he had been a captain in the Merchant Service previously. As a consequence of the rearrangements aboard such a small ship, the remaining space had to be extensively reassigned, with cabins' allocation based on rank. This situation, as we know, ended in disaster with the collapse of the expedition. Although it would be wrong to suggest that this was the reason for the mutiny, it is difficult not to consider that it was at least in part causal. In 1791, a second expedition was undertaken for the transport of breadfruit. This time there were two ships, HMS *Providence* under the command of the promoted Captain Bligh, and HMS *Assistant.* On their return to the UK they brought with them several botanical specimens, including fifteen orchids.

Earlier than the refit of *Bounty,* and a little earlier than when Fothergill was developing his techniques for transporting plants from distant lands, a tax was introduced that had a considerable influence on many areas of life, not least on glasshouse production. This was the glass tax, which was introduced by the British Parliament in 1745 and repealed in 1845. This tax should not be either confused or associated with the window tax, which was nothing to do with glass. Window tax, as it was called, was a method of counting the windows in a house for the purpose of setting a rateable value on the premises. Glass tax was specifically about the manufacture of glass, and a very complicated one it was at that. The complexity of the tax caused severe problems for all glass manufacturers, as it was a tax not on the glass itself but on the melt. This meant that breakages during manufacture that required a product to be re-cast would use the same glass, but as it was remelted, it would be taxed again.

As was pointed out, because of the repeated taxation of re-used glass, by the time the tax was repealed, glass tax amounted to 300 per cent of the value of the glass. During the period of its use, the tax was modified to exempt manufacturers of small glass ornaments and high-quality optical glass. This was important because, in the words of the president of the Royal Microscopical Society, the finest glass for lenses was made by Chance Brothers and Company of Smethwick, Birmingham. This exemption left window glass as the main target of the tax, which resulted in conservatories and glasshouses being very expensive indeed. Interestingly, pressure was brought to bear on repealing the tax, as it was recognised that the glass tax was reducing natural light in houses, which in turn was affecting the health of the working population. So when the tax was repealed in 1845, an editorial comment in the *Lancet* captured the feeling: 'In the financial scheme presented by Sir Robert Peel to the House of Commons we hail with joy the abolition of the duty on glass'. The editorial comment did mourn the continuation of the window tax for the same reason, but this one had to wait until 1851 to be repealed.

One glasshouse that probably would not have been built if the glass tax had continued was the Crystal Palace for the Great Exhibition of 1851. It was in 1850 that Chance Brothers and Co. received the order for 406,400kg (400tons) of sheet glass to glaze the large greenhouse that was designed by Joseph Paxton (1803–65). Paxton was an extraordinarily accomplished individual, starting his working career at age fifteen as a garden apprentice. By the time he was twenty years old, and after a number of moves, Paxton was head gardener at Chatsworth House, the home of the sixth Duke of Devonshire, William Cavendish.

It was in 1836 that Paxton approached the construction and layout of the glasshouses at Chatsworth. To create the large and airy spans that he envisaged for the great conservatory of Chatsworth, Paxton developed a new technique of prefabrication of cast and wrought iron load-bearing structures with laminated wooden superstructures. The glass was made in fixed sizes by blowing glass into a cylinder, cutting both ends off, slitting the glass cylinder lengthways and allowing it to flatten out under gravity while it cooled and set. Although the Crystal Palace is the best-remembered structure that is associated with Paxton, it was the glasshouses at Chatsworth that had the biggest effect on orchid cultivation. It was the great conservatory that was open to the public and had around 50,000 visitors a year during the nineteenth century. It is a common problem with glasshouses that they are difficult to heat adequately to maintain a constant temperature, and it was no different for the glasshouses at Chatsworth. The prohibitive cost of heating the great conservatory from a coal-fired boiler eventually rendered it unmanageable during World War I (1914–18), with the result that the heating was turned off. This left the structure to a slow process of decay that was almost impossible to reverse, with the result that in 1920 the structure was demolished, although the stone and brick supports are still in evidence in their original positions in the garden of Chatsworth.

While the stove house was in operation, the orchids at Chatsworth formed a ground-breaking collection of plants, both in scale and the manner in which they were grown. By 1836, the orchid collection contained around 300 species, mainly by acquisition of plants and collections from other individuals. By any standards this was a large collection, but this was not sufficient to satisfy the ardent gentleman-collector of the nineteenth century. What was needed were rare and exotic species; better still, new species never before seen in the West. To this end the sixth Duke was persuaded by Paxton to send John Gibson, a nineteen-year-old gardener at Chatsworth, on an expedition specifically to track down new and exotic species of orchids. Gibson travelled by boat to India and then on foot to the Khasi Hills, an area to the east of modern Bangladesh. He sent back many hundreds of plants for cultivation, many of which were orchids new to science. His plants survived by being packed in the newly developed Wardian cases. This was one of the first overseas excursions specifically for plant hunting, rather than being made by an explorer causally collecting for a commercial boost to their income.

It was a hundred years earlier, in 1732, that *Bletia purpurea* flowered at the garden of Sir Charles Wager in Fulham. The particular plant that flowered had been imported a year earlier by Peter Collinson. Collinson (1694–1768) was born into a Quaker household with a considerable business as woollen drapers. He developed a keen interest in gardening and from there into studying botany as a discipline in its own right. All the while he was making his living as a merchant dealing in woollen cloth. The wool trade was most profitable with North America, where the family firm developed a network of agents, and it was through these contacts that he gained access to many rare and unusual plants. These were either in seed form or as growing plants sent home on the long sea voyage from the New World. Although no orchid seeds were sent back, it was the seeds that led Collinson to realise the commercial possibilities of seed importation for private and public gardens; for example, he supplied seeds to Philip Miller, who was in charge of the Chelsea Physic Garden. The supplied seed was not, of course, orchid seed; at that time it would only be orchid plants that would make the journey home. Inheritance and genetics were unknown, so it still remained an assumption that only those plants that produced seed that looked like seed, would reproduce in that way. The work of Collinson, as it is recorded, seems to have fulfilled the note that he left tucked into his will:

> That he hoped he should leave behind him a good name which he valued more than riches; that he had endeavoured not to live uselessly; and that all his days he constantly aimed to be a friend of mankind.

This was also a time of distinct hierarchies; the multi-tiered class system was as ensconced as a rusty screw in wood. There was the class of which you were a part, delineated by money, and there was a class of which you were a part, delineated by birth. For the rest, these were the players, paid employees, rather than gentlemen. It was for this reason that areas with a thriving commercial culture based on trade, such as Liverpool, Manchester and Bristol, trading with the New World and bringing back rare and exotic products, including orchids that could survive the journey, also had a wealthy middle class. To these traders and investors of wealth went many of the newly discovered orchid species for their private collections, purchased from the returning travellers who had an eye for a plant of interest. They would have been fully aware that these exotic plants could be sold to those at home with money to indulge their hobby. Some of the newly imported plants turned out to be previously unrecorded and were consequently given a Latin binomial that fitted in with the newly accepted system of Linnaeus. So although they were not named by the growers, they were often named after them. Thomas Moss will be remembered in *Cattleya mossiae*, if not for being a Liverpool banker, or the Reverend John Clowes of Manchester as lending his name to *Anguloa clowesii*. There are many other such examples of solicitors and entrepreneurs who were the first to flower specific plants that had been bought as casual imports. An extreme example of this is found in *Cattleya*, which was named by John Lindley in honour of William Cattley, the first person to grow and manage to get *C. labiata* to flower in 1824. This particular plant species became part of an extraordinary tale of exploration and loss, which is detailed in Chapter 8.

One of the reasons that flowering of new tropical orchids was so often recorded was that, although brought into the country, even if they arrived alive, survival was still not guaranteed. Some would survive well, but a lot of species would flower and perish, the flowering being an almost last desperate act of propagation by the orchid as it found itself in quite the wrong conditions of temperature and humidity to survive. This was especially true for epiphytic species, a mode of growth previously unknown, except for a few parasitic species, such as mistletoe. Because it was an alien growth mode, when they arrived from overseas it was seen as natural to plant them in pots of various composts; understandably, none of this worked. It was for this reason, among others, that watercolours of tropical orchids were produced in quite large numbers as the nearest that most people would ever get to these extraordinary plants.

Chapter 3

PLANT HUNTERS BRINGING BACK PLANTS FOR SALE TO COLLECTORS

For as long as there have been people, there have been collectors, and orchids are just one thing that can be collected, but they were certainly an item that would give prestige to the collector. In this respect the collector is the person who owned the collection, rather than the collector in the field. It is, however, the collector in the field who underwent the privations, dangers and astonishment of discovery. It is the explorers and collectors tracking down rare orchids that provide the greatest interest, as it was they who found the plants that were so unusual and lovely that they would create a stir when they arrived home.

Many of these collectors, both professional and amateur, spent years overseas, collecting plants of all sorts, not just orchids. These long periods of self-exile were as much about the distances from home as pleasure taken in exploration of mountains and forests. With journey times to anywhere outside Europe in the nineteenth century being measured in weeks, and before the Suez Canal months, a return journey was not taken without considerable reason. Plants collected would be despatched home at irregular intervals and often not under the supervision of the collectors themselves. This would mean that, although there was much published material regarding the best way to pack and send plants, it was not often followed. In the early years of the nineteenth century it was routine for collections to be loaded on to boats at remote sites in the tropics, often far up the nearest navigable river, to be sent to the coast where they would undergo further handling on a quay waiting to be reloaded for shipping home. This very process of shipping would result in a high mortality rate among the plants, with problems ranging from waterlogging to standing in direct sunshine causing overheating. If plant seeds were being shipped, as long as they were properly packed survival would be very high, certainly higher than for live plants. Of course, orchid seed was rarely sent in the nineteenth century because of the recognised impossibility of getting it to germinate.

While most seeds are inert and generally robust, plants are a very different case, no matter how they are packed. In the most basic terms, metabolising plants require light and water. Without these two essentials a decline in plant health can be expected, resulting in a high mortality rate, only to be discovered when the plants are finally unloaded by the recipient on the other side of the world. Few of the collectors in the field left extensive written records about their travels, but we are lucky that some did. Very often those who were casual collectors did not leave any particular tales of their exploits, but those who would undertake specific journeys, whether for collecting plants or not, would write about their exploits, creating whole books based on the journals they wrote while away from home.

The collectors themselves came from a wide range of different backgrounds; some were motivated by money, some by fame, but they all had one thing in common: they were fired by curiosity. Sometimes this was scientific, sometimes adventure and sometimes exploratory. Whatever the motivation, the result was the same: plants, including orchids, coming back to the home country. These were accompanied by journals and very often illustrations that would depict the plants, especially orchids, in their natural state. These illustrations, usually either pencil drawings or watercolours, done in the field, were important, as photography was very limited in capacity for much of the nineteenth century. Watercolour paintings were of inestimable value to the owners of the nurseries who would want to be able to sell the plants for the best possible price to collectors who may not be familiar with the orchid, except by name alone. Indeed, even the nurserymen may never have seen the illustrated orchid themselves, as it may be new to science or extremely rare.

It is also worth noting that not all collectors in the field were focused on orchids. All manner of plants were of commercial value, but these were collected for what, in effect, was the mass market of garden plants. By contrast it was high-value sales of individual plants that made orchids so valuable; this was especially so in the first half of the nineteenth century when orchids became so very fashionable. One such general plant collector was Francis Masson (1746–1806), who travelled extensively in Southern Africa. Although he did not collect orchids, the records of his travels published in 1776 give a good indication of the trials and tribulations of the early explorers and plant hunters. His was a determined effort to collect plants for Kew Gardens, which, given the privations of thirst, wild animals and lost directions, is quite astonishing. One of the things that happened to him while crossing a desert region was that his oxen, the animals used for pulling his carts, became lame. It is clear from his description of the animals that what they had was foot and mouth disease. The animals recovered, as they often do, but in a much weakened state.

In the tales that were published by Victorian orchid hunters it is rarely pointed out that sometimes it is easy to collect plants. Someone who did this was Ed Kromer, who said that:

> Although one hears much of the deprivations, some species are more easily found – more or less from the comfort of a good hotel. Less often an expedition is needed that is just as dangerous as those of the gold prospector, African explorer or missionary.

Kromer was an American orchid hunter who was based in Europe. Details of his life are scarce and his published output small, but in a series of articles in the *Orchid World* of 1912 he described a journey to South America undertaken twenty years earlier in 1892. This was based around the search for the lovely mauve *Cattleya lawrenceana*, named in honour of Sir Trevor Lawrence, who was President of the Royal Horticultural Society at the time. *Cattleya lawrenceana* had been found on Mount Roraima, a plateau on the border of Brazil, Guyana and Venezuela, many years before in the 1840s by another orchid hunter, Schomburgk. It was about forty years later before a consignment of the plants reached the UK. Having spent two years in Brazil, Kromer was having a short holiday in England. His employers were quick to ask if he was available for a search back in South America for *C. lawrenceana*. The answer was 'yes' and so the planning started. The first thing Kromer did was to havc a set of trunks made for the journey – these were not for his clothes, but so that his equipment was kept in good condition on the journey, which began with a two-week sea voyage from England to Demerara, which he described as being a very pleasant journey.

He took a stock of goods for bartering, the composition of which is interesting and certainly of some surprise to modern notions of trade. Although this is not a complete list some of the choice items included:

- 1 dozen muzzle loading buck guns, purchased at $7 each.
- 1 dozen bags of shot.
- ½cwt gunpowder in ¼lb flasks (that is about 25.4kg in 113g flasks).
- 10 dozen boxes of caps.
- 2 boxes gun nipples.
- 1 dozen packets of fish hooks in various sizes.
- 1 dozen axes.
- 1 dozen cutlasses.
- 1 dozen American hatchets.
- 6 dozen butchers knives.
- 3 dozen pocket knives.
- ½ dozen saws.

The list goes on with combs, jewellery, thread, beads and coloured handkerchiefs. Kromer was a seasoned traveller, so we can be sure that he knew exactly what would be useful and necessary on his expedition, as all this material would have to be paid for and shipped across the world. Once they had arrived at Demerara, now in Guyana, Kromer spent a day or two provisioning for his journey to the interior. Moving up-river, his first stop was at Bartika Grove, where he was surprised to find a transformation from small settlement to a proper town, all due to the influx of gold prospectors. From there the journey continued, with substantial obstacles to be overcome, such as rapids where they would have to haul the boats out of the water and carry them overland past the obstruction. After eight days of travel he met a prospector who gave him a lot of useful information, as he claimed to have accompanied another explorer up-river to Mount Raimur some three years earlier. Eight days up-river may seem a long journey, but for Kromer and his troupe this was just the start. After three weeks of travel upstream he managed to hire some local help at a place called Potaring on the Curubung river, a local name not in widespread use. They spent three days making up packs of about 70lb (around 31kg) for the hired porters to carry, after which they left the river behind and started out on foot.

For the next three days Kromer and his group walked in the shade of the forest, the trees being so dense that they were unable to see the sky through the dense forest canopy. When they emerged from the jungle, they needed to get back on to the river, although Kromer does not say whether this was the same river or a different one. For this section of the river journey they used native 'woodskin' boats, described as being made from a single piece of bark removed from a specific type of large forest tree. After a considerable amount of walking through the forest and paddling upstream, they found some plants of *Cattleya lawrenceana* but not in large numbers. This was assumed to be because another collector, Seyler, had been through and taken most of the available plants, leaving only 400–500 decent plants for Kromer to remove and ship back to the UK. These were not left for him deliberately by Seyler, or whoever it was, it was much more likely to be the case that they were missed, or were simply too much to carry back to base. Although Kromer was adamant it was Seyler who had removed all but a few of the plants, as we shall see in correspondence by Seyler, this may not be the case.

Further travels by Kromer saw them finally arrive at the base of Mount Roraima in a town called Kamaiwawong, where they secured a house for a month, with the rent paid in advanced. The rent, such as it was, was paid in the form of some fish hooks, two handkerchiefs, a cutlass, a pocket knife, two mirrors and a mouth organ. While they were there, using it as a base for their local exploration, they collected many different species of orchid, as well as a few more of the *Cattleya* that they were especially interested in. One of the longer explorations involved them in scrabbling over rocks where they were amazed by bromeliads and pitcher plants before achieving 'what before ourselves only three other white men were favoured to see – the top of Roraima'. After this extensive expedition collecting orchids, they headed home, which involved a period of 25 days and nights of rain.

Kromer met with Seyler when he was travelling up-river and Seyler down, and it was Seyler who wrote to an orchid dealer in the UK complaining of the problems getting indigenous people as carriers and the continuous rain damaging their stock. Although Seyler and Kromer were ostensibly travelling in different directions, they teamed up for some of the collecting. Provisions were generally short and not easily available, especially after much of their food was lost in a creek. As a result they were without food for two and a half days until they got back to the jetty where they were going to load a boat with their collected plants. These plants were being carried by their porters in packs, which were gradually getting heavier as they got wet, so, unknown to Kromer at the time, the porters would open the baskets and throw out some of the plants to lighten their load. The expedition rested in Bartika Grove for three days and then finally made their way back to George Town after a total of 106 days. It was from George Town that they dispatched the plants back to the UK. Kromer was annoyed by being held up in this by a demand for $100 for an annual orchid collecting licence and a charge for export duty of 2c per plant.

In the detail of Seyler's letter to the UK dealer, who is unnamed, he largely says much the same regarding conditions as Kromer does. However, he also says that on a previous expedition he had travelled to Roraima and collected many plants except *Cattleya lawrenceana* because these had been 'utterly rooted out already by former collectors'. After much searching, by the time they had returned to George Town and taken stock of their situation, according to Seyler they had 900 *Cattleya* plants, one-third good, one-third medium and one-third poor quality, and the whole trip had cost between $2,500 and $2,900.

Details of values for consignments of plants are not always easy to come by, but we do have them for some expeditions. One such was headed by Robert Herman Schomburgk (1804–65), before he was knighted in 1845 by Queen Victoria. Schomburgk was born and educated in Prussian Saxony until, in 1828, he went to the USA. Although starting in a shipping office, he quickly became a partner in various enterprises. Unfortunately, due to circumstances beyond his control, collapse of his commercial activities left him financially worse off than when he started. His interests moved towards exploration of South America, where he made many discoveries of orchids new to science, but also of the giant water lily *Victoria amazonica*, which appears on the coat of arms of Guyana.

The expedition led by Schomburgk was funded by a consortium, effectively a group of subscribers that was managed by George Bentham, who was the Secretary to the Horticultural Society of London between 1829 and 1840. The subscribers were contracting to receive from the expedition sets of dried specimens and, probably more importantly, orchids. These were to be supplied in sets at the rate of £2 10s per 100, the number of sets being marked on the parcels. Schomburgk was rather put out by the financial arrangements, as, although his subscription fund paid for his expedition to South America, he had to cover the shipping costs of specimens himself. This was understandable because shipping would be a considerable expense, as the material was being sent by boat from Demerara to London. Besides dividing the material up into sets, there was also a scale of importance among the subscribers. This would not be an issue unless there was a shortfall in plants, at which point decisions would have to be made as to who got what. For example, one of the subscribers was Loddiges' Nursery who paid £10 on account, which was the cost of four complete sets of 100 plants each. There was also a recognised financial value to the consignment, beyond the perceived scientific and horticultural values, and it was with this in mind that, on the suggestion of Schomburgk himself, the consignment was insured for the sum of £150.

It is interesting to note that the impression of plant hunters being motivated by money and, to a lesser degree, fame, is easy to see. Sometimes, however, the moving force behind botanical exploration was rather different. One such was the botanical expedition of Hipólito Ruiz López (1754–1816) and José Antonio Pavón y Jiménez (1754–1840). These two Spanish botanists are usually just referred to as Ruiz and Pavón, where their legacy is most often seen as the original describers of species and genera. This takes the form of 'Ruiz & Pav.' tacked on to the end of a plant name. A good example of this is the orchid *Anguloa uniflora* Ruiz & Pav., bearing in mind that this is only one of several hundred plant descriptions of new species that they were responsible for. This particular orchid genus, one of a small group of tulip orchids from the eastern side of the Andes, was named in honour of Don Francisco de Angulo, the Director General of Peruvian mines, who had given help and aid to the intrepid explorers Ruiz and Pavón. Quite how this prolific botanical expedition came about is a story of politics and the changing times of eighteenth-century Spain.

In 1759, Charles III succeeded his half-brother Ferdinand VI as king of Spain, relinquishing his titles in Sicily and Naples that he had achieved by invasion in 1734, but still taking with him his reformers from Italy. He liked to see himself as an enlightened despot and was certainly keen on reforms, which he saw as an essential part of making Spain a significant power in Europe. The major reform that he wanted to introduce was simple. Spain was becoming increasingly dependent on its overseas' colonies to fund a large, and mostly unproductive, clergy and gentry, so it was time to make the home economy sound. Inevitably the introduced land reforms alienated both of these major land-owning groups. The new king also developed a practice of employing graduates in his bureaucracy rather than the hereditarily titled, developing a meritocracy. In a determined move he also ousted the Jesuits from Spain, temporarily crippling the education system, so this was reformed at the same time. It was these reforms and changes, allied to the understanding of the importance of having an intellectual input into Europe, that was the motivation for Charles III to sponsor three expeditions to his colonies. The first and by far the most productive of which was conducted by Hipólito Ruiz López and José Antonio Pavón y Jiménez, Ruiz and Pavón. Setting up the expedition was an interesting collaboration that did not fare well in the long term.

Determined to become world leaders in botanical exploration Charles nominated Ruiz as head botanist for the expedition. This appointment was made even though he had not completed his studies at Madrid University, where he was studying pharmacy. However, as part of his studies he had spent a great deal of time at the botanical gardens studying botany. So it was Pavón, not Ruiz, who was appointed as expedition pharmacologist. This was an important position, as rare and exotic herbs and spices, as well as cures for various ailments, came into the province of pharmacology. This close connection to botany extended to the pharmacopoeias of the period, as these were primarily books of plant descriptions with notes on their uses. The third senior member of the expedition was also in some ways responsible for instigating the whole project. This was a French botanist called Joseph Dombey (1742–94). It was an official French request in 1776 that Dombey should be allowed to study and collect samples in Peru; the Spanish Government accepted the idea, but only as long as there was a Spanish contingent as well, and also duplicates of all findings and specimens were to be given to Spain. So although the original idea was French in origin, it was a Spanish expedition that set sail from Cadiz in 1777, arriving at Lima, Peru, in 1778.

Dombey himself seems to have been quite a colourful character. He ran away from home to go to Montpellier to study botany, but graduated in medicine in 1768 and it was as a physician, rather than as a botanist, that he went on the expedition. In 1772 he travelled to Paris, again to study botany, after which he suggested the expedition to Peru and set the ball rolling on a very successful exploration of South America. After he returned from the Peruvian expedition he was paid a lump sum and an annuity by the French Government. In 1793 he was sent to the recently formed USA to help with metrication, a process they have still not embraced. He did not get as far as the USA, being captured by a privateer and incarcerated in Montserrat, where unfortunately he died.

Besides the three scientific members of the expedition, there were also two illustrators, Joseph Bonete and Isidro Gálvez. It was the illustrations that were the backbone of the descriptions produced by the expedition, as well as the huge numbers of specimens that were collected. These comprised about 3,000 specimens, and 2,500 descriptions and illustrations.

The expedition had its share of trials and tribulations, which included the sinking of the ship *San Pedro de Alcantara* in 1784. This happened off the coast of Portugal and took with it a large number of the specimens that had been collected by the explorers. They also lost a lot of material in 1785 in a fire. One of the ships carrying material was captured by the British and the contents diverted to the recently opened British Museum. Even during the uprising of the indigenous independent Inca Empire led by Tupac Amaru, the intrepid explorers cautiously continued their work, spending their time mainly in Peru and a little in Chile. Problems arose with Dombey, mainly as a dispute over publishing results and descriptions, which ended in Dombey leaving the expedition four years before the Spanish contingent returned home.

The outcome of the expedition was undoubtedly hugely successful. There were a lot of new plants discovered, which included many orchids, with many descriptions of species and genera new to science. These included genera such as *Masdevalia* and *Maxillaria.* These two genera were often confused because the original description was sufficiently vague to allow a great deal of interpretation by the collectors and taxonomists. During their expedition, Ruiz and Pavón discovered *Phragmipedium caudatum*, with long, ribbon-like petals, in Peru. Although this orchid was, and remains, a very rare, wild species, it formed the type description for the genus *Phragmipedium*. Although discovered in 1787, it was not until 1847, when a specimen made it to the UK to be flowered two years later, that it was formally described. Beyond these species' descriptions, of which there were many, a large, unified body of work was planned, *Flora Peruviana et Chilensis.* This was originally to be published in eight volumes, which for financial reasons was rescheduled into twelve volumes, of which only three finally saw the light of day during the explorer's lifetime. The story did not end there because the 100 plates destined for volume four, along with some for volume five, remained in Spain. So it was that 155 years later, in 1957, volume four was finally published.

Many famous collectors, botanists and explorers rarely collected orchids, and if they did it was almost by accident, certainly as an aside to their day-to-day activities. Indeed, one of the greatest botanists and explorers of the nineteenth century collected very few orchids. This was Sir Joseph Dalton Hooker (1817–1911), the son of another botanist, Sir William Hooker. Joseph Hooker explored and collected plants around the world, from as far south as the Antarctic and up through the tropics to India and beyond. He would often be employed as surveyor on these trips to produce maps of the ever-increasing Empire. His collection of plants was sent back to Kew or, more precisely, to his father who was the first director of the newly state-owned botanical garden, which had previously been a royal garden under the control of William Aiton. When his travelling days came to an end, Hooker took over as Director of the Royal Botanical Garden Kew from his father. During his stewardship of the gardens he came into conflict, both directly and indirectly via political intrusion, with Sir Richard Owen of the British Museum. It was Owen's contention that Kew should be under the control of the museum as the premier scientific establishment in the United Kingdom. The museum certainly had a large botanical collection, but lacked the one thing that Kew had – a botanic garden.

As can be imagined, plant collecting in the late eighteenth and early nineteenth centuries was not an intrinsically profitable activity. Making a living from collecting plants was a rare occurrence and from collecting orchids, even more so. Even though people were fascinated by the large and showy tropical orchids, it would be some time before desire for orchids by private individuals would be matched by the willingness to pay for them. In the interim, the large group of Europeans who were working overseas as colonial administrators and commercial managers would also be subject to a developing curiosity and desire for orchids. One such was Nathaniel Wolf Wallich (1786–1854). Wallich, like so many before and after him, was a surgeon and botanist: a surgeon to make a living, and a botanist by hobby and choice. He was born in Copenhagen and notwithstanding the intervening years retired to London, where he died. Although he studied at the Royal Danish Academy of Surgery, it was here that he gained much of his botanical knowledge, as his tutors were widely educated in botany, as well as surgery and medicine. Graduating in 1806, Wallich took a position as surgeon in India at Serampore in West Bengal. At the time that Wallich was appointed to his job at Serampore, it was a Danish colony and was referred to as Frederiksnagore. Sited on the Hooghly River as part of the Ganges delta, the Hooghly rises from the Ganges and flows down to the Bay of Bengal via Kolkata, then known as Calcutta. The importance of Serampore for trade in India was considerable, as it was a major inland port trading in spices, cotton, oil and sugar. Wallich set sail for his new post in India in April 1807, having to travel around the Cape of Good Hope, as it would be another 60 years before the Suez Canal was opened. During this period, political ramifications at home in Europe were becoming ever more complicated, and when the Danish alliance with Napoleon went wrong, the effects could also be felt on the other side of the world. One of these repercussions was that Britain, as part of trying to coerce the Danes to join forces against Napoleon, annexed many Danish outposts, including Frederiksnagore. When this happened the new authorities made many arrests, including Nathaniel Wallich. In his case, apparently due to his being recognised as a man of letters, he was released soon afterwards. During this period he was closely involved with the Botanical Gardens of Calcutta, where he became Superintendent in 1817. He was also a friend of Sir Stamford Raffles, founder of Singapore, and he helped in the design of the new botanical gardens that were being set up there.

Wallich was a collector of some renown in the hills of India. He was responsible for the discovery of *Paphiopedilum insigne* from the Sylhet region of Bengal, now northern Bangladesh. This species was never easy to find and, due to over-collecting in the nineteenth and twentieth centuries, it is now very rare indeed. Although originally found in Sylhet, records of it from that region soon ceased, but it was found some years later by William Griffiths in the Khasi hills of the Meghalaya region of India, which lies due north of Sylhet. The plant was sent to the Frederick Sander Nursery, from where it was sold, in 1890, for the large sum of £250. It was also in Sylhet that Wallich found *Paphiopedilum venustum* in 1816. The significance of this discovery was that it was the first of the genus to get to Europe, where it flowered in 1819. While Wallich explored extensively himself, he was also well known for the assistance he gave to the relatively large numbers of plant collectors heading north to the Himalayas. During the nineteenth century, the number of visitors was tiny in comparison with modern tourist rates, but a large proportion of the travellers in the area were there as collectors, both of plants and animals. One of the major forms of help that Wallich provided was in packing and dispatching plants to Europe, for which he had an enviable reputation for the survival rate for his cargoes.

Species of *Paphiopedilum* are often large and spectacular, but this is not the only aspect of them that has engendered excitement among growers and collectors. There was also the cachet of having a rare plant from a far distant land that few people have visited and the romance of all the associated dangers that this entails for the orchid hunter. Nonetheless, it was not always the orchid hunters who benefited directly from this trade. In 1840, Hugh Low, from Low and Company, Nursery, which was based in Clapton, East London, during the middle of the nineteenth century, went out to the Far East, exploring and collecting plants on behalf of the nursery started by his father, also called Hugh. In 1860, among a consignment he sent back from Sarawak there was a previously unnamed species of *Paphiopedilum*. This particular plant was a large species that found its way into the collection of Mr John Day, a collector who illustrated approximately 4,000 different orchids during his lifetime. When it flowered in 1862, it was described botanically by William Hooker who gave it the name *Paphiopedilum stonei*; thus the species was named not after Low the collector, nor Day who owned it, but in a more democratic way, after Robert Stone, the gardener who worked for Day and coaxed the plants into flower in the purpose-built stove house in Tottenham. The collector of the original plant, Hugh Low, stayed in the Far East and became a very successful administrator in the region, helping to abolish slavery and establish railways; he was knighted by Queen Victoria in 1883.

One of the many orchid hunters of the nineteenth century who had an alternative career was Colonel Robson Benson (1822–94). Here was a man who was an intrepid explorer and had a considerable influence on the orchids grown in stove houses throughout the UK. Stove houses were not an invention of the Victorians, having a much earlier origin, but it was the Victorians that developed them to their pinnacle of use. Although there were early references to putting tender plants in close proximity to a fireplace as a method of keeping them over winter, the first serious use of a stove for warming plants was associated with citrus plants being kept in the new status symbol of an orangery. An orangery was not a glasshouse as we would recognise it, but more of a large room, fully integrated into the building but with very much more glazing than normal. It was this glazing that set the scene for extravagance and conspicuous demonstrations of wealth. These eventually evolved into glasshouses that were heated by a stove. The increasing importation of tender species from overseas, especially plants that were much smaller than the more traditionally grown citrus trees, increased the interest in conservatories and glasshouses of more modest proportions than an orangery. Originally fuelled by wood, as coal became available this took over as the preferred method of space heating for these large and status-enhancing glasshouses. They were at this time always large, as these were strictly the province of the wealthy and the stoves were expensive to run.

Colonel Benson was not directly employed by anyone as a collector, but he was fully employed in the India Staff Corps as Commissary-General, and as a Colonel in the Indian Army at the time when he was collecting orchids. By the time of his retirement he was Lieutenant-General and moved to Perrymead Court in Perrymead, Bath, in 1881; the house has since been subdivided into flats. During his retirement from the army he became a magistrate and a local councillor, and after a long illness, he died in 1894. But it is his life that is so extraordinary, rather than his death. He was, at least according to his obituary in the *Bath Chronicle and Weekly Gazette*, Manager of the Botanical Gardens of Madras and Rangoon. What we do know for certain is that while he was in the Indian Staff Corps he was simultaneously making a considerable reputation for himself as a botanist, with specialist knowledge of orchids, which resulted in being elected Fellow of the Linnean Society.

Most of the orchids that he collected were either sent to the Horticultural Society in London or to Veitch Nurseries, although friends of his also benefited from his botanical largesse. His journeys through India and Burma were particularly productive, but most especially the area of Moulmein and the Arracan Mountains. Moulmein is now known as Mawlamyine and lies on the eastern side of the Gulf of Martaban in the south of the country. Rangoon, as it was, Yangon as it is now, stands almost opposite on the other side of the Gulf. His collecting seems to have been most prolific in the second half of the 1860s. Examples of many plant species were sent simultaneously by Colonel Benson to Kew and the Chelsea nursery of the Veitch family.

As would be expected from the geographical area, there were many species of *Dendrobium*, but his collecting success was not confined to this genus alone. Some of the best known of his orchid introductions are:

- *Cirrhopetalum retusiusculum* from Moulmein.
- *Coelogyne reichenbachiana* from the Aracan Mountains was sent to Kew and Chelsea, and both plants flowered in 1868.
- *Dendrobium bensonae* was sent from Burma and named after Mrs Benson.
- *Dendrobium crassinode* from Arracan, again flowering simultaneously at Chelsea and Kew in 1869.
- *Dendrobium crystallinum* from Arracan flowered at Chelsea in 1868.
- *Dendrobium cumulatum* sent from Moulmein in 1867.
- *Dendrobium infundibulum* sent home from Burma.
- *Dendrobium lasioglossum* was sent to both Kew and Chelsea and flowered in 1868.
- *Saccolabium bigibbum* – Colonel Benson sent this dwarf species directly to the Veitch nursery in 1868; it was widespread in Burma.
- *Sarcanthus chrysomelas*, a species known as much for its foliage as for its flowers was sent home from Moulmein.
- *Thuna bensoniae* came from the area around Rangoon, being collected in 1866. It flowered at Kew and Chelsea in July 1867. This plant was named in honour of Colonel Benson.
- *Vanda bensoni*, also from Burma, was sent to Chelsea in 1866. It flowered shortly after arriving at Chelsea.
- *Vanda coerulescens* was discovered at Bhamo in Burma in 1837, but it was lost until Beson rediscovered it in 1867. It flowered two years later in early 1869 at the Chelsea nursery of Veitch.
- *Vanda denisoniana* came from the Arracan mountains and was sent to the Chelsea nursery in 1868; it flowered the following year.

The dates between dispatch of these orchids and their flowering at the receiving gardens is often only a year, which tells us that these plants were mature when they were sent to the UK. Also, of course, it indicates that they must have arrived in good condition as well. We do not have information regarding how they were sent, but since the journey time was relatively lengthy, we can assume they travelled in Wardian cases or similar protective environments, which protected them against the worst effects of the sea journey. We may not have definitive information from Colonel Benson regarding his method of transporting plants, but we do from other plant collectors. One such collecting traveller was Robert Fortune (1812–80). Born in Scotland, he was indentured to a garden in Berwick before moving to the Royal Botanical Gardens at Edinburgh. At age 28, in 1840, he took a position with the Horticultural Society of London, later the Royal Horticultural Society, at their gardens in Chiswick. It was in 1844 that, according to Alicia Amherst in *A History of Gardening in England*, he started his career as traveller and plant collector, although he describes precisely his first view of the Chinese coast as being 6 July 1843. He was not working for a commercial concern at this time but as an agent directly paid for by the Horticultural Society of London to bring back plants from the previously closed country of China.

The Horticultural Society of London was formed in 1804 by a committee that had as its members, among others, John Wedgwood, son of Josiah Wedgwood, the pottery magnate, Sir Joseph Banks and the Superintendent of the Gardens at St James' Palace and Kensington Palace. As can be imagined, the newly formed Society quickly amassed considerable funds from its membership, which enabled it to acquire the garden at Chiswick from the Duke of Devonshire; the sixth Duke was himself President of the Society from 1858 to 1861. At its inception this was a club for gentlemen gardeners, so it would be the owner of the plot, rather than the digger of it, who would gain membership; as a result, the Society started life with a flourish. Such were the funds available from what was a newly formed society that the redoubtable Robert Fortune soon set off to China. Even though the journey took four months by sailing vessel and was at the whim of the weather, he undertook several such journeys between 1843 and 1861 with great success, sending his live plants home in Wardian cases. His exploratory travels were not just in China; he did, for example, send home *Phalaeonopsis amabilis* from the Philippines. This was bought rather than collected by him and for which he paid $1. He had to cut the plant down in size to get it into one of his Wardian cases for shipment when he got back to Manila, but it still turned out to be the largest specimen of the plant in Europe. In total he despatched a large number of these plants back to the Horticultural Society and 45 of these were distributed to Fellows of the Society.

Fortune had an interesting attitude to Chinese house plants, referring to them as pet plants and claiming that the only orchid that was grown domestically was *Cymbidium sinense*. This is a species that is widespread across the region, but of such delicacy and elegance that it would be surprising if it had not been a favourite for household culture. It was in China that Fortune came up against restrictions of movement for foreigners, which he decided to rail against by taking on the guise of a working Chinaman. Restriction of movement was a political manifestation of the uneasy relationship between the rulers of China, both local and central, and Europeans, whether visiting for trade or curiosity. Percolating down through society this also manifested itself in simultaneous distrust and curiosity on the part of the local people for this strange Westerner who wandered around the countryside. One of the ways in which Fortune tried to get around this problem, besides getting his Chinese-speaking helper to tell everyone he was 'perfectly harmless', was to pass himself off as Chinese. This took the form of more than just clothes, he had his head shaved and attached a wig that he bought, complete with plait at the back. It was this disguise that Fortune decided to wear when he travelled to investigate a town up-river from the coast that he calls Soo-chow and we would now call Suzhou. His motivation for this visit was an interesting one. While in the south of the country, and most especially while in Shanghai, he was told that 'fine pictures, fine carved work, fine silks and fine ladies, all come from Soo-chow', which raised his curiosity. There it would have rested, and indeed Fortune probably would not have considered visiting the town, but for one repeated statement made when he visited the plant nurseries of Shanghai. He was informed by the nurserymen of Shanghai that Soo-chow contained a great number of excellent flower gardens from which the dealers in Shanghai obtained most, if not all, of their stock that they had for sale.

Fortune was not alone in making the rounds of the nurseries wherever he could, as these were often the places from where rare and exotic plants could be obtained at little cost and without having to mount expeditions into unknown and frequently hostile territory. As a collector for the Horticultural Society, it did not matter so much where the plants came from, just so long as they were going to be of interest to the membership. With this in mind it seemed obvious that he should venture up-river to find Soo-chow and what were starting to seem to be mythical nurseries full of extraordinary plants.

Journeys such as this were not as straightforward as it might at first seem from our point of view, with satellite maps and high-quality atlases, as the exact geographical position of the town was not known other than 'upstream'. Allied to that vagueness it also proved difficult for him to find boatmen that wanted to take the foreigner beyond the accepted limits of travel away from Shanghai. These travel problems had their origins around about 1760 when the Chinese government decided to restrict trade with the outside world. In this context the outside world was mostly made up of the Western powers of Europe. So the government solved their dilemma by confining such commercial activities to the southern port of Canton on the Pearl River. The trading port of Canton is now called Guangzhou. This situation of strictly controlled access by foreigners continued until what became known as the First Opium War of 1839–42. At the end of this a treatise was drawn up that, even at the time, was recognised as a one-sided affair that ceded much to the British government, including opening up other ports to trade. One of these was Shanghai, which also gained a British Consular office. It was, therefore, in Shanghai that Robert Fortune found himself when he decided to travel, against the rules, to Soo-Chow. The local boat-owners were told by their officials that they could take Westerners down-river towards the sea, but only a mile or so beyond the limits of Shanghai in an inland direction. This restriction on local movement by foreigners was a bone of contention and after some local negotiation it was agreed that the foreign residents could travel a day's journey into the interior or, put more prosaically, as far as they could travel there and back in 24 hours. Needless to say, this was still not enough for Fortune, so once he had managed to find a boat he made excuses for its destination and gained a substantial supply of rice. He travelled in his Chinese costume and set a course in what he thought was roughly the right direction. It was only after 20 or 30 miles on the canal that he told his servant and crew what his real intentions were and, with the help of bribes, persuaded them to carry on with the project. The first night at anchor was not auspicious, as they were visited by cat burglars who stole his clothes and disguise and then set the boat adrift, all this without waking Fortune or the crew. He managed to retain some of his Chinese money and sent his servant into the local town for more clothes to hide his foreign appearance, after which progress resumed, so that they arrived at the outskirts of Soo-Chow on the following evening.

Next morning Fortune sent out his servant to locate the gardens and nurseries that were of interest to him; this was all with a view to buying from them plants of particular value to the Horticultural Society at home. Knowing that, strictly speaking, he should not be there, it was with some trepidation that he left the relative security of his boat. Once off the boat he was surprised that his disguise seemed sound and effective. He wrote that he was mostly ignored as he walked into the town, though by his own admission, the dogs were less easily fooled and he would be snapped and barked at until he left their territory. Sadly he discovered that he had been given some misinformation as to the number of gardens and nurseries in Soo-chow, but those that Fortune did locate were of considerable size. While he did not find any orchids, he did take back to Shanghai several new herbaceous plants, including an unusual double yellow rose. While he expressed the hope that these plants would appear in every garden in England, the rose was a failure as it showed a level of frost sensitivity that precluded it from much of the country. After considerable travels in the Far East, Fortune retired to London, where he had at least twelve species and one genus named after him.

Robert Fortune was, like many of the plant collectors of the nineteenth century, chasing the unusual and exotic, and if orchids came into their area of activity, so much the better, but they would rarely go out to deliberately look for them. Unlike Colonel Benson who searched specifically for orchids, general collectors were much more the norm. In this we are lucky in having the memoirs of Robert Fortune to indicate the lengths that collectors would go to in order to find new plants; we certainly don't have an equivalent for Colonel Benson. In his case he left no manuscript of his adventures, so it is only the legacy of his plants by which he is known.

With the growth in commercial nurseries, and a growing interest and enthusiasm among the middle classes for orchids and all things associated with orchids, which included the daring tales of adventurers, profit was in the air. As demand increased for plants that could at that time only be propagated by divisions, so the value of each plant went up. It was true that orchids had always been valuable in comparison with most other plant types, but it was also true that while modestly priced orchids were available, so, too, were ones of immense value. When the nursery of the Loddiges family finally closed in about 1852, the sale of orchid stock was well documented. John Day, who was at the time a novice grower, started his collection by buying around 50 orchids from the closing auction for an average of £1 per plant. These were grown on at his home in Tottenham in a purpose-built stove house where, as we described earlier, he cultivated and made drawings of these and other specimens that he acquired over the years.

Loddiges was a good example of the commercial fragility of nineteenth-century nurseries, where commercial margins could be very small. As a company, Loddiges had been set up in 1771 when Joachim Loddiges from Saxony bought a small seed merchants in Hackney on the outskirts of London. This was commercially developed by selling on seeds that travellers brought back from overseas' expeditions. Importation of seed was fraught with uncertainty, both in quantity and in the species supplied. The business passed to George Loddiges but when he died his son, Conrad, was faced with a commercial problem. Renewal of the lease on part of the land was not possible, as it was wanted by the owner to be sold for development in an ever-growing London. This put pressure on the remaining site, which was owned by Loddiges, to be sold at the same time. It was this slow decline due to long-term uncertainty that resulted in the final closure of the nursery 1852. Although complete closure of nurseries could be seen as an unfortunate side-effect of an ever-growing suburbia, many nurseries started with premises in what we would now consider to be central positions in London, such as Chelsea, often on the King's Road. All of these nurseries disappeared under commercial pressure from the area, but usually not with the complete demise of the company. By the nature of the business, it was relatively easy to move out to the suburbs, or even far out into the country, if provision for taking key staff could be made.

It was during the period of an increasingly well-off middle class who wanted to join in with the most exotic of hobbies that the Royal Horticultural Society held the first of their Orchid Conferences. It was held on 12 and 13 May 1885, with a report published in the journal of the RHS in the following year. The conference had been opened with an address by Sir James John Trevor Lawrence, nearly always called Trevor Lawrence. He was RHS President from 1885 until his death in 1913, thereby bridging a very important period in the development of orchid culture. He was a very keen orchid grower and while species were named in his honour, such as *Cattleya lawrenceana*, rather more unusually a genus took a derivation of his first name in the form of *Trevoria*. In his opening address, Lawrence described the range of countries to which a single orchid nursery sent collectors, more than 30 in all, while also making a comment on the prices that were paid for plants once they were shipped home. He had a special comment to make about auctions, which, as we know, regardless of what is being sold, can be hypnotic. He said in the conference report 'that every now and then foolish persons, like myself, are carried away by a momentary spirit of competition and give a great deal more for plants than in all probability they are worth'. He suggested that it is never a good idea to spend such large sums because one day a plant may cost £10 or £50, and the next day, when a collector sends over a boat load of plants, 'only as many shillings'. In contrast, he goes on to suggest that the hybridised plant, raised in this country, should be bought for a high price because of the skill and efforts of the plant breeder. This was a reasonable attitude in many ways as at the time there was no clear understanding of orchid germination, so the usual practice was of spreading seed around the base of the parent plant. We now know that this would be where the symbiotic fungi would be living, which were suitable for seed germination. Production of hybrids could be a very slow process: it took seventeen years from seed to flower for the first *Cattleya* raised in the UK. Although it may seem a reasonable claim that the hybridiser has a special skill, it remains uncertain as to whether you can compare the privations of the collector in the field with the skill of a hybridiser of orchids; they are, after all, very different activities.

There is a very good example of Sir Trevor's ideas on plummeting values due to large numbers of plants being imported. In the nineteenth century, a strange convention arose around *Masdevallia tovarensis*. This species arrived in Manchester from Tovar, New Granada, now Colonia Tovar in Venezuela. The town is very unusual in having been created by German colonists in 1843. Taking their architectural style with them, it looks like a transplanted German town and still retains this character. One of the original colonists sent a plant of *Masdevallia tovarensis* to a friend in Manchester, which was grown and flowered, the flowers being pure white. So striking was the plant that, once well established, it was divided and the divisions sold, grown on, divided and sold, all at great value, as they had all came from the single, imported orchid. So from this plant the convention arose for this species to be sold at the rate of one guinea per leaf. This was an obvious opportunity for collectors, so Fredrick Sander, a very commercially minded orchid dealer, grasped the possibilities by sending out Mr Arnold as a collector specifically to track down this orchid. With spirited disregard for the conservation of the hills of Venezuela, Arnold reputedly sent back to Sander's Orchid nursery 40,000 plants. Most of these were immediately sold at auction, sending the value down to less than a shilling a leaf.

A similar story came about with the orchid named *Dendrobium phalaenopsis,* which eventually became the variety *Schroederianum.* The original two plants, mauve dendrobiums, arrived at Kew from a collector called Forbes in 1875. These were grown on and one piece given to Mr Lee at Leatherhead and one to Baron Schroeder. When the collection of Mr Lee was dispersed at a sale, Baron Schroeder paid £35 for Lee's *Dendrobium phalaenopsis.* This was a very calculated purchase as it meant that Baron Schroeder now had the only two specimens in private hands. However, commercial practice came into play as Sander's nursery saw a possibility for commercial gain, all they had to do was track down where Forbes had originally collected the plants and find more. Although it had been originally reported to have been found in New Guinea, this seems to have been a deliberate ploy to hide the plant's true origin. Sander followed the described route on maps and decided that the island of Larat in the Moluccas, Indonesia, was the most likely site. This turned out to be exactly right. In 1890, Fredrick Sander sent out his long-term orchid hunter Wilhelm Micholitz to Larat to search, successfully, for *D. phalaenopsis.* Micholitz found a large quantity of orchids, which he collected, and then managed to lose the lot. This was not his fault as the entire cargo was lost when the ship they were loaded on was destroyed by fire while it was still in port. Upon his return to the island to further the search he discovered that a rich source of them was to be found in a local burial ground. After collecting a consignment of plants and shipping them home, one of the plants was seen to be attached to a skull. This particular specimen was not sold, although where it ultimately went seems to have been lost. Wilhelm Micholitz (1854–1932) worked for Fredrick Sander for about 30 years, but died in poverty. This seems to have been due to most of his money having been invested in German Government Bonds that became worthless after World War I.

When we talk of auctions and sales we have to be aware of the gulf of time between costs and currency in the nineteenth century compared with the 21st century. This gives us two considerations to wrestle with to help us put things into context. The first one is simple, given a cost from 1900, what would it represent in modern terms? Sometimes people try to convert the figure into a modern value by allowing for inflation, but this can be misleading, as it does not take into account the social context of any transaction. So here we will leave the reader to consider the rarefied costs of orchids by presenting the simple example of a skilled tradesman who, in about 1850, would earn around £2 10s for twelve days work.

The second aspect of costs is how they are expressed. Before February 1971, the UK had a non-decimal currency system, which is best described as odd, and it was certainly illogical. A brief mention has been made in the Introduction regarding guineas, but it is worth putting the whole monetary system into context. So here we go on an illogical ride through pre-decimal money. A pound was made up of 20 shillings, each shilling was made up of 12 pence, so a pound was 240 pence. There were added complications, such as a half-crown, which was expressed as 2/6d, or in words two shillings and six pence, and the guinea (gn), which was 21 shillings. This sub-structured nature of the monetary system resulted in a three-stage statement of cost, so £1 7s 6d is 1 pound 7 shillings and 6 pence; yes, pence were represented by a lower case d.

During the nineteenth century, sales of orchids were often on a large scale, as we have seen. Ships would come to port with a consignment for a particular plant dealer who wanted a return on his investment as soon as possible, which usually meant auctions. This was business, and a very lucrative business at that. For some auction houses rules regarding the state of the plants were imposed, which was the case with Protheroe and Morris of Cheapside in London. It was not unusual for them to hold sales where no flowering plants were present, although flowering examples were available. This was usually because there were too many plants in the sale for flowering examples to be given adequate space. For example, at their sale held on Tuesday 7 October 1884, there were 400 lots and no plants in flower were allowed.

Protheroe and Morris were not exclusively auctioneers of orchids, but they were a major part of the commercialisation of orchids, in much the same way as the orchid nurseries were, but by taking a different line. So while the nurseries sold what they had grown and developed, as well as imported, the auction houses would broadly sell two different types of plants: bulk sales of imported orchids, often straight from the boat and still wrapped for transit, and sales of orchids from collections. This latter type of sale was either to slim down a collection, or to disburse it completely. So it was on Thursday 22 March 1906 that what was described as 'rare and choice duplicate orchids from the Rosslyn Collection' came on to the market at an auction held by Protheroe and Morris. Although no longer in existence, at the time of the sale this was an extraordinarily well-known collection of orchids. The collection came from a house called Rosslyn in Stamford Hill north London and had been created by H.T. Pitt. As was written in *The Orchid World*, a monthly magazine for orchid growers, in 1912:

> It has been jokingly said that to have a large and important collection of orchids, one must also own the Bank of England. However, although only separated by about four miles, 'Rosslyn', for many years the residence of H.T. Pitt, Esq., possesses a collection of orchids as

> celebrated to orchidists as the Bank is famous to London. The association of Mr Pitt's name with that of orchids will be perpetually remembered.

Sadly, Mr Pitt is virtually forgotten, while his orchids are still remembered. A large part of this continued fame is associated with the 1906 sale.

At the 1906 sale there were 122 lots billed as the first sale of any plants from the collection. One of the aspects of orchid culture that Mr Pitt was involved in was culture of blotched and patterned varieties of *Odontoglossum crispum*, for which his plants received many awards and medals. At this sale, although it was not just plants of *Odontoglossum* that were sold, they were the ones that took the highest prices. *Odontoglossum crispum* plants fetched a range of prices, one made 54gn, another 70gn and a third 80gn. There were also several other *Odontoglossum* plants that sold for hundreds of pounds. However, it was one plant that staggered onlookers and resulted in the sale making a column in *The Daily Graphic* of 23 March 1906. This particular plant made a record of 1,150gn. It had been exhibited twice at the Royal Horticultural Society; the first time was in 1900 when it was good enough to receive a First Class Certificate, given to plants of outstanding excellence. By June 1901 it was exhibited again and, according to *The Gardeners' Chronicle* in August 1901, had actually got better, it being declared as the 'very best blotched *O. crispum* seen to that date'. The plant was bought by Mr Sander, of Sander's Orchid Nursery. That single disbursement of plants from Mr Pitt's collection made a total of £5,342, not only a very large sum, but also a testament to his skill and ability to produce varieties of a very impressive nature.

During 1899, the sale of a plant of *Cypripedium curtisii* (now regarded as synonymous with *Paphiopedilum superbiens*) caused quite a stir. This plant had been sent to the nursery of Veitch and Son in 1882 by Charles Curtis (1853–1928) who was working for them in the Far East, later to become Director of the Botanical Gardens, Penang. Not only was the overall consignment small, but no more specimens of this particular species were sent home, consequently making it a prized plant of an otherwise unknown species. Unfortunately its ecology and the exact site from where it came was unknown, but undaunted by the prospect of failure, Frederick Sander asked his collector, Mr C. Erickson, to search for the plant in Indonesia and the surrounding area. It was not, thankfully, a single-minded expedition, as it lasted more or less five years. There were many successful finds during the search, but after five years Erickson decided that it was unlikely that he would ever find *Cypripedium curtisii* and was prepared to cease looking for that species altogether. However, chance intervened and while he was on an expedition in the Barisan Mountains of Sumatra he stopped at a hut that had been provided for travellers. It was the following morning, while he was looking at the mountaineers' graffiti left by grateful travellers, much as we might sign a visitors' book, that he realised there was a picture of a *Cypripedium*, signed CC, which was assumed to stand for Charles Curtis. As far as Erickson was concerned, the search was now back on. After many days Erickson started to think that Curtis had produced his drawing just by way of decoration and not as an indicator of where the orchid was to be found. But, on the evening before the very day they were due to leave empty handed, one of his porters arrived back at camp carrying one of the plants.

As with any auction, the process can go wrong. This is not necessarily the fault of the auctioneer, or of the person who did the original appraisal of items for sale. In cases of sales of non-flowering orchids, the auction house would not have the expertise to pass judgement on whether either stated species or stated provenance were correct. There is a lot of trust involved and so mistakes happen. One such auction was held by Protheroe and Morris where what they thought they were selling were supposed to be plants of *Odontoglossum coeleste*. When the orchids were presented for sale, the audience agreed that they were, in fact, *O. ramossissimum*, a completely different species. The upshot of that was the abandonment of the sale.

Orchid sales that took place in the first part of the year, on the whole seem to have been rather more profitable than those later in the season. There was a good reason for this because, if a collector bought a plant early in the year, there was plenty of time to get it acclimatised and established to its new home before winter. With later sales, time could easily run out and the weather change before a plant was able to cope with the changing seasons. We tend to forget that in the nineteenth century, heating a stove house or orangery was a very expensive and labour-intensive task; as there was no thermostatic control, the wide temperature fluctuations put extra strain on poorly established orchids.

When companies such as Protheroe and Morris took on a large sale, as would occur for probate settlement, for example, when an entire collection was to be sold, they would decamp to the premises of the orchid collection. This is quite understandable, as the process of trying to move what may be a lot of very large plants to a sale room would be quite daunting, especially since it would involve trains, and horse and carts, neither of which could maintain a suitable temperature for cold-sensitive orchids. This was what happened with the Downside Orchid Collection in 1888. Over two days in July 1888, Tuesday 10 and Wednesday 11, the entire collection was to be sold in 640 lots to the general public. Interestingly, transport was a potential issue for customers as well, so the catalogue contained details of trains from Waterloo and London Bridge stations suitable to get interested parties to Leatherhead in Surrey in time for the sale.

The fate of a plant sold at auction is always going to be ruled by chance, but sometimes the orchid gets lucky and finds a long-term home. Indeed, sometimes the orchid will not only outlive the collector, but it will still be going strong when the auction house is not even a memory. When the Royal Botanical Gardens of Edinburgh decided to renovate their glasshouses in the 2020s, they needed to rehouse their collection, and so took the opportunity to carry out a stocktake so that they would have an accurate and up-to-date idea of what they had. It was at this point, during the stocktake, that an interesting observation was made. Many of the accession numbers on the labels were most definitely from times past. When the record for these numbers was looked at they had 44 orchids that were over 100 years old. Some of these orchids had been bought at auction from Protheroe and Morris in London and then sent by train to the gardens in Edinburgh, for example, *Stanhopea saccata*, *Stelis alba*, *Dracula bella*, *Masdevalia corniculata* and *M. demissa*, *Dryadella simula* and *Cochlioda noezliana*. All of these arrived in a single consignment on 27 March 1896. There were many other specimens of considerable age, some of which came from a local auction house, Lyon and Turnbull, at the start of the twentieth century. In this case Lyon and Turnbull, which had been founded in 1826, are still going strong, although they no longer carry out auctions of plants. There were also some plants that had been purchased directly from dealers, and Sanders and Sons were among the most regular and largest suppliers of orchids to the Edinburgh Botanical Gardens. This is a good example of something not often considered – how long these apparently delicate plants can live. We are used to the idea that trees have an enormous longevity, but forget that just because a plant appears to be less substantial and without woody parts, it does not mean that it will not outlive us. Although we know that the Edinburgh orchids have been grown under glass for more than a century, we do not know how old they were when they arrived. Realisations such as this make the wholesale destruction of areas for their orchids even more difficult to understand, but, as we shall see, there were philosophical ideas tied up with religion that help explain the contemporary attitude.

In the Presidential address of Sir Trevor Lawrence at the First Orchid Conference in 1885, he makes a very interesting observation. He says, in reference to orchid plants, that, 'I do not see, in the case of most of them, there is the least reason why they should ever die'. By his logic this is true; all, or most, of the plant is annually reproduced and can be divided and grown on, so there is no reason why they should ever die unless they are killed by errors of cultivation. In his next statement he acknowledges this possibility, 'I believe it is quite possible to give what answers to gouty affections and other diseases to plants by injudicious diet'. So even at the time when the Royal Botanical Gardens in Edinburgh were building up their collection, it was surmised that these were long-lived plants, although at that time there was no evidence for this. Even the terrestrial orchids of northern Europe have a longevity little guessed at by country walkers. Certainly, for orchids in the genus *Dactylorhiza*, such as the common spotted orchid and marsh orchid, they can live for at least twenty years, and it is usually disturbance and habitat destruction that causes their demise.

There is no doubt that during the nineteenth century and early twentieth century, the interest in tropical orchids was increasing. It was probably the social and political turmoil of two world wars, but, most especially, the degrading trench warfare of World War I, followed very quickly by the deaths due to Spanish Flu that highlighted the profligate expense of tropical orchids. The differences between those who could afford such things and those who could barely feed themselves threw into stark relief the social disparities of a class system based simply on heredity. But, as there is nothing that can be foretold with certainty, and berating the past will not change it anyway, during the years after World War II of increasing disposable income amongst the wealthy middle classes, interest in orchids and their culture grew unabated.

Chapter 4

THE RISE OF COMMERCIAL ORCHID COLLECTORS AND DEALERS

Almost imperceptibly through the nineteenth century the world moved from amateur orchid collectors primarily working on other things, such as diplomacy for the empire or exploration and surveying of new lands, to professional collectors working for clients at home. These were sometimes companies and sometimes wealthy individual patrons. Broadly speaking, a wealthy patron would have one or possibly two collectors directly reporting to them, whereas commercial companies may have employed collectors in many different parts of the world. As a commercial model this made a lot of sense, as sending back seeds of known plants, or ones documented by the collector if they were rare or new to science, would ensure many plants were produced. This was, of course, exactly what the nurseries wanted – large numbers of known species that could be grown in gardens by the increasing middle class, as well as the rare and new that would command a premium when grown for the first time. In the case of orchids, needless to say, seeds were not going to be an option until well into the twentieth century. Even then plants were going to be a better bet for the growers as they can be sold at a high price based on rarity, or grown on to be sold as divisions soon after arriving at a nursery greenhouse.

Into the newly developing economic environment of the nineteenth century, one company stands out as not only significant commercially, but as botanically important as well: this was Veitch and Sons. It was the Veitch Company that was a prime driver of the increasing interest in gardening with non-native species and the collecting of exotic plants, hardy plants for gardens and cold-sensitive plants for conservatories and parlours. Although some of the immediate Veitch family were also plant hunters themselves, they were predominantly the growers and sellers of plants that others had procured under their direction or as direct employees. Indeed, sometimes the impression is given that being a Veitch family member meant that the option of travel was open, as it was to all wealthy young men, but it came with a catch. While wealthy Victorians might go to visit Greek and Roman ruins in Europe, the Veitch travels should be taken far away in the tropics and, if possible, they should bring back some rare and exotic plants, not models of the colosseum.

The company started in 1808 when John Veitch (1752–1839) rented land at Budlake, not far from Killerton in Devon. Why it was here was coincidental with his employment history. Born in Jedburgh in Scotland, where his father Thomas was gardener at Ancrum House, it was the influence of his father that gained John a position as trainee gardener with the Lee nursery. In 1745, Lewis Kennedy formed a partnership with James Lee at the nursery called The Vineyard in Hammersmith on the Hurlingham Road. The Vineyard got its name because it had previously been the site of a commercial vineyard making burgundy. The house, still called The Vineyard, remains on the site with the largest private garden in Hammersmith. The gardening partnership became Lee and Kennedy, which at its height at the end of the eighteenth century and beginning of the nineteenth century was regarded as the foremost plant nursery in the world. Although not directly involved in the orchid trade, they were a very influential company with many new introductions, such as *Fuchsia* species from South America. These were to be sold at one guinea (gn) per plant (a guinea being 21 shillings). It was at the Hammersmith site that John Veitch completed his apprenticeship, after which he moved to Devon to work in the garden of Sir Thomas Dyke Acland at Killerton House, Broadclyst. So after his peripatetic start, this was why the Veitch Company and Nursery originated in Devon.

After having rented the land at Budlake, the ambitious James Veitch decided he needed to expand and gain the security of owning his own premises. The move to a permanent site nearer to Exeter was also influenced by the difficulty of running the company about eight miles (13km) from his home in Exeter. It would also be better to have premises closer to the centre of commerce, in this case Exeter. This original purchase of land was at Mount Radford, which included a house that he called Gras Lawn. This is a pun on the Welsh *gras* meaning grace. Gras Lawn still persists in Exeter but only as a road name. The land where the house stood was used later on to build the Princess Elizabeth Orthopaedic Hospital, which opened nearly a hundred years ago in 1927.

This site at Mount Radford was the start of the Veitch plant dynasty, which at its height was a formidable commercial enterprise, and over the years introduced 232 new species of orchid into cultivation. According to George Johnson in *The Cottage Gardener and Country Gentleman's Companion* of 1855: 'It was not till the bold and energetic course which has been pursued by a provincial nurseryman of England was adopted, that a new era of botanical discovery began'. This was in regard to the extensive range of plants that were made available by the Veitch family and specifically by the collectors that were directly employed by Veitch and Company.

The continued growth of the Veitch nursery was helped by the bold move of taking on new premises at Chelsea. This was made possible by the acquisition of the nursery of Knight and Perry in 1853, which was already sited in Chelsea. The Chelsea nursery was developed to such an extent that it was not possible for the company to control both sites with the same level of management from Exeter. As a consequence, the Chelsea part of the family traded as James Veitch and Son, while the Exeter end became Robert Veitch and Son. The company in Chelsea continued until 1914 when it ceased to trade, while the Exeter company carried on until 1969, at which time it was sold by the last of the family, Mildred Veitch, to St Bridget Nurseries.

During the active years, and they were very active years, Veitch were in the enviable financial position of being able to employ a large number of plant collectors in as many different parts of the world as it was possible to get to. These new collectors were chosen on the basis of their ability to cope with the trials and tribulations of travel in distant lands and, just as importantly, botanical knowledge. In times past, plant collectors had been more or less self-appointed and as such were inevitably going to be from one particular echelon of society where money was not an issue. Of course, this meant that they would be collecting for their own amusement rather than making a living. Even the sailors who took home plants with the intention of selling them to collectors were employed on board ship – they were working for a living. The administrators and clergymen, missionaries and even the military who collected plants were all dilettantes compared with the professional collectors for whom financial remuneration from sales of plants was necessary for a living. This new form of democratisation of plant collecting was essential to the commercial development of companies such as Veitch. For a commercial company it was no longer possible to rely on casual imports; not only were new and novel species of orchid required, but they were wanted in large enough numbers to make profits. In the nineteenth century it was not just the manufacturing industry that was cutting a dash making individuals both rich and famous, it was all manner of commerce that was doing so, amongst which were the nurserymen.

It was during the time of James Veitch and his son James Veitch junior as he was known, that expansion from Exeter to Chelsea took place, and it was during this period that many, though not all, of the employed collectors were sent out on what can only be described as perilous adventures. Although not a collector himself, James Veitch junior was very active as a committee member of the Royal Horticultural Society and Gardeners' Benevolent Fund, and very well liked. It was upon his death, due to heart disease at the age of 54, that a sum of £890 18s 4d, a large pre-decimal amount, was put into the hands of trustees, the annual interest being put towards prizes for the advancement of horticulture in the form of the Veitch Medal, which is still awarded today under the stewardship of the Royal Horticultural Society. The Veitch dynasty was not just limited to the commercial side of horticulture, as two of the members of the family were active plant hunters themselves.

John Gould Veitch (1839–70), great-grandson of the founder John Veitch, was involved in the business at Chelsea from an early age. We can assume that he was encouraged by his parents in his propensity for adventure, which started with a trip of exploration at the age of 21. While we might imagine such trips as being easy in the modern world, with aeroplanes and mobile phones, in the middle of the nineteenth century, once out of sight of land, you were going to have to rely entirely on your own resources and ability to cope. Although navigation was a precise science, its application was not always easy, nor the outcome accurate.

So it was that in 1860 John Gould Veitch took a plant-collecting trip to the newly opened country of Japan, arriving in July at Nagasaki. For the previous 265 years the *Bakufu*, which we would call a military government, had ruled Japan using a form of *Sakoku*. This was an isolationist policy where all trade and relationships with foreign governments were severely controlled by the *Tokugawa* shogunate. Broadly speaking this was during the Edo period based on a feudal system that ran from 1603 until 1867. John Gould Veitch spent about a year in Japan collecting plants to be dispatched home so that they could be assessed as to their suitability to be grown in the gardens of Britain. While he was there he made much of the various opportunities the country afforded. No doubt being attached to the household of the Japanese envoy, Sir Rutherford Alcock, no matter how loosely, must have been a considerable advantage to a traveller. It was probably this association that helped him to become one of the earliest Europeans to climb to the top of Mount Fuji, one of the three holy mountains in Japan, the other two being Haku and Tateyama. We know this because Sir Rutherford Alcock was himself the first Westerner to ascend Mount Fuji in 1860. This was a time when there was considerable antipathy towards foreigners in Japan. In fact, Alcock's Japanese interpreter was murdered outside the legation, and the year after, in 1861, the legation in Edo was besieged by a group of *ronin*, or masterless *samurai*, which was repulsed by the action of both Alcock and his staff. It remains unclear as to whether J.G. Veitch was involved in this action but, given his exploratory and enterprising nature, it would not be out of character.

Even while all this was going on around him, Veitch found time to explore and send home plants to his parent's nursery, the modestly titled Royal Exotic Nursery in Chelsea. He left Japan with his plants going in one direction towards Europe and himself in another direction towards the Philippines. The apparent objective of this extension to his voyage was to send home as many new plant species as it was possible to do, but primarily various examples of *Phalaenopsis* orchids. During the nineteenth century these were well known and greatly sought-after orchids that would fetch high prices. It would be another 150 years, more or less, before orchids of this genus could be bought at DIY stores and supermarkets for little more than the cost of an oven-ready chicken. Although this was a successful trip collecting *Phalaenopsis*, it is certain that with hindsight the highlight was the discovery of *Paphiopedilum philippinense*. This spectacular orchid was sent to the Chelsea nursery in 1861 where it was coaxed into flower in 1865. This particular plant, although a triumph for the collector, was not the plant that was primarily being sent home, that being a *Vanda*. What had been searched for and found was a species of *Vanda*, which, it turned out, had the *Paphiopedilum* established on its roots. Veitch had been searching for *Vanda* for some time without success and it was only by chance that, when they ran the boat ashore in a secluded bay, the sought-after orchids were discovered growing on the rocks. One of the other successes that John Gould Veitch had was in collecting *Goodyera macrantha* from Japan. This is one of the few orchids that is mainly grown for its variegated foliage rather than its flowers. After his success in both Japan and the Philippines, it was time for John Gould Veitch to return home.

When he arrived home he settled for a very short time before being motivated again by commerce and the love of travel. So it was that in 1864 John Gould Veitch started on another voyage to the Far East. This time he set sail for Australasia. Yet again, this was a very successful voyage, especially from the point of view of the orchids that he sent back to England. Among these were several different species of *Dendrobium*, which arrived at the Chelsea nursery in 1865, all the way from Cape York in the far north of Queensland. One of the plants that Veitch sent back was *D. gouldii*, which received its name in honour of John Gould Veitch. Using his middle name was hardly surprising as there were already many plants bearing the Veitch name, including orchids such as *Coelogyne veitchii* and *Masdevallia veitchiana*. So to make it personal it needed his personal identifier and there had already been a John Veitch, his great-grandfather. Of course, this family confusion was about to be compounded as John Gould Veitch named one of his sons James H. Veitch. There had already been two previous members of the family named James Veitch, and to add to the complexity, the other son was named John Gould Veitch, the same name as his father.

After his successful trip to the southern hemisphere, John Gould Veitch returned home in February 1866. Unfortunately, only a year later, at the start of 1867, he became ill with a lung infection, the precise nature of which remains unknown. What we do know is that he made a partial recovery until, in 1870, he started to haemorrhage from the lungs and he died shortly afterwards, aged only 31. It was his son, James Herbert Veitch, who seems to have inherited the desire for travel, as he left for Naples towards the end of 1891. Although he was ostensibly collecting, there were few orchids sent home and he returned to Chelsea in 1893.

We know that the two branches of the Veitch empire had premises in Chelsea (James Veitch and Son) and Exeter (Robert Veitch and Son), and it was from the Chelsea branch that Peter Christian Massyn Veitch (1850–1929) ventured forth. Later on, in 1880, he joined the Exeter branch of the family business, taking over control of the nursery. He was generally known as Peter C.M. Veitch and was the 'Son' referred to in the company name. He had an interesting career, much of which, before his arrival at Exeter, involved travel far and wide. Like all the Veitch family, Peter started as a trainee nurseryman learning as much about the intricacies of the business as about the plants themselves.

It is from descriptions of his various positions that we know the Veitch nursery was very well ordered, being made up of different departments. So he started in Trees and Shrubs before moving to the New Plant Department, these two jobs taking two years between 1876 and 1869. It was at this point that his travels started with a trip to Germany in 1869, not long after the federal unification of Germany under the watchful eye of Bismark. The idea of the journey for Veitch was to learn new techniques at a 'seed house' where plants were, as the name suggests, grown from seed. He went from there for a further six-month sojourn at a French seed house, again to learn and develop new techniques of culture. After these two trips he returned to Chelsea where his education in the business progressed. By 1875 it was thought the right time for his major overseas' trip to start. This was a long journey to Australasia and the Far East, ostensibly to visit clients but, as we have seen, once unleashed in the field, the Veitch family always collected plants.

His initial destination was Sydney, Australia, but soon after landing he was offered a place on board HM Schooner *Renard* bound for Fiji. This type of boat was constructed to be both a light draft and lightly armed, specifically so that it should be able to cruise amongst the 200 or so islands of the South Pacific. The ship upon which Peter travelled to Fiji was about 121,920kg (120 long tons) with a crew of 28. Peter spent several months aboard *Renard* visiting many of the Fijian islands, while collecting plants to send back to the Royal Exotic Nursery in Chelsea. After several months around Fiji, Peter Veitch found another berth, this time on a trading vessel heading towards the South Sea Islands. Just like so many plant collectors before and since, his plant collection went one way and he went the other. His collection of plants destined for Chelsea did not fare well, being entirely lost in a storm at sea. In the meantime Peter carried on with visits to Australia in the last three months of

1876 and New Zealand in 1877. The plants he despatched this second time, which he had collected in the South Sea Islands, did find their way back to England, including several species of *Dendrobium*, one of which, *D. petri*, was named in his honour, as was *Spathoglottis petri*. In the middle of 1877, he went back to Australia and then in August on to New Guinea. It was at the start of this voyage that he was shipwrecked on the north coast of Australia and, again, his collection was lost. He survived this disruption to his travels and in early 1878 returned to Chelsea with his remaining plants, collected in Borneo in conjunction with F.W. Burbidge.

There was at this time another collector who had been working directly for Veitch in the Far East for some time, F.W. Burbidge, which is why Peter was instructed to join him in his plant collecting endeavours in Borneo. This instruction came from what was to all concerned Head Office and we don't know how much of this was due to the cost of repeatedly ringing the Lutine bell for Peter's lost collections and how much was to try to make light work of collecting in Borneo, an extremely difficult area of the world. It took Peter until November 1877 to reach Labuan, an island on the north-west coast of Borneo. Early the following year, having accompanied Burbidge on many excursions and made several of his own, Peter headed home to Chelsea, where soon afterwards he transferred to the Exeter nursery, eventually taking charge.

Fredrick William Thomas Burbidge (1847–1905) was a collector for Veitch on one particular expedition that turned out to be of great value to the company. He had trained and distinguished himself at the Royal Horticultural Society Garden at Chiswick and at Kew Gardens, at that time still titled the Royal Gardens at Kew. His stated aim was the introduction of a pitcher plant that was known to come from Borneo, although it was not known exactly where, and Borneo is a very large island – larger than Madagascar and more than three times the area of Great Britain. It would take a skilled botanical eye to search out likely sites on an island of that size. He was obviously very capable in this as his search was successful. As well as collecting many fine orchids, such as *Phalaenopsis mariae* and *Aerides burbidgei*, he also sent home an orchid species that momentarily received its name in honour of Burbidge, *Dendrobium burbidgei*, although now it is called *Dendrobium bicaudatum*. When Burbidge returned from the Far East, in 1879, he was given an appointment at the Botanical Gardens at Trinity College, Dublin, as Curator, and five years later as Keeper of the College Park. Many other awards came his way until he died of heart failure due to a serious heart complaint aged only 58.

It was in 1891 that James Herbert Veitch (1868–1907), the last of the Victorian Veitch adventurers, travelled away from Chelsea in an easterly direction in pursuit of new and exotic plants to send home for the public to marvel at; also, in his own words, 'to eat the Mangosteen'. This is a thick-skinned fruit that tends to have a more local market than many fruit from the tropics. One suspects that Veitch was either saying this in hindsight, since he would be unlikely to have tasted this fruit until he arrived in the area, or he had heard about it from family members. Although he travelled widely between 1891 and 1893, visiting Japan, Korea, Australia and New Zealand, his collection, and consequently introduction, of plants was quite small. It was certainly not on the scale of those commercial collectors who had a need to justify their expenses to their employers at home. His seems to have been more of a tropical grand tour, with the possibility of collecting should the chance arise. Upon his return home, in 1903, J.H. Veitch started back at work for the company but, according to contemporary accounts, he had a nervous breakdown and became simultaneously withdrawn and offensive to customers. This had inevitable commercial repercussions and the business entered a decline. By the end of the nineteenth century he decided to embark upon a history of the Veitch business and although initially intended for private circulation, it was published under the title *Hortus Veitchii*. This was published in 1906, only a year before J.H. Veitch died aged 39. With his decease, control of the business at Chelsea fell to his brother, John Gould Veitch, not to be confused with his father who was also John Gould Veitch.

One of the most well-known of the collectors who worked for Veitch was Ernest Henry Wilson (1876–1930). Although it is true that Wilson went on to great success in his own right and his work for Veitch became a small part of his career, it was the Veitch nursery that gave him his first taste of travel to distant shores. So well known did he become for his travels in the Far East and China that he became known colloquially as 'Chinese' Wilson. Although he is sometimes described as having been born in Birmingham, this is incorrect. He was born in Chipping Campden, Gloucestershire, and while still a child his parents moved to Shirley, which is south of Birmingham and where the confusion arose. His professional association with the fine city of Birmingham started with him becoming a trainee gardener at the botanical gardens in Edgbaston at the age of sixteen. He excelled in the gardens and also at night school, where he studied botany as an academic subject. It was inevitable, therefore, that he should quickly move on, and consequently he found himself both working and studying at Kew Gardens. It was only a couple of years later that the Veitch Company approached the director of Kew Gardens, Sir William Turner Thiselton-Dyer, to see if they had anyone suitable for a lengthy journey to China. This was a common manner for finding suitable people for special or unusual jobs: you ask someone who might know a candidate. In this case, the Director of Kew suggested that the 23-year-old Wilson was just the person.

The purpose of the journey, like most botanical trips funded by commercial nurseries, was to collect plants that would be hardy in UK gardens and, better still, simultaneously new to cultivation. This represented a subtle shift in emphasis, away from large-scale greenhouse cultivation towards open garden planting. As a commercial idea this made a great deal of sense, as the development of both the underground and overground train system had created a large hinterland around central London of suburbs with gardens. The newly built estates for the burgeoning middle classes all had gardens and the new suburbanites had both the time and resources to be tempted by exotic and unusual plants for them. So although Ernest Wilson had great success in his plant-hunting career, which extended far beyond the six-year sojourn he spent employed by Veitch, his orchid hunting was relatively modest in comparison with his collection of garden plants.

Starting off in April of 1899, Wilson travelled to America where he visited the Arnold Arboretum in Boston to find details of the sorts of trees, shrubs and plants that he could expect to find in China. From America he proceeded to Hong Kong in June of the same year. At this time China was part colonial and part imperial, so he went from Hong Kong to a French enclave at Tonkin. This was predominantly to find a member of the Chinese Customs' Service by the name of Dr Henry who was an expert in Chinese flora. Considering the scale of China and the wide geographical latitudes it covers, it is likely that this was something of an exaggeration. Henry was not at Tonkin when he arrived, so he carried on for Szemao in Yunnan in June. Unfortunately, by the time Wilson arrived at Laokai on the way to Szemao, it became unsafe for him to proceed further due to an uprising in Mengtsze. This local difficulty resulted in several weeks delay, so it was not until 24 September that Wilson finally met Dr Henry in Szemao. Having conversed at length with his local mentor, Wilson almost immediately started collecting plants and sending them home. In 1902 he returned to England, but only briefly before returning to China in 1903. His second trip for Veitch was to an area nearly 1,000 miles (1,609km) west of his original trip, taking him right up to the Tibetan border. Part of the journey was hampered by bad roads and severe weather, as well as every explorer's nightmare – lack of food. After his fifth year as collector for Veitch, Wilson returned home and, although his orchid introductions were few, they included the slipper orchid *Cypripedium tibeticum*, a hardy orchid that first flowered in the UK in 1905 and is now grown in gardens. Between the first expedition and being sent back to China, Wilson married a girl from Edgbaston who he had met while in training at the botanic gardens.

After working in China for Veitch, Wilson worked as a collector for the Arnold Arboretum, part of Harvard University in the USA. In 1910 he made a return visit to the Min Valley in China collecting plants, but in a landslide had his leg very badly damaged, which resulted in him having to be carried, with his leg in a splint made out of his camera tripod. He always walked with a limp after this accident, his 'lily limp' he called it, as he had been searching, successfully, for regal lilies at the time. In 1919 he was appointed Associate Director of the Arnold Arboretum. The story of E.H. Wilson does not end well as, while returning home with his wife, Helen, from a visit to his daughter, his car skidded on a greasy road surface, the car crashing through a fence and plunging 40 feet (12m) down an embankment. His wife was killed outright with Ernest surviving a little while longer, but dying later in hospital.

It is interesting to note that Wilson seemed to have an easy manner and sympathetic attitude to the Chinese with whom he was dealing, which paid dividends in his collecting activities. This is in stark contrast to Charles Maries. Although not specifically a collector of orchids, his methods and attitude as a plant collector is an interesting example of Victorians abroad. While Maries had an illustrious career, both at the Chelsea gardens of Veitch and as a garden designer in India for the Maharajah of Durbhungah and Maharajah Scindia of Gwalior, laying out palace gardens, it was his plant-collecting excursions in Japan and, more especially, China that demonstrates his colonial attitude. In this he was not unique, but it is unusual to have it described by a third party, especially his employer. In the summer of 1878, Maries travelled from Japan to China. In Japan he had been quite successful, but in China, according to Veitch, 'he was not sufficiently gentle, and was often threatened and occasionally robbed of his baggage'. By way of an aside, it was also the case that Maries lost many of his samples in a shipwreck and suffered sunstroke.

Of all the collectors that worked for Veitch during the nineteenth century, probably the most well-known orchid collectors were the Lobb brothers. These were two brothers, William and Thomas. William (1809–1864) was the elder of the two with some years over Thomas (1817–94). Although they both worked for the Veitch Company, they travelled in opposite directions to each other in search of new and exotic plants for the pleasure of the British public. William was, like his brother, very proficient in the garden, but he was also acutely aware of the botanical knowledge surrounding the plants he was growing. In 1837 William joined the Veitch nursery in Cornwall, where he was sent to Redruth and the garden of Stephen Davy. After he had been there for three years it was reported as being a very efficient and well-run establishment. This most definitely established his bona fides as a very competent horticulturalist. So it was that, although he was a very valuable member of staff, he could not be held back. It was this very skill and knowledge of botany, along with a recommendation from his brother Thomas, who had worked for Veitch for a number of years already, that fitted him perfectly for the post of overseas' plant hunter.

Other than who should be sent overseas as an independent representative of the Veitch organisation, the other big question that Veitch had to answer was where should William be sent on his first exploratory trip. At this time there were few people who had travelled widely enough to be able to make any helpful suggestions regarding the best place to go in search of new and exotic plants. In this context, the places that could be visited would be described in wide brushstrokes by continent, such as Africa or South America, so how would it be possible to decide where in the world to start? The answer to this was surprisingly straightforward. Instead of trying to find an explorer who had accomplished what at the time would have been virtually impossible, speak to botanists who had already received plant samples from around the world and therefore knew where best to go in search of exotic blooms. Veitch had been in correspondence with just such an individual, Sir William Hooker (1785–1865), who had become financially independent after receiving a considerable legacy. Hooker was well-travelled, but more than that, he had a wide knowledge of botany and plants from all over the world, from areas he had never visited, as well as those he had, by virtue of receiving plants and plant specimens from travellers in every part of the globe.

Hooker had his own first experience of plant hunting in Iceland. This was on an ill-fated expedition during political unrest, the outcome of which was that he lost his collection of plants due to fire, caused by sabotage on board his ship. This did not put him off his chosen profession and by 1841 Hooker had become the first director of the newly formed and state-run Kew Gardens, where he founded the herbarium. Herbarium keepers are sometimes not given the credit they deserve for their knowledge, putting the specimens into taxonomic groups and geographic associations. Information such as this, in conjunction with the collection date, can tell us a great deal about how well a plant family is represented in an area, as well as the conditions needed for it to flourish, flower and survive. So with this level of knowledge, and as a friend and correspondent of Veitch, he was the ideal person to approach for help when deciding which country William Lobb should start with to find the next great commercial plant. Hooker suggested that a suitable destination would be South America, as it was already known to be a place of immense botanical diversity, barely tapped by previous visitors.

As the whole process of setting up and running a commercial overseas expedition was new to both Veitch and Lobb, the financial implications of having a man in the field were unknown. So after Veitch had booked the passage from Falmouth to Rio de Janeiro for William, he arranged for money to be available to him on quite generous terms. Lobb could draw on funds to the amount of £400 annually from many of the major cities of South America. This sum really was a generous amount as about that time a skilled mechanic or an 'overlooker' at a cotton mill in Manchester could expect to earn about £70 per annum and a coal miner about £1 a week. This sum of £400 was, of course, to provide for everything on the expedition, which included all the unknown costs such as horses, guide hire and, most importantly, the stowage and passage of samples to be sent home to the Veitch nursery in Exeter.

By his own admission, James Veitch knew little of the life of either of the Lobb brothers before they arrived at his nursery. This is not in the least surprising as the paternalistic dynasty that was the Veitch empire, like most Victorian industry, had little personal interest in their employees and it would have been seen as rather intrusive to enquire. So although Veitch neither knew nor cared for the origins and past of the Lobb brothers, the fact that William spent much of his leisure time in the study of botany while working for Veitch had not gone unnoticed.

When William first arrived in Brazil he made his way to the Orgaos Mountains, where he started as he meant to go on, discovering many new and unusual orchids that had only infrequently been seen in England before. It may have been his intention to increase the stock of tropical orchids available at the Veitch nursery, but his plant-collecting career changed direction to become much more focused on hardy plants, especially shrubs and trees that could be grown outside in British gardens. Although working mostly in southern climes, his activities at altitude resulted in large numbers of hardy trees that could withstand the climate of the lowland areas of the northern hemisphere, as we have it in the UK.

The biggest and most continual problem for the independent traveller in the nineteenth century was risk to health, either as infectious diseases or broken limbs. Close on the heels of which came loss of specimens, which for many plant hunters figured as more important than their own safety. For William both these vicissitudes, risk to health and specimens, dogged his collecting. He was severely ill when crossing the Andes to Chile, a route he took trying to avoid a boat trip round Cape Horn. Further north, in Ecuador, he had to take refuge on the island of Puna when an epidemic of yellow fever took hold on the mainland. Unfortunately, while he was quarantining himself, the agent that had been charged with despatching his collection to the Exeter nursery managed to forget them. So when William had left Ecuador for Panama he was unaware that his samples were daily losing their value in the corner of a warehouse. By the time he arrived in Panama City, however, he received a message from Veitch to say the plants had not arrived. These were from the Peruvian Andes and contained several interesting orchids. While he was in Panama City, William had a case of dysentery. In the 21st century this is a very unpleasant condition, which can be caused by either bacterial or parasitic infections; it has a fatality rate of about 4 per cent, even though treatment is available. When he had recovered, William felt obliged to return to Ecuador to try to find out what had happened to his lost consignment.

Returning to Ecuador, William Lobb found his plants from the Peruvian Andes in a sorry state. They were still more or less where he had left them, in a warehouse, but remember this is Ecuador, a country that straddles the equator. Even at the coast, temperatures are such that it is always pleasant and often very hot, so rotting is a problem. This is what William returned to – Wardian cases with rotten frames. His carefully packed seeds and herbarium specimens had not fared any better as they had been attacked by ants. All in all, a collection of plants and materials that was no longer worth sending home. According to the records of the Exeter nursery, more glass was sent to William so that he could reconstruct the Wardian cases – presumably the rotting frames had resulted in cracked glass as the frames gave way. With the new shipment of glass came a request that he should make another collection of the plants that had been lost. He was already reduced in general health and stamina by illness but nonetheless he returned to Peru to make another foray into the Andes in search of more examples of the plants that had been lost. It was in 1844, after this new collection had been made, that he arrived back in England. According to Veitch, he was back in rude health by 1845 and working in the Exeter nursery, but not for long. He started out again for South America, this time his brief was mainly to collect trees and shrubs. These, of course, are easy to transport as seeds rather than plants, which is diametrically opposite to orchids that, as we have seen in earlier chapters, were virtually impossible at this time to be raised from seed.

When William Lobb returned again to his port town of Exeter in April 1845, he was reunited with his brother Thomas after eight years. William was a restless soul and a year later he was off again, directly to North America, where he was charged with collecting seed from useful trees. These were collected, literally, by the sack load and despatched home from the western half of the country. In 1854 he returned to California, even as he was exhibiting many signs of chronic disease. Although it is impossible to be certain, it would seem from the description of his condition that this was syphilis. His contract with Veitch ended in 1858, but Lobb decided to stay in California, sending occasional material, seeds or herbarium specimens back to contacts in the UK, not just to the Veitch nursery but to many of the people he had met in his professional life. His last letter to his family was in 1860 and what happened between that and his death in 1864 is unclear, but his death was recorded as being associated with paralysis, which would fit in with the idea of cerebral syphilis. That he was neglected in his later years can be seen in *Hortus Veitchii*, where it is said, incorrectly, that William died in 1863, whereas it was 1864.

While William Lobb was working in the Americas, mostly collecting plants suitable for garden cultivation from cooler areas of the Andes, the Rockies and other high-altitude places, his brother Thomas was on the other side of the world. Thomas signed an agreement on 11 January 1843 to go searching for plants on behalf of the Veitch nursery in Exeter. While most contracts refer to hours and remuneration, this one outlines the plan of campaign that Thomas Lobb should undertake in the search for plants, which should only be sent back to James Veitch and Son of Exeter. The idea, as outlined in the contract, was for Lobb to travel to Singapore from where he would make his way to his 'principal destination' of China. At that time it was not always clear whether Europeans would be welcome in China, so included in the contract was the caveat that if China appeared unfavourable, then Lobb should have the liberty to investigate any of the islands that he considered likely to reveal new and interesting plants. At the same time as awarding the discretion of sites to be explored to Thomas, it does say in the contract that next to China the most promising place would be Java. When he arrived in Singapore it became quite apparent that China was not entirely hospitable for a botanist, so it was to Java that he turned his attention.

The journey through Java was immensely productive, but in a quite different way to the success of his brother William. Thomas was in an area of intense and continuous heat, tempered only slightly by seasonal changes in temperature and rainfall. It was immediately clear that this was the perfect country for the collection of rare and exotic orchids. Thomas set forth with such determination that it resulted in a trip lasting from 1843 to 1847, and the introduction of many new orchid species, including numerous species of *Phaelonopsis*, *Dendrobium* and *Vanda*. Although this had been a very successful trip, just like his brother, Thomas was a determined plant hunter and would travel endlessly in search of his quarry. So it was that after only a year back in Exeter, Thomas Lobb set off again on his travels. This time he would be searching and collecting in India, Nepal, Burma, the Philippines and Sarawak, which would take him away from home from 1848 to 1853. His expedition started with his arrival aboard ship at Calcutta, now Kolkata, on the north-east coast of India. This was another very productive trip, as he moved through the jungles of the East. He collected a large number of orchids for the stove houses of Britain, which was developing into a very valuable market, as the fascination with these plants increased throughout the reign of Queen Victoria.

While his brother had suffered in the cold of the high Andes and the Rockies, Thomas had other problems. Jungles can be dangerous but, generally, the danger does not lie with large carnivores, but with microscopic organisms that would like to make use of a mammal, such as a man, as a breeding reservoir. We think of diseases such as malaria as being carried by mosquitoes, and in terms of them being the vector between reservoirs; this is so, but we, the mammalian host, are just as important for the survival of the parasite as the mosquito is. So the biggest risk to working in jungles is being bitten by small animals such as insects and the best defence against disease is not to let them do this. They may not have a specific disease to spread, but messy feeders such as horse flies can leave an easily infected wound. Once infected, treatment would be difficult anywhere, let alone so far from rest and clean materials with which to dress such lesions. Even though it had been initially suggested in 1840 that infectious disease was caused by microorganisms, this was a scientific observation and rather more of a speculation than a fact that could be acted upon. Consequently, with the travels of the Lobb brothers, the biggest dangers were going to be broken bones and infected wounds, whether from insect bites or scratches and scrapes.

Thomas seems to have been untouched by the possibilities of tropical disease and such tribulations until his last voyage. He returned from his second expedition in 1853, only to dash out again to the Far East a year later. So, in 1854, Thomas was in Java again, and although not searching for orchids specifically, he did make some spectacular finds and brought home many rare plants. From this journey he returned to Exeter in 1857, but again, not for long. By 1858 he was back searching for plants in Borneo, Myanmar, Sumatra and the Philippines. It was in the Philippines that some sort of accident took place that curtailed the activity of Thomas. Details about the accident are sketchy at best, but what we do know is the outcome. The injury received in the Philippines resulted in the loss of a leg through amputation. Again, information is unclear at this point as to geographically where the amputation took place, the various reports being wildly different – some saying it was in the Philippines, while others claim it was back in Cornwall after he had returned home. The entire event, which would loom large in anyone's life, was described by Veitch many years later thus: 'As the result of exposure in his work, he had the misfortune to lose one of his legs, a circumstance which induced him to settle at Devoran in Cornwall'. It does seem to be a rather casual description of a significant event, but the understatement probably reflects the practice of the times.

Thomas survived in retirement for many years, apparently living from the sales of herbarium specimens. There remains a small mystery regarding his retirement, as he became generally a home-bird but was induced to travel from his home to visit his ex-employer, James Veitch junior in 1869. Although referred to as 'junior' this was simply to distinguish him from his father James Veitch, but by this time 'junior' was already 54 and had given up his interest in the Exeter nursery in 1864. The subject that had persuaded Thomas to travel from his Cornish home seems to have been either a dispute over compensation for his leg injury or a return to plant hunting. We will probably never know; it could have been a simple social visit as they had been on very amiable terms while employer and employee. What we do know is that while Thomas Lobb was staying with James junior, James had a heart attack and died. Thomas went on until 1894, retired but not forgotten. His obituary was published in June 1894, within two months of his death at the end of April.

As was alluded to earlier, disease and accident were the lot of the plant hunter, I say were, but in many ways it still is. The difference is that in modern times help is often little more than a telephone call away. In the nineteenth century, while undersea telegraph cables joined continents, personal communication was still limited to how far you could shout. So it was that accidents and disease loomed large in the lives of the professional collectors working for Veitch.

It was disease that cut short the career of Richard Pearce who worked for Veitch very successfully between 1859 and 1866 in South America. During this period he was mainly collecting begonias, rather than orchids. It was in 1867, a year after returning from his trip, when he was in London that he signed up with Mr William Bull. This was to go back to South America, now being recognised as a seasoned traveller in those parts, to collect orchids. However, on 13 July, as he arrived in Panama he was taken ill with what was described as a bilious remittent fever and died shortly afterwards on 17 July. The most likely cause of his fever and death would be malaria, bilious fever being a common description of the condition as bilirubin in the blood causes jaundice with yellowing of eyes and skin.

Other collectors whose lives were shortened by tropical adventures include David Bowman. He was in the pay of the Veitch nursery just for the year of 1866. He was born in Scotland where he trained as a gardener before moving to the gardens of the Royal Horticultural Society at Chiswick as foreman. In early 1866 he had been tempted by Veitch to undertake a collecting expedition to South America. It probably did not take much persuasion, as for someone who had been growing exotic plants from far distant lands to be given the opportunity to go there himself and see them in their natural habitat would be unmissable. He sent plants back to Veitch, including one that now holds his name *Dieffenbachia bowmani*, a small shrub grown as a house plant here, but as a medicinal plant in its home range. He went on to collect and send home plants for the Royal Horticultural Society until, as he was preparing to sail for England with a collection of plants from around Bogota, he was robbed. His natural inclination was not to return empty handed, so he decided to stay on to make good the losses. Unfortunately, not long after the robbery he contracted dysentery and died soon afterwards in June 1868.

Gottlieb Zahn was a German collector for Veitch whose specific charter was to collect orchids and, most particularly, *Miltonia endresii*, also known at the time as *Odontoglossum warszewiczii*, but now known by the even more unwieldy *Miltoniopsis warszewiczii*. This orchid, a native of Central America as far north as Guatemala, was known and described, but had not been successfully kept in the greenhouses of England and so was highly sought-after as a challenge. This was a normal way of going about the commercial business of horticulture in the nineteenth century – if a plant dies, just import more. Unfortunately Zahn failed in his attempt to locate a supply of the plant he was searching for. He had started in Panama in 1869 and within a year was proceeding north to Costa Rica when he perished by drowning.

Between 1870 and 1878, J. Henry Chesterton worked for Veitch in South America. His was an unlikely start for a career as a plant hunter, as he was originally a valet to a well-travelled gentleman. Like many independent travellers of the time, he wanted to return home with some new plants to cultivate, so he required information regarding the best way of bringing home plants from far distant lands. Who better for him to approach than Veitch, well known as an importer of exotic plants? It was not, of course, the 'well-travelled gentleman' who learned how to do the packing and looked after the health of the plants, it was Chesterton. When he returned to London he had, by Veitch's own agreement, a superbly packed and healthy collection of plants. It was this that induced Veitch to suggest that he travelled to South America on their behalf, exclusively in search of orchids. He was given the task of specifically seeking out what was described at the time as the 'scarlet *Odontoglossum*', *Odontoglossum vexillarium* or *Miltonia vexillaria* but now known as *Miltoniopsis vexillaria*. The Veitch Company had a long association with this particular orchid as it was first seen in the wild by David Bowman and also later by another Veitch collector, Gustave Wallis, but neither of these collectors had managed to introduce it into the UK. Chesterton successfully found the orchid and introduced it to the Chelsea nursery, where it flowered in 1873. He sent home many other orchids, some in large numbers. When his contract with Veitch ended in 1878 he stayed on in South America for many years, still collecting orchids. During this period he sent a note to Veitch to say that he had been quite ill, but was determined to leave his hotel in Puerto Berrio, Colombia, for a collecting trip up the Magdalena River. Unfortunately he quickly relapsed and was barely back on shore before he died. The precise cause of his death was never stated, but the nature of the relapse suggests malaria.

Gustave Wallis originally came from Hanover, a state in considerable political turmoil until the unification of Germany in 1871. After trying various occupations, he trained as a horticulturalist in several different gardens in Germany. From one of these he was sent to southern Brazil to help with a branch of the German horticultural company. Unfortunately the parent company folded, which left Wallis far from home and without any means of support. By great good fortune he managed to find himself funded by a private plant collector for whom he travelled widely in South America exploring the Amazon and its tributaries. In 1870, Veitch persuaded Wallis to undertake a voyage to the Philippines, this time specifically to search out orchids but, most especially, species of *Phalaenopsis*. This trip was not a great success, probably because it was an area previously unknown to him, and with no contacts it was always going to be difficult to find what he wanted. Consequently, in 1872 he was directed to New Grenada. This was a Republic made up of Colombia, Panama and parts of Costa Rica, Ecuador, Venezuela, Peru and Brazil, basically a country that straddled the borders of the modern countries. He was far more successful on this expedition, so he managed to send back to Veitch many fine orchids. Once again the intrepid explorer stayed on after his contract had come to an end and proceeded to explore Central and southern America.

Aerides houlletiana a species native to Thailand, Vietnam, Laos and Cambodia.

Self-portrait of Albert Millican from *Travels and Adventures of an Orchid Hunter* (1891). A woodcut by Gustave Guggenheim from a photograph by Millican.

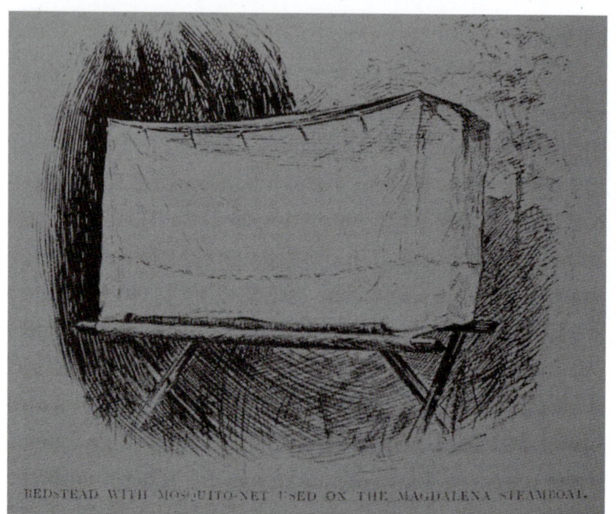

A mosquito net as described by Albert Millican in *Travels and Adventures of an Orchid Hunter* (1891). The woodcut by Gustave Guggenheim was based on a photograph that Millican had taken on board the *Magdelena* steamboat.

Anguloa uniflora, the type species of the genus, originates from Venezuela, Colombia, Peru and Ecuador in deep shade. It was originally described by Ruiz and Pavon in 1798.

Cattleya labiata from *About Orchids* by Fredrick Boyle (1893). A lithograph by Vincent Brooks, Day and Son, a well-known lithograph producer, who created posters for the London Underground and illustrations for *Vanity Fair.* This illustration was by Henry George Moon (1857–1905), originally used in *Reichenbachia* volume 2.

Cattleya veitchii, named in honour of H.J. Veitch, this is regarded as a hybrid between *C. schilleriana* and *C. coccinea*.

The Blue Plaque at Birmingham Botanic Garden recognising the training of Ernest 'Chinese' Wilson.

An illustration of a *Cymbidium* from *Manual of the Mustard Seed Garden*. This is a manual of Chinese painting and an early example of colour printing. The first part was published in 1679.

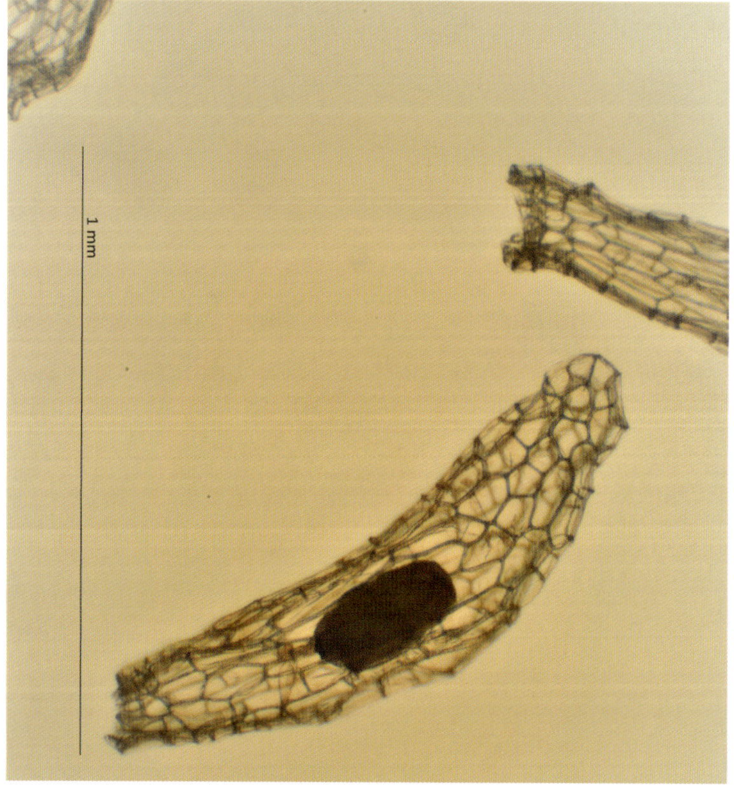

Seed of the UK native species *Anacamptis morio*, the green winged orchid. The scale bar represents 1mm.

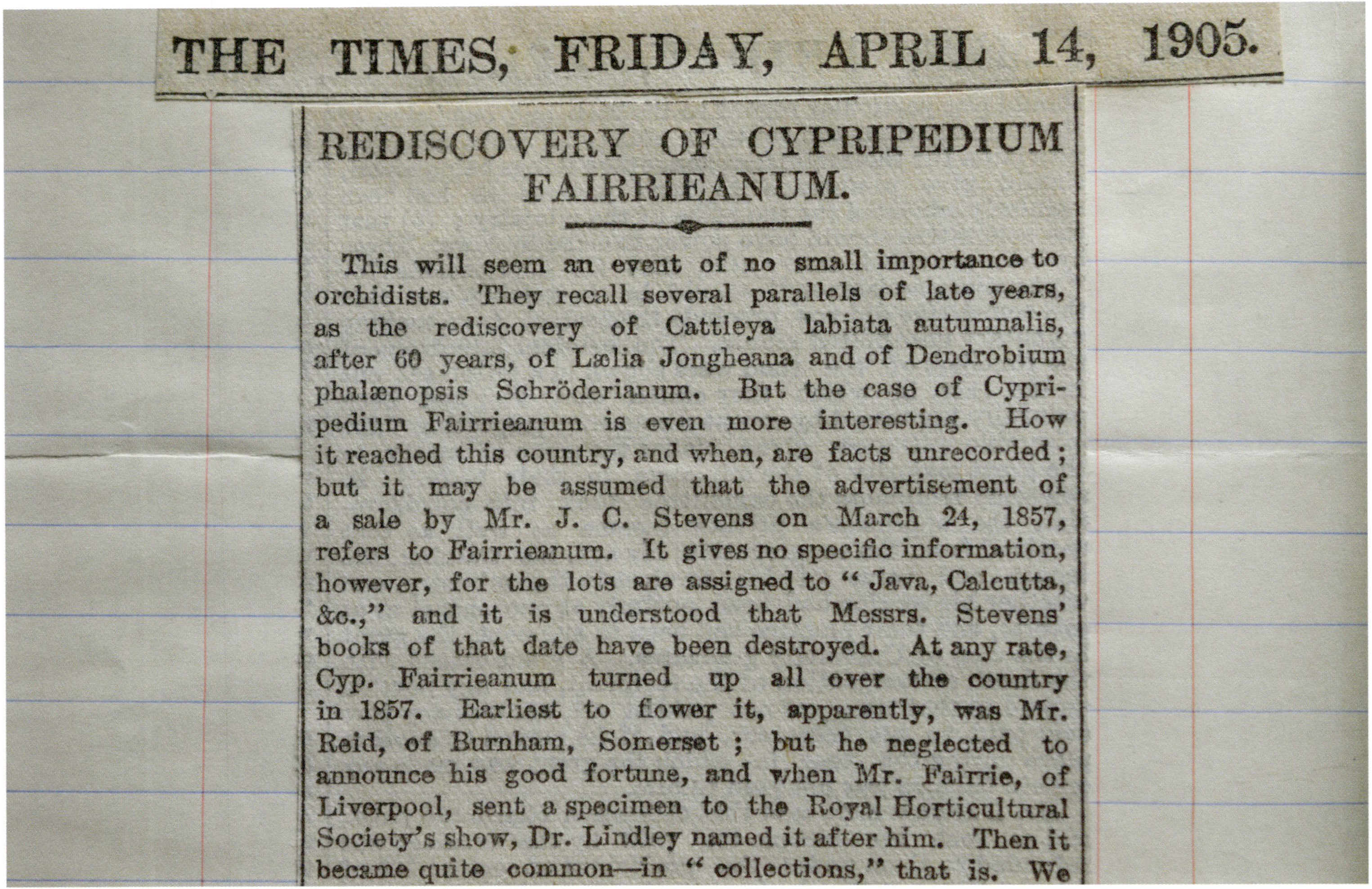

THE TIMES, FRIDAY, APRIL 14, 1905.

REDISCOVERY OF CYPRIPEDIUM FAIRRIEANUM.

This will seem an event of no small importance to orchidists. They recall several parallels of late years, as the rediscovery of Cattleya labiata autumnalis, after 60 years, of Lælia Jongheana and of Dendrobium phalænopsis Schröderianum. But the case of Cypripedium Fairrieanum is even more interesting. How it reached this country, and when, are facts unrecorded; but it may be assumed that the advertisement of a sale by Mr. J. C. Stevens on March 24, 1857, refers to Fairrieanum. It gives no specific information, however, for the lots are assigned to "Java, Calcutta, &c.," and it is understood that Messrs. Stevens' books of that date have been destroyed. At any rate, Cyp. Fairrieanum turned up all over the country in 1857. Earliest to flower it, apparently, was Mr. Reid, of Burnham, Somerset; but he neglected to announce his good fortune, and when Mr. Fairrie, of Liverpool, sent a specimen to the Royal Horticultural Society's show, Dr. Lindley named it after him. Then it became quite common—in "collections," that is. We

Press cutting from *The Times* 1905 describing the rediscovery of *Paphiopedilum fairrieanum*.

A REDISCOVERED ORCHID

The *Cypripedium Fairieanum* was sent in 1857 to London. From the day of its first discovery until recently not a plant was found. The original stock of plants in Britain dwindled until only one specimen was left. A member of the Tibet Expedition discovered a whole bunch of the plants.

Magazine illustration of *Paphiopedilum fairreanum* accompanying the rediscovery of this species. The editorial team have reproduced the photograph upside down.

Phragmipedium humboldtii. A native of the area from Mexico south to South America.
Photograph courtesy of Dr D.C. Morgan.

Paphiopedilum insigne. This is the type species for the genus. Due to collecting it is now very rare in its wild range of the Indian States of Assam, Meghalaya and adjoining areas of Bangladesh.

Mr. Kromer, and the Interior of his House.

An illustration from *Orchid World* (1912). The plant hunter Ed Kromer, right, and possibly his companion, another plant hunter, Seyler. They are sitting in the house with a local man, the house having been rented for a month in exchange for various goods, such as fish hooks and knives.

St Anne's Church viewed across Kew Green next to Kew Gardens. Founded in 1714, after rebuilding it is now largely nineteenth century. Buried in the churchyard are Sir William Hooker, the first director of Kew Gardens, and Sir Joseph Hooker, the second director of Kew Gardens.

Angraceum sesquipedale. Having seen the orchid, Charles Darwin described the pollinator as a large hawk moth with a proboscis capable of reaching nectar at the end of the spur. This was before the moth, *Xanthopan morganii*, was discovered.

Odontoglossum crispum illustrated in *Reichenbachia* and re-used in Boyle's *About Orchids*. This was painted by Henry Moon (1857–1905). Originally 21in by 15in (53cm by 38cm), it was reproduced much reduced in *About Orchids*.

Laelia anceps subspecies *Schroederiana*. Now synonymous with subspecies *Dawsonii*. This is from the illustration that appeared in *About Orchids* in 1903. A native of Mexico, it was named in honour of Baron Schroeder. The subspecies of *L. anceps* was reviewed by Heinrich Reichenbach in *The Gardeners Chronicle* December 1902.

Portrait of William Curtis on the frontispiece of the first volume of the *Botanical Magazine* of 1793.

Galeandra baueri, from Mexico into South America. This is from *The Orchidaceae of Mexico and Guatemala* by James Bateman. This orchid was named *baueri* in honour of Francis Bauer who was an artist at Kew Gardens from 1790 to 1840. He is buried at St Anne's Church, Kew Green.

Masdevallia veitchiana. An unusual orchid named in 1868 in favour of Dr Jose Masdeval and also James Veitch.

Mountain Chair.

A carrying chair as illustrated being used in *Three Years' Wandering in The Northern Provinces of China* by Robert Fortune written in 1847.

A demonstration of air pollution, which would choke orchids as well as people. Claude Monet painted this picture of Waterloo Bridge from the fifth floor of the Savoy Hotel. The first chimney on the right is a flour mill, the tower in the centre is the shot tower of a lead works, further left, obscured by smoke, are the steam cranes of the docks where orchid consignments were unloaded. Detail of the painting in the Hugh Lane Gallery of Modern Art, Dublin.

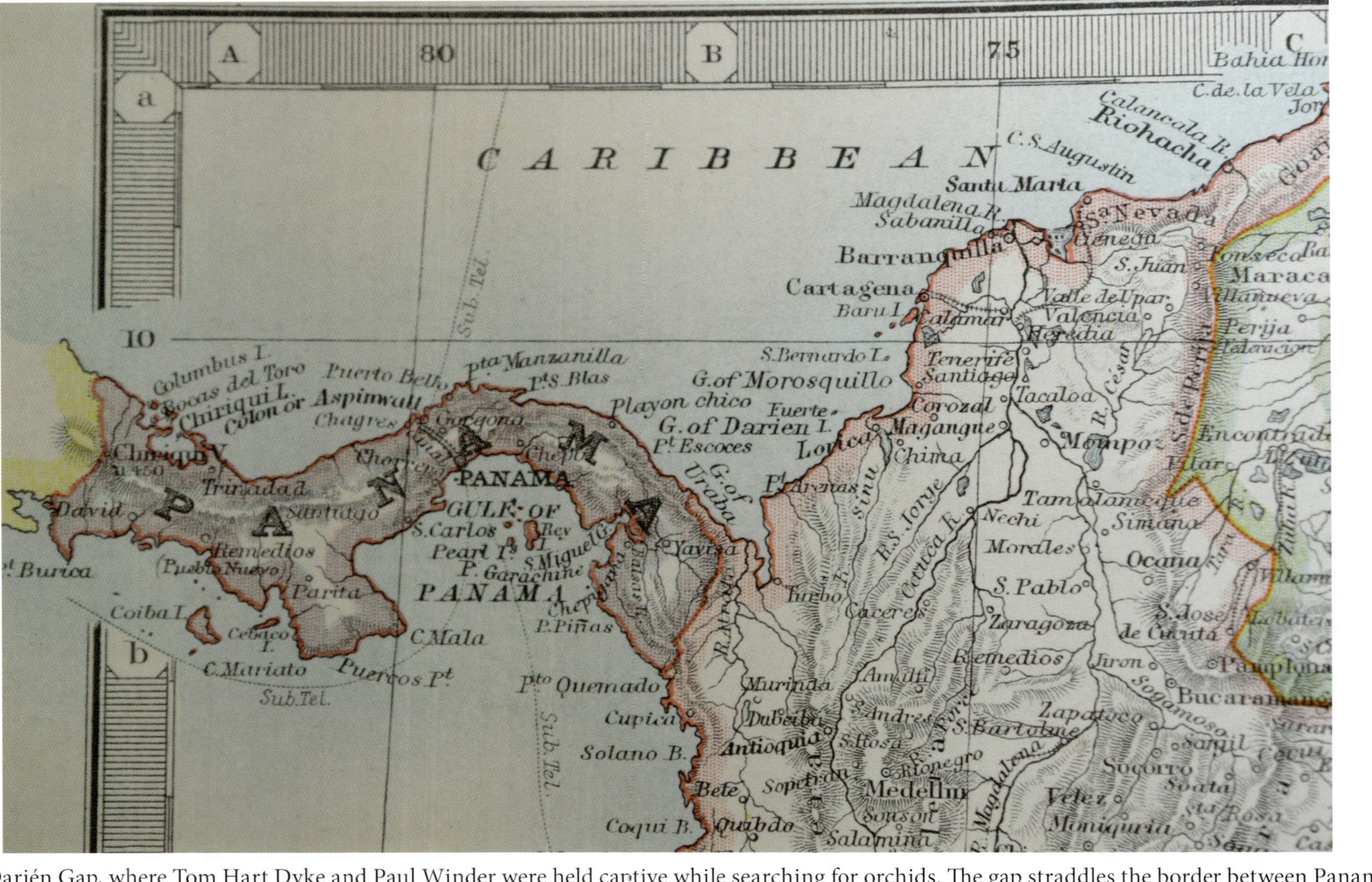

The Darién Gap, where Tom Hart Dyke and Paul Winder were held captive while searching for orchids. The gap straddles the border between Panama and Colombia and is made up of mountains, swamps and enormous biodiversity. This map is from 1894.

An illustration of *Angraceum sesquipedale* and a suggested moth pollinator. This was published in *Quarterly Journal of Science* October 1867 in an article by Alfred Russel Wallace supporting Charles Darwin's suggestion that an unknown long-tongued hawk moth was the natural pollinator.

A river scene on the Huangpo River, Shanghai, as shown in *Three Years' Wandering in The Northern Provinces of China* by Robert Fortune, published in 1847.

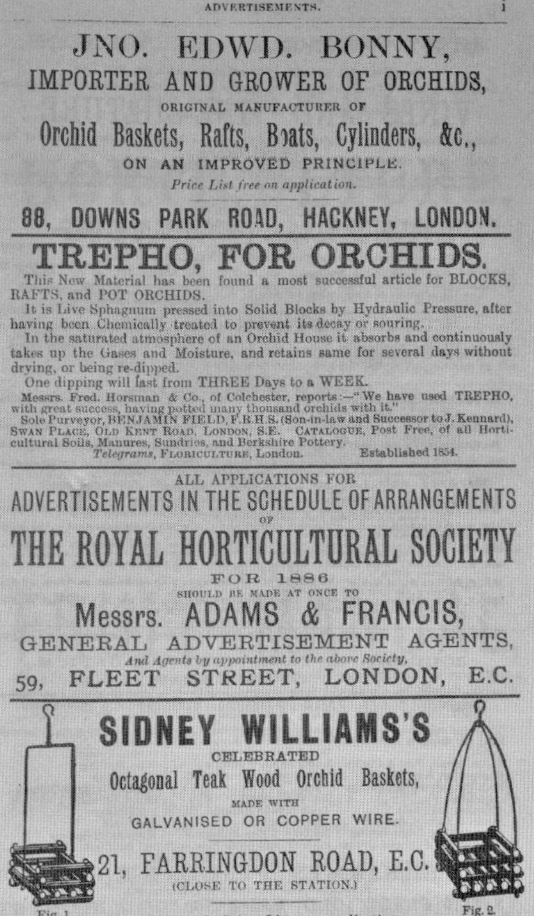

ADVERTISEMENTS. i

JNO. EDWD. BONNY,
IMPORTER AND GROWER OF ORCHIDS,
ORIGINAL MANUFACTURER OF
Orchid Baskets, Rafts, Boats, Cylinders, &c.,
ON AN IMPROVED PRINCIPLE.
Price List free on application.
88, DOWNS PARK ROAD, HACKNEY, LONDON.

TREPHO, FOR ORCHIDS.

This New Material has been found a most successful article for BLOCKS, RAFTS, and POT ORCHIDS.

It is Live Sphagnum pressed into Solid Blocks by Hydraulic Pressure, after having been Chemically treated to prevent its decay or souring.

In the saturated atmosphere of an Orchid House it absorbs and continuously takes up the Gases and Moisture, and retains same for several days without drying, or being re-dipped.

One dipping will last from THREE Days to a WEEK.

Messrs. Fred. Horsman & Co., of Colchester, reports:—"We have used TREPHO, with great success, having potted many thousand orchids with it."

Sole Purveyor, BENJAMIN FIELD, F.R.H.S. (Son-in-law and Successor to J. Kennard), SWAN PLACE, OLD KENT ROAD, LONDON, S.E. CATALOGUE, Post Free, of all Horticultural Soils, Manures, Sundries, and Berkshire Pottery.
Telegrams, FLORICULTURE, London. Established 1854.

ALL APPLICATIONS FOR
ADVERTISEMENTS IN THE SCHEDULE OF ARRANGEMENTS
OF
THE ROYAL HORTICULTURAL SOCIETY
FOR 1886
SHOULD BE MADE AT ONCE TO
Messrs. ADAMS & FRANCIS,
GENERAL ADVERTISEMENT AGENTS,
And Agents by appointment to the above Society,
59, FLEET STREET, LONDON, E.C.

SIDNEY WILLIAMS'S
CELEBRATED
Octagonal Teak Wood Orchid Baskets,
MADE WITH
GALVANISED OR COPPER WIRE.
21, FARRINGDON ROAD, E.C.
(CLOSE TO THE STATION.)
Illustrated Price List on application.
Fig. 1. Fig. 2.

A page of advertisements from the *Journal of the Royal Horticultural Society*, Vol. VII, No. 1, the report of the first RHS Orchid Conference. Suppliers of ancillary equipment recognised the value of orchid growers and were keen to attract their business.

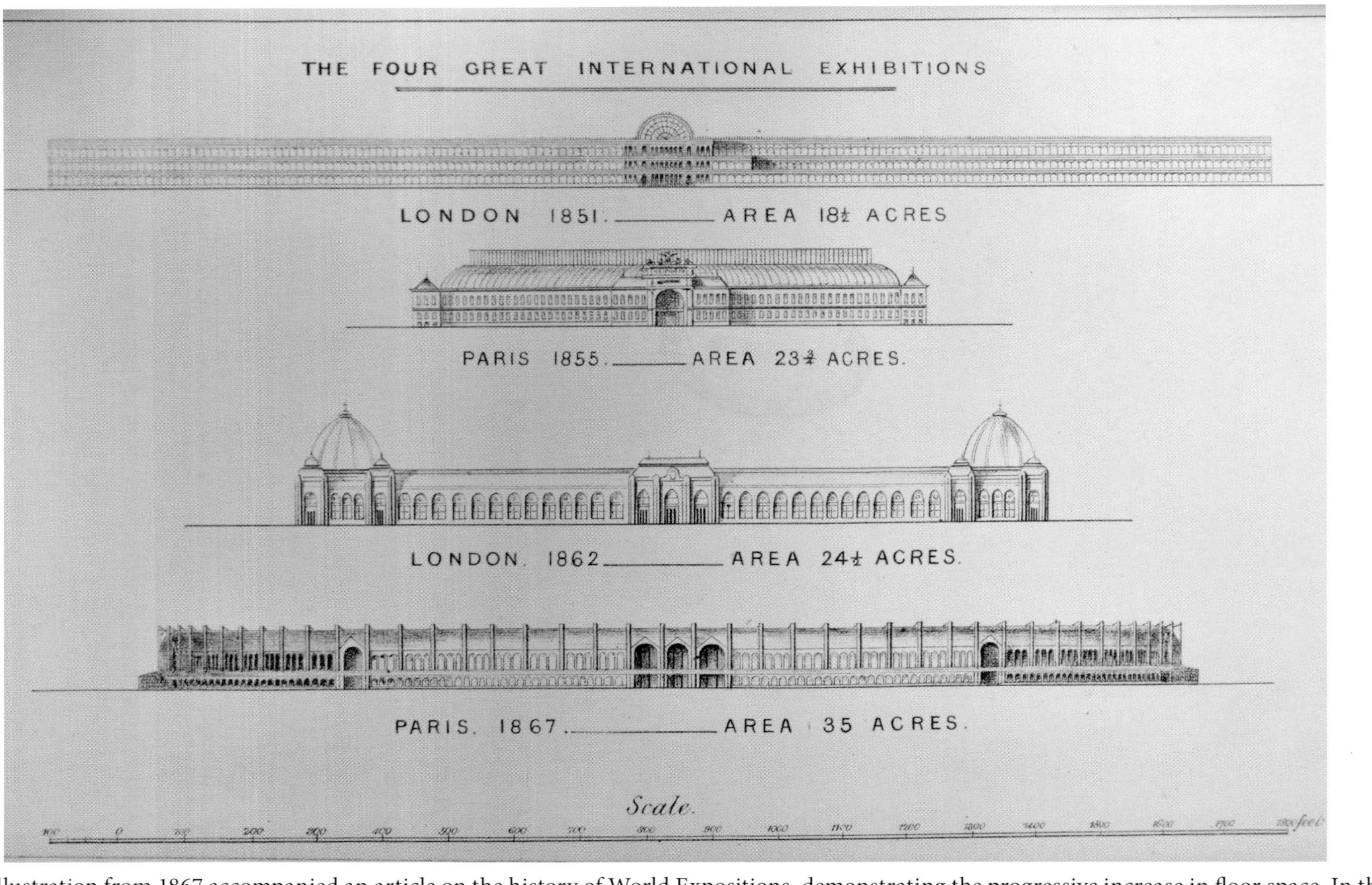

This illustration from 1867 accompanied an article on the history of World Expositions, demonstrating the progressive increase in floor space. In the 19th century there was a competitive feeling about the size of the main pavilions, starting with the Great Exhibition in London of 1851.

After leaving the employment with Veitch, Wallis was known to be ill with fever in Panama, from which he did recover, but his insistence upon travelling as soon as he thought himself fit enough proved his undoing. He died in the hospital at Cuenca in Ecuador in June 1878, not apparently directly as a result of his relapsing fever, but because of a bout of dysentery, which proved to be one thing too many for his ravaged health to recover from.

Being a plant hunter for the Veitch organisation was always seen as something to aspire to, the benefits being seen to far outweigh the risks. One such aspirant was David Burke, who started at the Chelsea premises of Veitch as a young gardener, but was keen to travel as a collector for the company. He was initially sent with another collector to Borneo, which produced a good crop of plants that were sent back to the company. At the age of 27 he was sent by Veitch to British Guiana, now Guyana, from which he returned with many orchids, amongst which was *Zygopetalum burkei*, a new species that was named in his honour. Burke was unusual in not seeming to specialise in a specific geographical region. For this reason, he then went back to the Far East, again searching for orchids. Almost as though he was ricocheting around the planet, between 1894 and 1896 there were three trips as an orchid hunter in Colombia. After only a short respite at home following his Colombian trips, in 1896 he headed out to the Moluccas, again in the Far East. It was there on one of the islands, Ambon, that he died in 1897. It was recorded that he liked to live both with, and like, the natives he was amongst and it was unkindly suggested at the time that this was in some way associated with his death.

There were numerous collectors working for the Veitch Company during the nineteenth century and into the twentieth, as the commerce and the optimistic attitudes of the Victorians took hold throughout society. Although we still have commercial garden centres and specialist orchid growers, often working on very large scales, it was the Veitch nurseries that laid down the basic plan. Prior to them creating the idea that plants could be a large-scale commercial product, the people involved in the marketing of garden and house plants tended to be very local and generally worked on a much smaller scale. Also, they were more often seed merchants rather than sellers of plants, simply because seeds were so much easier to deliver than plants. Seeds and plants were regularly being advertised for sale in gardening magazines, which in themselves were a newly developing market. During this period Great Britain had developed a certain social distance from mainland Europe, but it had not always been so. Although on the extreme western edge of Europe, Great Britain was very definitely a part of it. We think now of the European Union as being the bridge linking societies, but this is the necessary product of a century of wars and petty nationalism. Most histories covering the last three centuries tend to deal primarily with succession and politics, calling themselves social histories. What is less well recorded is not how the states interacted at the military level, but how the people of those states interacted. During the period up to World War I, the ease and regularity of movement of individuals between states is quite surprising. We may now have regular holidays abroad, but this has always been the case for those with funds to take themselves on The Grand Tour of Europe. The free flow of people and ideas, the easy movement of individuals for work without hindrance was an accepted norm until the start of the war-torn twentieth century, and with this movement of people came the movement of orchids across Europe as collectors sent them home and they were passed on as original plants or divisions to other nurseries and growers throughout the continent.

A collector from whom we have a first-hand account of their activities is Albert Millican, who was a dedicated Victorian orchid collector. He wrote about his activities in South America in *Travels and Adventures of an Orchid Hunter*, published in 1891. Like Robert Fortune before him, his descriptions of his activities are as much a travelogue as a description of the plants he collected. However, there is a considerable difference between Millican, the orchid hunter, and the more general plant hunter that Fortune was. Part of this was based upon the need for the plant collector to have a wide knowledge of botany to be able to recognise a plant of potential for the commercial market. The orchid hunter has the relatively more straightforward need to only know what orchids are and how to recognise them in the field. Admittedly Orchidaceae are a very large family, but the plants and the flowers do tend to follow a limited range of forms. This difference between botanist and hunter manifests itself in another aspect of their profession in that the orchid hunters were aware of the very large sums of money that could be made from a consignment sent home for sale. The rarer the species, the more money that could be made. This created a certain amount of animosity between orchid hunters and a ruthless attitude to the possibility that there may be plants remaining that could undermine their exclusivity and, therefore, their value.

Most of the collecting that Millican did was focused on the hot-spot for orchids that is Colombia, although his activities were not confined to that country alone. During the period from 1887 to 1891 he made five expeditionary visits to the northern part of South America. One of the aspects of the writings of Millican, which is sorely neglected, is that he had a deep vein of satire underlying many of his descriptions. These have often been taken at face value, which is a shame because their humour gets lost, even though he is using satire and irony to make a valid point. The first paragraph of his book gives an example of this.

> Having fully made up my mind for a long sea voyage, and taken my ticket for anywhere and everywhere beyond the seas, I provided myself with a stock of knives, cutlasses, revolvers, rifle and

overflowing supply of tobacco and newspapers and started on the third Saturday of the eighth month of Her Majesty Queen Victoria's Jubilee year.

Travels and Adventures of an Orchid Hunter, Albert Millican (1891)

This is the first sentence of Millican's book and gives a good flavour of the style, if not the accuracy and precision to be expected. The idea that he had simply decided to travel is not quite the whole story, which can be discovered by looking in more detail at the dedication of the book to R. Brooman White. Richard Charles Brooman White was the son of Susannah Brooman and Richard Brooman. When his father died, Susannah married John White. The house in which they lived was Addarroch in Scotland and upon the death of John White the house was left to Richard on the understanding that he would append White to his name, hence Brooman White. His mother went on to marry for a third time, this time into a titled family, while Richard became a great authority on tropical orchid cultivation. With his interest in orchids and large personal fortune, it was possible for Brooman White to personally sponsor Millican on his orchid-collecting expeditions.

In South America, while travelling through Colombia on a steam-powered paddle boat on the Magdalena River, he describes the provision of on-deck sleeping accommodation, including the provision of mosquito nets. Although since the last century we have associated mosquito nets with the prevention of malaria, this was not always so. Relapsing fevers were well known and had been since the first natural philosopher had noted down another person's symptoms. One of the commonest of these relapsers is malaria. The causal agent of malaria was not known until the organism, a protist, was seen inside red blood cells from fever patients in 1880. It was even suggested in 1881 that mosquitoes were the vectors of malaria, but it was not until 1897 that Ronald Ross demonstrated the life cycle of the protist, including the phases in humans and mosquitoes. So when Millican was travelling, the mosquito net was not really associated with disease prevention.

There are a lot of exciting tropical diseases that are transmitted by insects, many of which can be controlled by mosquito nets as a simple physical barrier that stops the pesky vector from biting in the first place. Many of these insects are not particularly bothered what species they bite; very often they are content with other mammals for their blood meal. One of the insect-borne diseases of great significance in South America is Chagas disease, caused by a trypanosome parasite similar to the African equivalent – sleeping sickness. The vector of Chagas disease is not a fly as in sleeping sickness, but a triatomine blood-sucking insect called a kissing bug. It gets its romantic name from its unromantic habit of biting a sleeping person around the mouth. Anyway, this is quite a large insect and easily excluded from nocturnal contact by the use of a mosquito net. It was not as a disease-prevention mechanism that mosquito nets were provided for Millican, it was for comfort, so that they were not being kept awake and constantly pestered by biting insects, or as Millican put it '... and keep the hungry hordes at a safe distance'.

The journey undertaken by Millican was certainly very different to the modern experience, as he was offered various sorts of livestock for sale at every port. It was not just a straightforward offering of livestock either – they were selling monkeys, turtles, tortoises and parrots. Many of these offered species were sold as food, kept fresh by being kept alive. One such food that Millican ate *en route* up the Magdalena was described by him as a large lizard about three and a half feet (about a metre) in length. This we can be fairly sure is one of the species of tegu that is found in South America. These are large lizards ranging in size from about 1 to 1.3m (3¼–4¼ft) in length and are ecologically the equivalent of the monitor lizards from the Far East.

When Millican, our Victorian orchid hunter, had travelled some distance up-river, he decided to take a break from his cruise to finally get to grips with the rainforest. It was at the disembarkation point of Puerto Wilches that he tried the cooked tegu, describing it as quite palatable but there was 'trouble skinning the scaly gentleman'. This casual attitude to the wildlife extended to shooting alligators sunning themselves on shore from the boat, in this case not for food, apparently, but just for sport or fun or boredom. One species that was occasionally shot for food was referred to as a 'large black duck', which was most probably the wild Muscovy duck. Quite how it got the name 'Muscovy' is lost in the mists of time since it was never a native of Moscow or wider Russia. What is interesting is that while Millican calls the cooked meat of this duck tough and unsavoury, this is exactly why it has been domesticated. The meat is nearer to beef than that of ordinary domestic ducks, in both texture and flavour; besides which, as they are significantly larger than the mallard-derived domestic duck, one duck feeds more. Another species that he describes but leaves us without definitive identification was a food fish that the local helpers herded into the shallows of the river, whereupon they dispatched them with machetes. Using his description and the illustration of a scale from one of the fish, it seems likely that these fish were *Salminus affinis*. This may not be a correct identification, as he describes having seen the same fish at seven feet in length (over two metres). This is most likely an assumption on the part of Millican that the very large fish, having a passing resemblance to the fish he had eaten without pleasure, must be the same species.

Once Millican had left the boat at Puerto Wilches and provisioned himself and his guides with local produce, it was time for him to start the big adventure of searching the forest for those orchids that would justify his entire expedition. Initially his searches did not find any plants suitable for his attentions, but there is no concealing his delight in the plants and animals he comes across. This was in stark contrast to his casual use of the pot-shot, while on board the boat, to randomly shoot animals in passing. It is interesting that, although they were nominally following a trail, it was at various points either overgrown or blocked. This occlusion of trails makes transit through a forest, even with a guide, very difficult. More than that, the current author knows that without a track it is not only extremely difficult to traverse a forest, it is almost impossible to back-track without dead reckoning using a map. Maps were a facility that Millican did not have access to simply because a lot of the continent had still to be surveyed; in fact, some of it still does. When he reached the towns of the Andes, one of the orchids that he came across in great profusion was *Cattleya mendelii*. This is still a very popular plant as it is an easy one to grow and it flowers well. Along with *Cattleya* orchids he also found another orchid, *Sobralia leucoxantha*, a large plant with pretty white flowers.

His search for orchids of all sorts was rewarded with a spectacular display of the epiphytic *Cattleya mendelii* that he described as being worth the journey from Europe alone. He collected some plants that must have been very old, as they had 500 bulbs and 100 spikes of flowers. Even though these were massive plants, he got them ready for packing and organised to send them home to England. As Millican travelled further into the Andes he came across the point at which *C. mendelii* gave way to *C. warscewiczii*. So profuse was this epiphyte on some trees that the only thing visible was the profusion of white and mauve flowers with a splash of scarlet from a small *Epidendrum* that shared the space. As he moved inland he arrived at Bogota, which he thought to be a very well-appointed city of considerable wealth, which he demonstrated by reference to being able to buy Peak Frean's biscuits and Benson's watches – J.W. Benson was a premium London watchmaker of the nineteenth century and one of the very few such manufacturers that was not Swiss.

During one of his trips inland, Millican gave a rare example of a practical use for an orchid product. The locals rolled tobacco leaves into their own version of a cigar and to stick the end down they used a little of the sap of *Schomburgkia* orchids, a genus that was named after Robert Schomburgk who spent many years exploring Guyana. Millican regarded this orchid as little more than a botanical oddity.

Collecting was all about removing the rarest and most sought-after orchids and, if they were rare and unusual, they would fetch high prices once shipped home. This led to the temptation of removing all the plants from an area, and giving in to this temptation by the collectors was what so often happened. Removal of all the plants was one thing, but knowing most of them would not survive was quite another, as it was used as the excuse and justification for such destruction. Survival of the collected plants was always going to be an issue. They had to be carried to the coast and packed aboard ship with a significant death toll at every stage, with few plants ever reaching the shores of England alive. A simple description of trying to get the epiphytic *Cattleya trianae*, found by Millican at 4,000ft (about 1,220m) above sea level, down to the coast for shipping home serves to illustrate this. The plants were transported by man and beast to the town of Honda on the Magdelena river, 600 miles (965km) from the sea. This was as far up-river as the steamboats could traverse before being stopped by rapids and the shallowing of the river. From Honda, travel was down-river to Puerto Berrio *en route* to the ocean, where the plants were moved from one ship to another before traversing the ocean. Millican noted in his journal that it was at Puerto Berrio that there was a rough wooden cross dedicated to J.H. Chesterton, the orchid collector for Veitch.

Long before Chesterton met his end he had made the acquaintance of Rosa Carnegie-Williams, who was travelling with her husband and maid, Hills, during 1881. She was very keen on orchids herself and on her return to the UK wrote about her travels as *A Year in the Andes: or A Lady's Adventures in Bogota*, which was published in 1882. In this almost annotated diary she has an entry for 7 October where she visited what she described as the headquarters of Messrs Shuttleworth, Carder and Co. This was a small country house that had been set up for the purpose of cultivating the orchids ready for export to England. Both Shuttleworth and Carder had previously been collectors in Colombia for William Bull, a botanist who had a nursery on the King's Road in London. By 1882 they were independently shipping plants directly for auction by Stevens, auctioneers in Covent Garden and by 1883, although they were still despatching plants directly for auction, they were also selling from their premises on Park Road, Clapham.

While hardship was a common factor for all collectors in exotic destinations, outright aggression was a rarity. Such an event did happen to Millican as he was collecting orchids. For those among us more used to the safety of modern travel, we would have been alerted to the potential problem by being told, when trying to find a crew to take canoes up the River Opon, that six well-armed men would be required. While travelling on the river they were on the receiving end of a shower of misdirected arrows. They could tell the direction from which they had come, but were unable to see even a rustle in the undergrowth. Things went well with Millican and his crew for the next four days until after they had camped and spent a day very successfully collecting plants. That evening they found themselves under attack with one of his group being mortally wounded by being hit with three arrows. Millican and his team took shelter behind trees so that the attackers were coaxed out of hiding into the light of the campfire, at which point the remaining five let loose a volley of rifle fire. The ending of this adventure was that they had to bury their companion in the forest where he had died and returned without further interference from the Opon indigenous people. Millican also suggested that for as long as the Opon indigenous people were in residence, the orchids of the upper reaches of the river will remain undisturbed, certainly by him.

While Millican was delighted to return home and obviously took pleasure in his return, he was drawn back to tropical America by his curiosity and desire for exploration. Before giving way to his urge to travel again in the tropics, he spent many months touring the country giving talks about his travels and promoting his new book. Unfortunately his luck ran out on his final trip as an orchid collector, in 1899, when he was stabbed to death. Like many events, the details are only truly known by the perpetrator and victim; what we can read in various accounts is that he was killed by rivals and, possibly, while stealing rare plants himself. It seems unlikely that this was correct as he was a hunter in the forest and in his writings never gave any indication of being an orchid thief in fact or by implication.

Chapter 5

INCREASING INTEREST IN ORCHIDS FED BY EVENTS: THE GREAT EXHIBITION OF 1851 AND PAXTON'S GLASSHOUSES

With the increased and easy availability of orchids from the end of the twentieth century onwards, it would be natural to imagine that orchids are as popular now as they ever were. This would be a mistake. Sales of *Phalaenopsis* may have increased from the days when individual plants were venerated as rare and exotic, but this is as nothing to how it was in Queen Victoria's reign. Surrounded by mystery and with an air of the exotic, the very nature of orchids, enhanced by their extraordinary biology, rendered them the stuff of legend. Combined with their undoubted beauty, often seen as beacons caught in a shaft of light in the dark forests of tropical exploration, orchids from the tropics of empire were almost destined to cause a stir in Victorian society. There was another side to the fascination with orchids, which was in part perpetrated by the orchid hunters themselves.

As far as we know, it was not a deliberate process of misinformation that suggested orchids were parasites. What seems to have happened was that casual mention of the strange things that had been seen and the strange process of finding these flowers gave rise to the idea. No doubt this was enhanced by rumour and exaggeration. All this was sparked by such floral beauty being found in deep, dark forests where the flowers stood out against the stark backdrop of the undergrowth. As epiphytes growing on trees, some of these plants would have been found in flower high above the ground, apparently without contact with the soil far below, although we now know that soil accumulation does happen in the tree canopy by accumulation of leaves and moss, held in place by the roots of epiphytes. With the Victorian assumption of there being no soil to support the plants, an automatic assumption would then be made that they were in some way parasitic. This would be a natural assumption since the only epiphytic species we have in northern climes is mistletoe, which is parasitic. It was a bit of a step from there to the idea that they were predatory, but aerial roots and the almost pugnacious appearance of some flowers, like *Paphiopedilum*, all helped not so much to fuel the idea, as to not contradict it. This idea of predatory plants – a completely wrong idea – was a product of fiction. It was because of the romance and exotic nature of orchids that it was easy to use them as a subject of power and anxiety – they were victims of their own success. Once they had been built up as weird and enigmatic, they became ideal targets for writers of fiction to utilise as perpetrators of evil intent, almost but not quite sentient, but definitely craving flesh. Writings by some authors were seen as deliberately commercial enterprises, taking advantage of the stories surrounding orchids as predators and parasites, even at the time they were being published.

One convoluted story that was developed to increase sales of an imported orchid species was promulgated during the 1890s. It may well have had elements of truth associated with it, but which bits are hard to discern as the tale became exaggerated in parts and pointedly incorrect in others. The author of this tale was M. Hamelin who was searching for a specific orchid, the lovely pure white *Eulophiella elisabethae* in Madagascar. From his own account he clearly found his quarry and although he never gives a precise location, he does say that he had taken all the plants from the area that were suitable for transport and relocation to Europe. This was done deliberately so that it would be some years before any more became available. He also freely refers to the commercial element of his enterprise, along with the hazards of collecting. He writes: 'If an amateur pays 100s [£5] for a plant of *Eulophiella*, he owns a great prize for a trifle of cost'. He points out that the cost he refers to is the loss of plants in a storm and the sacrifice of human life in collecting them.

It is at this point that Hamelin's story becomes a mixture of fact and fiction. The remaining plants were supposedly protected by his brother-in-law against anyone but Hamelin himself from collecting them. Hamelin explains that the rather strange reference to his brother-in-law stems from the chief of the tribe with which he dealt, sending the chief's brother-in-law with Hamelin as guide. Unfortunately his guide, the chief's brother-in-law, was mauled by what was described as a Madagascar lion, and died of his wounds. This left Hamelin with a dilemma of protocol; as he put it, marry the widow or be 'greased and burnt'. In such a position he did the pragmatic thing and married the widow, thereby making the chief his new brother-in-law. Reports of this traveller's tale appeared in both *The Gardeners' Chronicle* of 1893 and *The Orchid Review* of a year later in 1894. There is a difference between the two reports in the press that is sometimes missed. *The Gardeners'*

Chronicle takes the whole story seriously, requiring further investigation, while *The Orchid Review* has a rather more humorous attitude to a mangled attempt at naming the voracious animal that mauled the chief's brother-in-law.

The Gardeners' Chronicle took its responsibility for the contents of what was published in its pages quite seriously by engaging the counsel of Mr R. Baron from Antananarivo, the capital city of Madagascar. This was quite unusual, as although some form of peer review was seen among some scientific journals it was by no means universal; for example, *The Lancet* did not introduce it until 1976. The other point, of course, is that peer review is usually anonymous, whereas Mr Baron was quite happy to append his name to the review, which if not printed in full, was certainly extensively quoted. The editor does say that they had decided not to publish the strange tale of Hamelin until they had corresponded with a botanist familiar with Madagascar. Mr Baron was not one to mince his words and says in a general sort of way, 'Many, nay, most of the statements made are purely imaginary'.

The predatory animal that was said to have mauled the brother-in-law of the tribal chief was described as being *Protocryptoferox madagascariensis* by Hamelin, the Madagascar lion, 'which crouches in the forks of trees... and watches for its prey'. Baron simply writes of this statement that 'the latter part is pure and unmitigated fabrication'. In *The Orchid Review* of 1894 fun is poked at Hamelin for this strange portmanteau name for his ferocious animal. The actual name of the animal is *Cryptoprocta ferox*, which is the binomial for the fossa, an endemic species of carnivore from Madagascar, which does not get longer than a metre, not counting the tail. The writer in *The Orchid Review* calls it a civet, which is not strictly true, but it is done for comic effect rather than zoological exactitude, as demonstrated in this extract: 'Poor little Civet! Was not thy name of *Cryptoprocta ferox* sufficiently terrible, that it must be thus garbled, and the number of letters doubled, save one?' According to Baron in *The Gardeners' Chronicle*, Hamelin had discovered a new and interesting orchid somewhere in Madagascar, 'The rest is largely and purely Romantic'.

Regardless of the truth or otherwise of the writings of Hamelin, the content was calculated to raise awareness of his orchids in the hope of increasing his revenue from their sale. It may have done this, but it did more than just stimulate local interest in Hamelin's plants. Such stories, created with a hint of truth and an unknown level of embellishment, fuelled excitement in all things associated with orchids and their adventurers, increasing the mystique in which they were held. The development of lurid fiction, never pretending to be anything other than fiction, depicting predatory and parasitic orchids, all added to their allure. In purely practical terms there were other aspects of orchid culture that made a significant difference to how they were viewed and the most important of them all was the ability to keep them alive. It was the influence of the Wardian case, a small, glazed carrying case, used primarily for the transport of plants, that gave the hint that a large-scale glazed area would make it possible to keep tropical orchids healthy, but better still, it would allow for plants to be propagated. As we have described in Chapter 2, larger glass structures were hampered by a punitive tax on the manufacture of glass. Repeal of this tax made it possible to make enough glass to glaze massive stove houses at a reasonable cost, and the greatest of them all was Crystal Palace built for The Great Expedition.

The Great Exhibition of 1851 was significant in many ways, but not least because of the very wide social scale upon which it operated. This was almost inevitable given the number of people that visited the exhibition, and the building and stands that it contained. It is said that about six million people visited the exhibition, which constitutes approximately a third of the population of Great Britain at the time. The exhibition was started and later on run by a commission that had been established at the beginning of 1850, so they had just over a year to complete the process of designing and building the entire project. By March of that year the committee was ready to accept submissions for a building to form the centrepiece of the exhibition, which was tentatively going to be erected in Hyde Park. Rather than just have an open 'anything goes' competition, there were some specifications that had to be met, although these were both vague and open to interpretation. The primary restriction was that the building should be temporary, as it was intended that it would be moved from the park after the exhibition. Besides this, and closely associated with it, the building should be simple to construct and should be cheap both in materials and labour costs of construction. There was one other restriction that focused the minds of the individuals entering the competition and that was the opening date of the exhibition, which was 1 May 1851. Entries came in from around the world, totalling 245 altogether. The range of structures put forward was as varied as the number of entries, but of them all the most interesting two were for glass and iron buildings. One was from France and one from Richard Turner in the UK. Both of these were far too expensive for the committee to consider, as this was supposed to be entirely funded by public subscription. Turner's estimate of costs ran to £300,000, which ruled his design out completely, although he was most definitely not happy with this and made his feelings clearly known to the committee. As the French entry was interesting but, again, far too expensive, they were for a while floundering.

The lack of a suitable entry that was both affordable and could be dismantled afterwards resulted in the exhibition committee putting forward their own design for the public to comment on. Their design was for a brick building, which was ridiculed in the press. It was at this point that Joseph Paxton became sufficiently interested in the project to submit a late design. The first sketch of the idea that would result in renaming an area of London as Crystal Palace was made on a piece of pink blotting paper in a board meeting of the Midland Railway Company; the original paper is now on show at the Victoria and Albert Museum. The detailed plan that Paxton finally provided of an iron and glass construction on a gigantic scale was seen as a credible idea because Paxton had proved his skill having already designed and built the largest glass building in the world at Chatsworth House in 1836. This was the conservatory, sometimes called the Great Stove House in reference to the means of heating it.

It took Paxton just two weeks to produce and cost his design, which came in at £85,800. By comparison, a building project more or less contemporary with the Crystal Palace was Nelson's Column in Trafalgar Square, which was built between 1840 and 1843 and cost £47,000. Cleverly, the builders chosen to construct the Crystal Palace were Fox, Henderson and Co. who were familiar with the use of cast-iron components, being primarily builders of railways and bridges. Perhaps the most surprising thing about the project, considering its size and cost estimate, was that it was completed on time and within budget. This was notwithstanding a sudden change to the plan so that a high atrium could be installed, allowing for the retention of a group of large elm trees within the building that would otherwise have to have been cut down. The possibility of these trees being felled had been a point of considerable public outcry, so retaining them was a marked public relations' event, as well as an acknowledged improvement in the aesthetics of the building. Glass was provided by Chance Brothers of Smethwick, a company of innovative glass-makers; for example, they made lenses for lighthouses and were the only company able to provide the opal glass for the clock faces of Elizabeth Tower housing Big Ben. They had introduced new techniques for making crown glass – the spinning of a disc of molten glass so that centrifugal expansion gave flat panes. Chance Brothers had a stand at the Great Exhibition where they showed to the public a crown glass disc of 66in (1.6m) diameter.

The Great Exhibition, like so much that was done in Victorian Britain, was all about optimism and what was possible. It was this attitude and a belief in the Empire, along with the Crystal Palace building itself full of exotic plants, which helped to fuel interest in growing orchids. A glasshouse on the scale of Crystal Palace fired the imagination of individuals who decided that they could have a glasshouse of their own, although one on a much smaller scale. One of the most significant improvements that the glasshouse industry embraced was the use of cast iron. Although large sheets of glass were available, by modern standards they tended to be thick and consequently heavy; they were also of uneven thickness. Interestingly, it was this uneven thickness – an artefact of manufacture – that gave rise to the now discredited urban myth that glass flows. This hoary old tale came about because while glass was known to have no crystalline structure, what was not realised was that it was an amorphous solid. In the nineteenth century it was thought that, since all solid material was assumed to have a crystal structure and glass did not, it couldn't be a solid. Consequently, by logical reasoning it must be a thick, slow-moving liquid. This idea was supported by finding large, old, plate windows that appeared to be thicker at the bottom than at the top. Making an irrational jump, it was assumed that the glass was slumping slowly downwards. Had they asked the glaziers they would have been told that the glass starts out thicker at one edge and this was the one that was automatically put to the bottom as an aid to balance.

It was the weight of glass that was the driving force, away from wooden frames for glasshouses and towards iron. To support the weight of the glass a wooden frame needed to be thick enough so as not to flex and to support the glass, which being of varying thickness also varied in weight. If a wooden frame was to do this job it would blot out a significant proportion of the light. It was the strength and stiffness of cast-iron beams, as demonstrated at the Great Exhibition, that gave it a major advantage over wood for the smaller scale domestic market.

In the third edition of the newly created and published *The Gardeners' Chronicle* of 1841, priced at 6d, a stove house in the private garden of Mrs Lawrence is described with plans and layout. This had an interior pond, designed to maintain the humidity for the orchids that she grew. There was at the time a certain competitiveness between her and the Duke of Devonshire as to who could cultivate the finest and best of plants, including orchids. Such was the fame of her garden in society that not only did the Duke of Devonshire visit along with Paxton, who was his head gardener at the time, but she was also visited by heads of state, including Queen Victoria and Prince Albert. Louisa Lawrence was married to Sir William Lawrence, a surgeon, and they had five children, two of whom died in childhood. One of the sons, Trevor, became a surgeon and also developed a fascination for horticulture and all things orchidaceous. In fact, he went on to become the President of the Royal Horticultural Society. In the position of President he gave the opening address at the first Royal Horticultural Society Orchid Conference held in May 1885.

With all the information regarding famous orchid collections being given in the newspapers of the time, it was no wonder that growing orchids was seen as a status symbol. Later on, in 1841, as its circulation grew, edition thirteen of *The Gardeners' Chronicle,* was starting to pick up advertisements, an essential part of any financially viable magazine. These were initially simple descriptions of what was on offer and usually at this stage not illustrated, but there was one notable exception to this for a second-hand glasshouse. It was unpriced and described as 'nearly new' with a cast-iron frame with the dimensions of 30ft (9m) long, 18ft (5.4m) wide and 10ft (3m) high. This was a large glasshouse, but it was not the dimensions that make it so interesting, but the way it was described as having glass that was the same as was used at the Great Chatsworth Conservatory. This was obviously a significant selling point as the buildings at Chatsworth were very well known and the Great Conservatory especially so for a very good reason. Until the building of what came to be known as the Crystal Palace for the Great Exhibition, Chatsworth was the home of the largest greenhouse in the world. It stood at 227ft (68m) long, 123ft (37m) wide and 67ft (18.6m) high. It had been started in 1836 and finished in 1840, and was one of Joseph Paxton's designs. The scale is easily appreciated by there being room for two carriages to pass each other on the main route through the glasshouse. There was also an upper gallery to view the trees from above. This was a true stove house, being heated by eight boilers sited underneath the glasshouse and fired by coal. The fuel was delivered by a private underground train and the boilers were controlled so that the temperature ranged from temperate at one end through to subtropical at the other end, the gradations being delineated by doors and partitions. As can be imagined, although the growth of orchids in a house of this type would be exceptional, it was also a very high-maintenance building. This had repercussions when coal became more expensive during World War I, so the Great Conservatory fell into a state of dilapidation. By the time that it became possible to restore the buildings, it was no longer seen as desirable for both financial and social reasons. As a result it was finally demolished in 1920, leaving only a low brick wall – a scar defining a bygone age.

As time went on and the obvious range and circulation of magazines and newspapers, such as *The Gardeners' Chronicle*, increased, illustrated advertisements became more frequent. All manner of horticultural equipment appeared in illustrations, from rolls of wire mesh to ploughs. Of greater significance to the orchid grower of the day were advertisements for glasshouses and stove houses, as well as the boiler systems to run them. By 1860, we can see that while great stove houses such as Chatsworth were being heated by coal, smaller systems were available that used the recently available gas supply. This was a system started in 1813 by the Chartered Gas Light and Coke Company and confined to London, so for many years it was not even an option for country houses.

At this period of the nineteenth century, all of the illustrations used in advertisements were woodcuts. Indeed, well into the twentieth century, advertising material was an artistic product and even photographs when they were used would be re-worked by a commercial artist for publication. With the development of a market for glasshouses came the primary task of the advertisement, which is to make the product desirable. So all of these early illustrations were probably taken from plans of products that may never have been built, but acted as a tantalising vision of what you could have in your garden. Samuel Hereman, of Pall Mall East, was even supplying simple triangular-section glasshouses that could be easily dismantled and moved with the owner should their tenancy lapse. With the shortest advertised Hereman stove house available of 30ft (9m) in length, these were still both large and, at £33, a considerable investment. It can reasonably be assumed that smaller houses were available, but what they wanted to sell were the larger ones, which looked better in advertisement anyway.

With all the new technology becoming available in the Victorian period, like stove heating and iron-framed glasshouses, there was an increasing interest in tropical orchids developing throughout Europe. There was also a large increase in the numbers of people travelling overseas. These trips were either for pleasure, simple exploration or commerce, and this was also helping to develop an understanding that not all orchids from the tropics needed, or required, a hot and steamy atmosphere. Plants were being brought back from these journeys, some of which lived at high altitudes in cooler and drier areas of the globe. Even with the changing face of society and an ever-increasing middle class, keeping orchids was an expensive business. The building of glasshouses was an expression of wealth, in the same was as expensive watches and preposterous cars became in the twentieth century. Once built, it was important for the owner of the glasshouse to have the finest and best plants, and orchids fitted this perfectly.

During this period and late into the twentieth century, printed works were the only method for the wide dissemination of knowledge, so it is hardly surprising that throughout the last 200 years there has been a proliferation of books on growing and looking after orchids. In more recent years this has even extended beyond tropical orchids into terrestrial northern European species. What is generally regarded as the first book about orchid culture was by John Charles Lyons, *Remarks on the Management of Orchidaceous Plants,* of 1843. This book was an attempt to move orchid culture away from being the preserve of the very wealthy and into the hands of the middle classes. This was a bit of an uphill struggle, however, as at the time he was writing, buying any orchid was an expensive and risky business, as just owning one did not guarantee it would survive or flower. Not wishing to relinquish control of his work, and being an enterprising individual, Lyons set up his own publishing house, Ledeston Press, specifically to publish his works. Over the following years there were many books published on the same subject by a wide range of authors, all claiming special knowledge of how to grow orchids and the best way to get them to flower. What they did gradually promulgate was the understanding that just because these plants came from the far south, mainly the tropics, it did not mean that they all required hot and steamy conditions. It was realised that they came from such a wide range of climates that the conditions they needed to thrive were equally varied, and even that a winter resting stage was important for them. The democratisation of both the printed word and education engendered the right conditions for the development of the gardening magazine market, which was also developing during this period, feeding on the growing enthusiasm for gardens and at the same time adding to this enthusiasm.

Education and the ability to read had a long, if informal, history in the UK, with much being done by the Sunday School Movement that was allied to the Churches. It was assumed that by teaching such things as the catechism, knowledge of reading, as well as morals, would be transferred to other aspects of life. It was only in the first half of the nineteenth century that the state began funding schools, although this was in no way a complete system. The well-off still utilised public schools over state schools, which very often came with an automatic entry to one of the ancient universities, regardless of merit. However, in the 1860s, industrialists were becoming increasingly vocal on the subject of education. Their argument in favour of education was the same as it has been ever since – that it was vital to the nation to have everyone educated if the UK was to maintain its excellence in manufacturing. Such an argument by those who generated the wealth of the nation carried considerable weight and so, in 1870, the first piece of educational legislation, the Education Act, was passed into law. This was a modest achievement as the only significant aspect of it was that there would be school boards, which would build and manage schools, although the already existing voluntary schools would continue as before. It was not until ten years later that the 1880 Education Act introduced compulsory school attendance, with every child between the ages of five and ten being expected to attend school. Unfortunately, ten years after the bill had been passed attendance was still only about 82 per cent in that age group. Nonetheless, throughout the nineteenth century, literacy was increasing, and a literate and progressively better educated workforce would read books on all manner of subjects, including the cultivation of orchids.

As part of the increasing interest in orchids, their cultivation and, more specifically, their biology, one of the intriguing aspects that captured people's imagination was pollination. Orchids were so unlike any other group of plants that it was sometimes hard to understand exactly what the pollinators could be and why the flowers needed to be so complicated. Into this arena of complicated orchid biology came Charles Darwin, who had already made a name for himself in 1859 with the publication of *On the Origin of Species*. It was a little later, in 1862, that Darwin published *The Various Contrivances by which Orchids are Fertilised by Insects*. This was followed many years later in 1885 by the second edition, which, by his own admission, was a long time after the first edition had gone out of print. In the interim, Darwin had been in correspondence with Fritz Müller (1822–97), a German biologist who had taken up residence in the south of Brazil where, somewhat confusingly, he was a mathematics' teacher. He had become an ardent supporter of Darwin and his ideas on evolution, which also influenced his own ideas about the origin and function of a form of mimicry that now bears his name.

Müllerian mimicry is the interesting situation where toxic, foul-tasting or well-defended species take on a similar appearance to each other, even though they are not related. Müller worked on various species of butterfly to develop his ideas to explain mimicry. Müllerian mimicry results in a predatory species learning from an interaction with one of the group that every species looking like that will be as difficult to handle or toxic; the knowledge of one is transferred to all similar species. This is the type of mimicry that is used to explain the universal black and yellow of the wasps, you don't need to recognise the species, the warning is implicit in the colours. Darwin's correspondence with Müller was particularly useful as it was of a very practical nature, having been gained by Müller as a biologist in the field.

A similarly famous contemporary botanist who gave Darwin ideas and pause for thought about orchid pollination was Robert Brown (1773–1858). He, Brown, had recognised something of a paradox by suggesting, in 1833, that all orchids had an orchid pollinator. If this was the case it became difficult for him to reconcile this with all the capsules on a dense flower spike producing seeds, this being the condition that would normally only be expected if the flowers were self-pollinated. Brown was a highly accomplished botanist and microscopist and it is for an aspect of his microscopy that he is best remembered. It was his acute observation of pollen grains that was significant, as he noted that small sub-cellular organelles, which were released from the pollen when suspended in water, moved in a random manner but without any apparent external force. Published in 1828, his paper on this subject, with an extraordinary long title, gave rise to what has become known as Brownian motion, a phenomenon that has attracted a lot of mathematical analysis, both statistical and physical, over the years. Both of these papers by Brown, on orchid pollination and what became Brownian motion, demonstrate an interesting aspect of scientific publication in the nineteenth century: both are very long by modern standards. This was not unusual at the time and the premium given to space in modern publications was not an issue in Victorian England. This has the interesting result that, in many of these writings, details are given of events and problems not necessarily considered important to the scientific content, but of potential interest to the reader anyway. What such extraneous details do is render the whole article as a window on to the world in which the scientist worked and the different standards by which they operated.

When writing in book form, the nineteenth-century naturalists and scientists were quite happy being conversational with their readers, and Charles Darwin was no exception to this. So, in his second edition of *The Various Contrivances by which Orchids are Fertilised by Insects*, he relates the tail of *Angraecum sesquipedale*. This orchid is native to Madagascar with flowers that Darwin so very clearly and evocatively described as being 'like stars formed of snow-white wax'. These self-same flowers have a spur at the back of the flower of, as he puts it, 'astonishing length'. At the end of this spur is a nectary and the conundrum with regard to this orchid was two-fold. The first was what could be the pollinator of this orchid and the other was what could possibly reach the nectar at the end of the spur? While we realise that the nectar is a lure, it was not always obvious that this was the case in orchids. When Darwin was asked about the pollination of this orchid, he thought through the possible answers. Using his knowledge of both plants and insects from around the world he postulated the existence of a sphinx moth, what would now be called a hawk moth, that had a tongue that was between ten and eleven inches long (about 22–25cm). The existence of such an insect was regarded as extremely unlikely when it was first suggested because most of the known species of hawk moths had tongues that were about the length of the body. This limit on tongue length was associated with the need for moths and butterflies to coil up the proboscis when not in use. So with his detractors thinking Darwin was wrong, the situation continued until Fritz Müller reported having found a sphinx moth in south Brazil that had a proboscis that was just about the correct length. This only demonstrated the possibility of very long-tongued hawk moths, as Brazil is a long way from Madagascar, where such an insect had still not been seen. It was said that the moth rolled its proboscis in a spiral of about twenty turns, which, of course, raises the question of what the mechanism is for the moth to be able to extend the tongue to its full length. It was some time later that a substantial hawk moth, *Xanthopan morganii*, was discovered to be the natural pollinator of the orchid *Angraceum sesquipedale*, with a very long proboscis capable of reaching the nectar at the end of the flower spurs. While Darwin's insight and clarity of thought is undoubted, this did not easily translate to the written form, so his writing style can be quite hard going in places for the modern reader.

This complicated ecological relationship of moth and orchid was recognised by Darwin as being a dependency such that, as he put it, if the 'great moths were to become extinct in Madagascar, assuredly the *Angraceum* would become extinct'. He also noted the converse, though not in such dire tones, noting only that the loss of the orchid would be a serious loss to the moth, the assumption being that while the moth is the only pollinator of the orchid, the orchid is not the only supplier of food to the moth. Such accounts of complicated interactions between plant and insect would be a source of wonder in any family of plants, but in orchids it hit a new mark, underlining the mysteries surrounding tropical orchids and their life-styles. For orchid collectors, rather than collectors of garden plants, the complex life of orchids was all part of the pleasure and mystique of growing them. Better still, reading about the complexities of orchids, as much as what was not known as what was, surrounded the plants with yet more mystery and romance, which increased their desirability.

It was this complicated relationship between orchids and insects, with orchid plants seen as simultaneously unprepossessing vegetation and spectacularly beautiful flowers, that drove forward the appearance of orchids in literature. It is probably true that as a group orchids have appeared more often than any other plant family in fiction. On the other hand, considering the size of the family, the appearance as a proportion of the number of species is probably not so high. However, what does stand out is that, although orchids have no truly parasitic or predatory members, they are very often represented as both. They also appear as sinister motivators of explorers and adventurers. One such of these stories is *The Priceless Orchid* by Percy Ainslie, published in 1892. In this story, the protagonist, Jack, is informed of the task to find the eponymous plant on page six, but does not locate the orchid until page 193. The space in between these fictional beginning and ending events is filled with various adventures, making the orchid merely a vehicle for an adventure story such as would be found in any amount of tales of daring action. There are a number of interesting aspects to this book, most notably that while the search is apparently for *Cattleya dolosa*, the subtitle of 'A Story of Adventure in the Forests of Yucatan' rules out finding it at all, as it is only known from central Brazil. We can accept such bending of biological distributions in the same way that we can guess that Ainslie never visited the tropics or he would be unlikely to have said, 'The drowsy hum of the mosquitoes lulled Jack into a dreamy state'. I don't think mosquitoes have ever lulled anyone into a dreamy state. All these are just fictional devices to enhance a story that the *Spectator* said in a short review of December 1892: 'There is enough of the unexpected in the narrative to make it a decidedly interesting story'.

While *The Priceless Orchid* was primarily an adventure story where the orchid itself was only a small player, at the other extreme are stories where orchids become the central player in a tale of horror. Although only a short story, *The Flowering of the Strange Orchid* by H.G. Wells is a good example of a predatory orchid plant taking centre stage in a story. Originally published in 1894 in a magazine and in book form in 1905, Wells refers to the real orchid genera of *Vanda* and *Dendrobium*, but also a fictional one. By using a name, *Palaeonophis*, which he had made up but close to *Phalaenopsis*, it gave the story a verisimilitude of truth. In *The Flowering of the Strange Orchid*, Winter Wedderburn buys a collection of dormant orchid bulbs, hoping that one would be new to science. One of the bulbs sprouts, producing a flower with a heady scent that drugs anyone near enough to smell it, after which the aerial roots move into action, sapping the blood from the victim.

An earlier version of the idea of a predatory orchid was published in *The Strand Magazine* in 1898. This was called *The Purple Terror* and was written by Fred Merrick White when he was not quite 30 years old. It tells, in what can only be described as melodramatic Victorian prose, the story of jingoistic Americans travelling through Cuba who anger a local man. This results in him leading them to a tree where a predatory orchid grows, which was famed locally for capturing unwary travellers that sleep beneath the branches of the tree. This short story is an early example of being able to make plausible a carnivorous plant by referring to it as an orchid, that most enigmatic group of plants.

Such stories were going to fuel the interest and even excitement associated with orchids. Some of them, such as *The Priceless Orchid* may even have encouraged individuals to become explorers, although that can never be proved. The converse is also true, rare orchids that seemed able to produce the most wonderful blooms from ragged foliage would have helped set them firmly in the world of fiction.

One of the results of this spiralling interest in all things orchidaceous was what has been occasionally referred to as 'orchidomania' or 'orchidelerium'. This has been used, incorrectly, to align it with the phenomenon of tulipomania that happened among the Dutch a century earlier. Tulipomania involved a relatively large number of people in the Netherlands for the short period between 1634 when it started and the beginning of 1637 when prices collapsed. The particular social conditions that created the strange state of tulipomania have been long debated, but what is undeniable is what took place. This was an enormous increase in the price of rare tulip bulbs, these being seen as an investment. There are, however, several reasons why it was short-lived and could have been seen-through right from the start. The bulbs that were bought were seen as an investment, but it is a truism that once propagated, by bulb division or better still by seed, the value of the initial investment would decline rapidly, as every owner could propagate their own. Ignoring this turned a normal set of transactions into what was, in effect, a pyramid-selling scheme and became regarded as the first example of a speculative bubble, where the price exceeds the intrinsic value of the product. The differences of this with orchidomania, if it can be described as such, in the nineteenth century are considerable. The first major difference is that while high prices were sought and paid for orchid plants, the orchids were bought by the individuals who would grow them because ownership was only part of the process, consummation of their investment was when the owner managed to get the orchid to flower. There was pride in ownership, not just money to be made. The other aspect was that while tulips could be grown from seed, with a few exceptions, orchids at that time could not.

With an interest among the wealthy for more and more orchids from ever more distant tropical lands, the arrival of *Remarks on the Management of Orchidaceous Plants* in 1843 written by J.C. Lyons was quite a revelation. Although this was an early publication in the history of orchid management, it was not the cultivation notes that were most significant, but the attitude to cultivation that was to make a difference to their popularity. John Charles Lyons was born in 1792, the only child of Irish parents; his father, though Irish, claimed Huguenot descent. He was educated in England at a boarding school and then at Pembroke College, Oxford, from which he did not graduate as he inherited the family property in Ireland. There is no doubt that he was a practical man, as he built the boilers to heat his glasshouses and also, on a more delicate scale, built clocks. Considering his emphasis in his work on cultivating orchids, his indifference to the plight of the starving during the Irish famine of 1845–49 sits somehow at odds with his almost egalitarian attitude to orchid cultivation. In *Remarks on the Management of Orchidaceous Plants* he makes much of the modest cost of plants and the ease with which they can be grown if his instructions are followed. Lyons definitely had a different attitude to previous authors by assuming that the reader would be the grower, rather than the person who would inform their gardener on the content of the books and journals they read. This was in contrast with previous writings that had, by implication if not statement, suggested that orchids were for the wealthy and titled who would employ a gardener to do the actual work. So although it was a wealthy clientele that initially supported high and inflated prices, it would be the less well-off with a more modest disposable income that would not only keep orchid growing as a hobby, but would develop the myths and legends of rare and exotic orchids from around the globe, from countries that they were only familiar with in atlases. This exotic element also made stories of giant orchids and predatory species all the more plausible.

The proliferation of printed material during the nineteenth century made it easy for individuals to purchase books and the proliferation of books was closely associated with the availability of mass-produced paper. Until the end of the eighteenth century, paper was made by hand, more specifically, page by page. In 1799 this changed with the patent being issued in France for a continuous paper-making machine. At a stroke, paper-making had been mechanised and was no longer carried out sheet by sheet. The original inventor was unable to develop it at home in France due to a commercial dispute with his partner, so he sent the idea to England. In London, finance was secured by two brothers, stationers by trade, Sealy and Henry Fourdrinier. They improved the paper-making machine to such an extent that it became known as the Fourdrinier machine. The first one was installed at a paper mill in Hertfordshire in 1803, with others quickly following. This continuous paper-making process was essential for a burgeoning book market to keep the costs down, but more than that, the ideas in the design of the equipment paved the way for other machines that would produce a continuous product from a dissociated or molten material like glass or steel. There is no doubt that with the advent of what became mass-produced books, dissemination of information about orchid culture became readily available. Nonetheless, it seems likely that there was another aspect to the fascination for orchids, which played a considerable part in their popularity.

In his seminal work *The Orchidaceae of Mexico and Guatemala,* which achieved fame for its size as much as for its content, James Bateman wrote lyrically in the introduction regarding the charm of orchids. It was here as well that he seems to have coined the term orchido-mania. In true nineteenth-century form, the sentence runs for many lines extolling the delights of orchids and then concludes with:

> ...in short, which might attract the man of pleasure by its splendour, the virtuoso by its rarity, and the man of science by its novelty and extraordinary character. It is, we are convinced, on this principle we can attempt to understand the *Orhido-Mania*, which now pervades all (and especially the upper) classes, to such a marvellous extent.

Once coined and later contracted to orchidomania it became an accepted description of collectors. Similar words that appear from time to time are orchidelirium and orchidfever. These are in many ways pejorative terms, used to belittle the status in some way of those who grow these plants, as if what they do is in some manner an illness.

The idea of a collective mania, rather than a private one, and it was never clear whether the phrase 'orchidomania' referred to an individual or the group consciousness of the age, was often applied in a negative way. As a term it has certainly been misapplied at various times, mainly by those that see the word and do not consider the social context of the time in which it originally appeared. The origin of our modern ideas of collective mania, of any sort, can be traced back to at least the start of the nineteenth century and the work of Gabriel Tarde (1843–1904), but really formed into a coherent idea with Gustave Le Bon (1841–1931) who wrote *Psychologie des Foules*, a book that was translated as *The Crowd: A Study of the Popular Mind* in 1896. In this he describes a fixed belief, of the second type as he calls it, thus 'these are transitory the beliefs, changing opinions, the outcome, as a rule, of general conceptions, of which every age sees the birth and disappearance'. Put more concisely, fads and fashions come and go. Such fashions are dependent upon a public, that is the crowd, but for the individual the situation seems rather different. It is the idea of keeping up with others that fuels this obsession, as does the development of aspirational desires. No doubt to some extent a fascination with orchids did have a root in this, but for all growers with a greenhouse it would have been a status symbol to be able to say they had an orchid, the most difficult of plants to grow. This, then, was less a mania than a statement of ability, the ability to grow the best and most difficult.

Chapter 6

COLLECTORS, ILLUSTRATORS AND BOTANICAL MAGAZINES

Before the advent of photography, more specifically in this age of digital images, which are so easy to capture and so easy to manipulate, the very best images of orchids were those rendered by artists. It was botanical art that familiarised people with orchids from overseas. There were only two ways that a plant could be seen in full flower: the first was to visit a botanical garden at the right time of year and witness the natural exuberance of blooming, or to gaze on the rendering made by a botanical artist. In this respect it is very easy to lose sight of the change that photography has made. In the twentieth century and onwards, photographs of almost every species known to man have been photographed multiple times. In the nineteenth century, a rare and exotic orchid may flower, or have only been seen in flower once in the wild, and painted at that exact moment, captured in watercolours, but only as a single image. This, then, was the immense value of botanical illustration: it had a pre-eminent position in recording an orchid, not only in its flowering glory, but of the seed pods and mode of growth, as well as the associated plant species found with it. It was often a well-executed watercolour illustration in conjunction with a dried specimen that was used as the basis for a full botanical description and appending a name to a plant.

When field guides are being used, the painted illustration still has a major contribution to make. This value to the person trying to identify a species in the field resides in the nature of variation within a species. Photographs are the record of an individual, not of what the species as a whole looks like. With drawn illustrations the emphasis can be directed to the diagnostic features and taken away from the less relevant. The reason for the takeover of images by photography from watercolours comes back to one of cost. With modern techniques of digital photography the cost of photography has come down even further, as the image cost is amortised over the capital cost of equipment, rather than disposables, as is the case with film cameras. Notwithstanding the cost of equipment, each image has an insignificant cost associated with it. In contrast to this, the time and skill required to produce a good-quality watercolour image of an orchid is significant. Consequently, it needs a financial investment out of proportion to the cost of the published work, whether that is book or magazine. It is also true that there are not many people who can produce a suitable watercolour image at any price. There are quality productions of non-photographic works published on a regular basis, but these do tend to be expensive in comparison with photographic productions. Photographic illustrations also have a disadvantage in that photographs do not have an intrinsic top and bottom, so if the publisher is not familiar with the subject, they can easily be printed upside down. Hand-painted watercolours of orchids destined for publication nearly always come with a signature and often a hand-produced caption on the plate itself, making accidental inversion a most unlikely event.

Photography as a publisher's tool only became available long after the invention of photography itself. Initially, book and magazine illustrations were woodcuts or engravings, depending on the required detail, which could then be hand-coloured to add extra interest to the finished product. Colouring would also add some cost to the final publication, so was not routinely used unless the subject needed it, which, of course, orchids do. Simple black and white, halftone, printed images started appearing in newspapers and periodicals around the middle of the nineteenth century, but they were of varying success and the technique used to produce the image would vary with time and development. While publishers were searching for a sound and reliable technique that could reproduce photographs, this was as much motivated by cost-saving for the publisher as it was by a desire for the instant and 'from life' images of great events. In books, the spill-over from magazines and newspapers took shape right at the end of the nineteenth century, in the 1890s. These early photographic reproductions did tend to be of relatively low resolution and also in black and white. This last aspect is not so surprising as it was only black and white photography that was being used outside studios. Alternatively, the aspect of early photographs that is sometimes missed is that cameras were expensive and there was no such thing as a budget lens. With camera lenses conforming to Keplerian optics, that is the image being projected on to the film in what to us would be upside down, it is possible to have few, very high-quality pieces of glass in a lens. Coupling this with a film format much larger in size than the later 35mm, which became the standard in the second half of the twentieth century, gave very high-resolution black and white image. These images could easily stand up to modern scrutiny, until that is, they are printed using a screen to change the original continuous tone image into a halftone one for publication.

So while photography and printed photographs struggled to make headway until the twentieth century, magazines and gardening papers were well under way a century earlier, relying on woodcuts for illustrations. To reach a large market, gardening magazines would need to appeal to the bulk of amateur gardeners. This was not going to happen for some considerable time after the establishment of a gardening press, as buying a gardening magazine moved from a casual purchase when funds allowed to a feeling of needing the magazine for new and exciting information.

The first gardening magazines were aimed squarely at the professional gardener or, more specifically, the employer of the professional gardener who would then pass on any relevant information to the employee. There are many reasons for this, not least the perceived level of reading ability of agricultural workers. We know that in 1800 male literacy was at about 60 per cent and female literacy at 40 per cent. By 1900, literacy was at 97 per cent for both sexes. This figure does not tell the whole story, as the reading age would vary widely, depending on the education level and, of course, reading practice. Whether it was coincidental or one drove the other, one thing we do know that affected the rise and development of the gardening press was stamp duty on printed material. This was a flat charge based on the number of printed pages and the amount of advertising, so cheap magazines and papers had a disproportionate part of their cost made up of tax. This tax was started in 1712, when there were more pamphleteers than newspaper publishers. The taxation level was increased further in 1797. Under pressure to reduce regulation of the press, and to increase literacy among the general population, it was reduced in 1836 and finally abolished in 1855.

Besides the primary market, which must have been relatively small, there was a perceived need for gardening advice for amateur gardeners who had greater than average gardens and resources. The corollary of this was that people with small gardens were not really catered for. This was a time when a lot of those moving into suburban areas found they had a garden, which they had never had before. What they wanted and needed was basic advice. When individuals wanted broad help with gardening they tended to have to resort to books, and they were fine for this, but there was a developing market for something different. This unquenched thirst in the market was for magazines that were instructional and, just as importantly, gave details of all the new plants that were arriving from overseas. This flow of new species, which included, to a very small extent, orchids, was gaining momentum and becoming difficult for the nurseries to disseminate information about. The large numbers of exciting new plants not previously seen in the UK that were becoming available could only be sold if they were known about by the general public. Consequently, it was the advertising of these imported plants that made the commercial production of papers and magazines viable. With the growing interest in gardening there was also an increase in the need for sheds and greenhouses, which also featured extensively in the advertising sections of the new magazines.

Notwithstanding the punitive newspaper tax of the time, one of the earliest and longest running magazines was *Curtis's Botanical Magazine*. This was first published, under the name of the *Botanical Magazine*, by William Curtis in 1787 at the relatively high cost of one shilling (Chapter 3 has more details about pre-decimal currency), but even at that price the initial run sold a reported number of about 3,000 copies. This exceptional magazine is of particular interest for two main reasons. The first is that it started as a beautifully illustrated magazine upon which its reputation was based and it continued in that vein. The second reason for its importance is that it ran in its original form until 1983, after which, with a small break, it was taken over and re-launched by Kew. It should not be imagined that it was only illustrations that made the name of *Curtis's Botanical Magazine*, as it also carried details of stove houses and greenhouses, which were still quite rare at the start of the nineteenth century.

There were many other gardening magazines produced in the early nineteenth century, many of which had a very short life-cycle. Whether this was directly due to newspaper duty or not is uncertain, but it could not have helped. These magazines had names such as *Botanical Register*, *Botanic Garden*, *Floral Cabinet* and *Botanical Cabinet*. *Botanical Cabinet* was started by Conrad Loddiges as an unashamed publicity vehicle for the plants and products that were available from his nursery – a sort of early catalogue, but one that you paid for. All of these magazines were expensive and generally not what a modern audience would call a gardening magazine. They were illustrated documents designed for the most part to keep, while simultaneously being very text-dense. So although they were magazines, they were worlds apart from the modern manifestation of a magazine. These were meant to be read and acted as a source of enlightening entertainment, as well of specific gardening information. It was this aspect of 'keep it for reference' that has left us with a surprisingly large number of bound copies in private hands, which come up for sale from time to time. Needless to say, those that do come on the market tend to be of great value, commanding significant prices. One of the other aspects of these early magazines was that they did not conform to the modern idea of a weekly or a monthly publication. They tended to appear irregularly, presumably the timing of publication being dependent upon when there were enough pages to print a complete magazine. They also tended to be on subscription only, requiring six months' or a year's payment in advance.

An alternative to an irregular or unpredictable publishing rate was to have the magazine launched as a quarterly and this was exactly how the *Gardener's Magazine* first appeared. First published in 1826, it was produced as a professional gardener's magazine, which was started by

John Loudon (1783–1843). The early circulation was astonishing at 4,000 since the cost of it was 5 bob – a bob being slang for a shilling. Over a relatively short time, production of the magazine became more frequent and at the same time the price came down. When it became a monthly magazine, it was 1s 6d. Even with the increasing success of the magazine, by the time of his death Loudon was in severe personal debt. Although it was originally designed specifically for professional gardeners, after his death, his wife wrote that she had considered that it had also encouraged amateur gardeners as well. In the way that the term was used, the idea of professional and amateur sticks strictly to the idea of paid or not paid for the work. One of Loudon's stated aims was to put right the perceived problem of neglected agriculture after the Napoleonic wars. It had become quite clear that between 1803 and 1815 the war against Napoleon had reduced the agricultural workforce considerably. Because at the time agriculture was human-driven, and there was no replacement for manpower, loss of people from the workforce meant less agriculture. This was also true of gardens that had previously employed gardeners. As a direct consequence of this drop in the available workforce, there were a lot of neglected gardens and orchards. It was, therefore, Loudon's intention to increase knowledge of gardening as a practical activity, as well as to make money from his magazine. He was also very interested in the proper training of gardeners, a subject that was included in his magazine alongside reports of flower shows. *Gardener's Magazine* was setting a precedent and a model for later magazines, even though it only lasted from 1826 until 1843.

John Loudon was entrepreneurial in his business attitude, but had a tendency to be rather loose with other people's work at the same time, there being suggestions of plagiarism. For this he received considerable criticism, the suggestion being that his writing was not original and he was just putting forward ideas as his own, which were not. But, as Joseph Paxton pointed out, Loudon was not the first to write on a subject implying the ideas were original and their own.

The formulation and continuation of many of the gardening titles available in the nineteenth century were totally dependent upon the vision of the magazine founder, who was most likely also the editor of the magazine. Just as in more recent times, when ownership and editorial policy changed, so, too, could the emphasis of the magazine. For example, the grandly titled *Horticultural Register* moved more towards natural history when the magazine had a change of editor in 1835. This not only seems to have changed the direction of the magazine, but also seemed to help it to lose its way, with the result that it folded in 1836, having only started in 1831. This, of course, is a phenomenon that is familiar today when magazines alter direction and lose readership. Of course, this was not the only cause of a magazine to collapse and during the nineteenth century gardening magazines came and went quite often.

This was especially so during the first half of the century. Niche publications were especially susceptible to this. For example, the *Gardeners' and Foresters' Record* ran for only three years.

The nineteenth century was a particularly fertile time for gardening magazines with a large potential readership and on the basis of this they were seen as good financial prospects. There were several people during this period who were serial editors, frequently starting papers and magazines. Such an individual was George Glenny (1793–1874), at various times a watchmaker, florist and publisher. During the nineteenth century he started several papers such as the *Horticultural Journal* and *Gardeners' Gazette*. There were several titles started by Glenny that developed and changed both name and direction at various times. As a florist and grower of cut flowers himself, Glenny also started floral societies. Probably the most significant of his activities, and certainly the most influential, was that he started the *Gardeners' Gazette*. This was a weekly newspaper costing 6d that started in 1837 and continued in this form until 1844 when it went through the first of a number of name changes. However, the original *Gardeners' Gazette* broke new ground as the first such newspaper for gardeners, rather than landowners. Glenny was known as an argumentative individual, who made public his dislike and disdain through his magazines. As originator, proprietor and editor, Glenny continued his open animosity in the pages of *Gardeners' Gazette*. Such was his argument with John Lindley, who at the time was Assistant Secretary of the Horticultural Society of London, that in 1839 Glenny was banned from the Horticultural Society shows. Eventually Glenny sold the paper, staying on as a paid editor for a while until he resigned and John Loudon became editor.

The weekly publications that George Glenny started showed the way forward to other publishers. Even so, during Queen Victoria's reign, there were a lot of new publications starting, most of which only ran for a short period before folding. The great success of the gardening newspaper format started by George Glenny almost inevitably spawned copies and rivals. Without a doubt, one of the most significant and long-lived of these was *Gardeners' Chronicle*. This was a publication with a most interesting history, surviving the vicissitudes of the twentieth century with two world wars, not by subscription or being associated with a society, but because it educated and entertained. It ran as an independent title from 1841 until 1969, when it was merged with the *Horticultural Trade Journal* and lost its identity. This extremely popular gardening paper was a vehicle for many articles on orchids and orchid care. This may seem unusual for a general interest paper, but the whole of the gardening press had helped to not only increase interest in gardening among those who did their own, rather than employing a gardener, but also changed attitudes. So although orchids were still very expensive, they became an aspirational plant, as did owning a glasshouse. Although not prolifically illustrated, and certainly not in colour, *The Gardeners' Chronicle* gradually became very well known for its advertisements of all sorts. These ran from classified advertisements for gardeners wanted, through to stove houses and glasshouses, many of which were designed by Joseph Paxton. That it was not heavily illustrated helped to keep the costs down, which is easily seen when compared to other magazines that were sold, like today, on the basis of their illustrations. So *Gardeners' Chronicle*, which was started by Joseph Paxton and John Lindley in 1841, with sixteen pages of text and advertisements, was sold at 6d. By 1876 this had come down to 5d and by 1898 it was 3d, reflecting the reducing cost of paper and printing. By contrast, *Paxton's Magazine of Botany*, edited by Joseph Paxton, had four colour plates and sold at 2s, that is, four times the price of *The Gardeners' Chronicle* at 6d. Similarly, the *Pomological Magazine*, all about fruit and edited by John Lindley, also had four colour plates and cost 5s. Of course, circulation may have been a big influence on the cost of the magazine. By 1851, *Gardeners' Chronicle* had a reported circulation of 6,500 weekly.

Content of *The Gardeners' Chronicle* reflected the interest in orchids of the two founders, Lindley and Paxton, with such articles as 'Orchids for the Million', a long series of articles described in more detail in Chapter 7. There were also regular reports of the costs of orchids at the auction house of J.C. Stevens in Covent Garden. These were mostly newly imported plants and although they did not reach record prices, they were certainly high. So, in 1851 plants were mostly sold at around £1 each, although some went to well over £7, which was quite a sum at the time. Although they were recorded in *Gardeners' Chronicle* as plant-selling auctions, they were equally well known during this period, and even more so now, as auctioneers of natural history specimens, curiosities and antiquities. One such curiosity would have been the covered van that was 'built expressly for the conveyance of Plants to and from the Flower Shows' that they had for sale.

The increasing awareness of orchids generated by *The Gardeners' Chronicle*, and other general gardening magazines and newspapers, was underlined by reports on the Horticultural Society orchid shows. This also brought up a point in correspondence to the editor regarding the raising of plants. An observer of the shows is quoted as saying, 'After all, one sees year after year nearly the same plants'. This is in line with the observation that success seemed to go with the larger plants at the expense of equally well-grown smaller plants. It would be expected that well-grown plants will simply get bigger and, therefore, every year effectively get 'better' by the standards of the shows, which, of course, is why they win. This situation changed towards the end of the nineteenth century, as there were not so many new, large plants coming through, because imports that did arrive were smaller, often with only a single growing shoot and would take many years to become fine, established plants. The other aspect of these show results that can be seen is that, even with different plants, the same names keep appearing. This is not to imply that it was a closed shop, but simply that there were hurdles for the aspiring grower to overcome and these were primarily associated with the time required to produce a large plant. There would also be questions of heating and space, and it should not be forgotten that for many of these stove houses they were kept at higher temperatures for plants and with greater expense than most of the population could afford in their own houses.

During the nineteenth century, in all manner of gardening magazines, the number of advertisements for stove houses and greenhouses of all sizes, built either in the style of, or influenced by, Crystal Palace in Hyde Park, was huge. This clearly indicates that the Great Exhibition and Crystal Palace were creating a market for these products among the middle classes who wanted to be a part of gardening society. *The Gardeners' Chronicle* of Saturday 3 May 1851 describes how wonderful the whole event was, having been opened by Queen Victoria on 1 May 1851. Later, in the same issue, the associated *Agricultural Gazette*, which was a fully integrated part of the paper, also reported the opening of Crystal Palace in Hyde Park. They were rather more fulsome in their description:

> The Palace of Glass is open. The Queen of England in her Glittering robes, and attended by her plumed and diamonded courtiers and gorgeous array has been there, enthroned like an Arabian 'Fair One', in her 'Hall of Light'.

All of the illustrations found in the newspapers and magazines during the nineteenth century were woodcuts or, rarely, engravings, until what was probably the first photograph appeared on the cover of *Harmsworth Magazine* in 1898. It was a long and tortuous process of development that took photography through to becoming the mainstay of print magazines.

Although recognition of light-sensitive materials had been noted for centuries, it was just that, light sensitive, there was no notion of forming an image using the rudimentary chemistry. Although, quite rightly, the subject of photography concentrates on light-sensitive chemistry, it should be remembered that the camera itself is just as important. Until an image could be formed in focus in a flat plane, no amount of chemistry was going to create a picture. During the eighteenth and nineteenth centuries, optics advanced considerably, making available high-quality lenses for telescopes that leant themselves to be adapted for cameras. Early photographs, the ones made after experimental trials, are of very good resolution. This is due to two major influences: the quality of the optics and the size of the picture. The most popular size of camera film in the twentieth century was referred to as 35mm. This film was 36mm × 24mm, which is very much smaller than the half-plate film of

11cm × 14cm and even smaller than a plate camera with a film size of 16.5cm × 21.5cm. So good-quality optics and large film format means high-resolution images. Getting the photograph on to a page, though, is quite another story.

The first printing of black and white photographs in magazines and books started early in the twentieth century; if it was felt necessary, these could be hand-coloured. Later on colouring would involve multiple wood blocks, each with its own coloured ink that would need to be accurately overlaid on the same image. Before colour photography was routinely used in books and magazines, the use of black and white images for displaying orchids was tried, but it had limited appeal. The reason for this is that orchid plants are normally grown for the flowers, so in black and white it would only be the shape that was represented. Since orchid flowers are sought for their colour, it seemed reasonable that a water-colour of the flowers would serve far better as an indication of its beauty. Even in the 21st century there is both scope and desire for the crafted image of plants that goes far beyond the photograph. An example of this is Chris Thorogood of Oxford University Botanic Garden, who researches a parasitic plant with the largest flower in the world, *Rafflesia*. While doing this he also creates painted images, as well as photographs, of the flowers. These help put them into scale and context with a clarity hard to match with a photograph.

With the rise of the general gardening magazine market, so arose, in parallel, a specialist plant magazine market. Setting up and publishing a magazine was simultaneously an expensive and complicated business. At the time, digital assistance was unknown, and typesetting and printing were skilled and expensive activities. The compositor would produce the page of type as a whole from individual letters, formed on metal backing blocks, which are then called sorts. These were then formed into lines in the composing stick, which were then bound together into a page frame. The skill of the compositor included being able to read the type right to left, made up of back to front letters. Changes in technology were designed to make the whole process quicker, easier and more accurate, up to the modern computer-generated type, but during the heyday of the orchid magazines, it was the compositor who kept the presses rolling.

Many of the orchidologist magazines were relatively late to the table, starting after the perceived high point of the excitement engendered by orchid hunters and the plants that they sent home from far-flung parts of the world. One of the reasons for this was that, while news of rare orchids appeared in general magazines such as *The Gardeners' Chronicle*, and even the general press, these were exceptional cases reflecting exceptional plants. The bulk of those who were actually growing orchids were still the well-off, and the total number of people growing orchids still quite small. While the general public were mesmerised by orchids and those who were lucky enough to grow them, most were not growing them.

Those who were growing them were obsessed with the new and exotic flowers, so the overall market for specialist orchid magazines at that time was really quite small. As the nineteenth century progressed and the middle classes expanded, so too did the number of individuals who grew orchids, and slowly, little by little, did the market for orchid magazines.

With the intense interest in orchids and their cultivation, stimulated by tales of travels in far distant places, specialist orchid magazines started to appear. These were encouraged indirectly by books such as Fredrick Boyle's *About Orchids*, of 1893, which had started out as a collection of modified essays that had originally appeared over several years in several periodicals such as *The Standard, Saturday Review, St James's Gazette, National Review* and *Longman's Magazine.* He does describe them to be 'no more than chat of a literary man about orchids' and while much factual information is imparted, the literary aspect does tend to interpret some of the information loosely. In a similar way, the very influential *Orchid Growers Manual* published in 1853, ran for many editions and certainly influenced individuals to take up orchid growing. There were many such beautifully illustrated books, which increased the interest in growing these plants. Although in the early part of Victoria's reign these were all about tropical orchids, curiosity helped to gradually shift interest among the more botanically inclined towards our native species. Needless to say, this did not detract from interest in tropical species, but somehow added to it. This was epitomised in *British Orchids, containing an exhaustive description of each species and variety* by Angus Duncan Webster published in 1898. Although he did pass comment on some aspects of orchid importation, he was more than happy to dig up wild orchids for his garden, a local form of orchid hunting that certainly made inroads into the local orchid populations to their long-term detriment.

All of these magazine articles, and books that have often been based on them, gradually created the idea that a magazine dedicated to orchids would be of both financial and spiritual value. The earliest of this new breed of publication was *The Orchid Review.* This is seen as the first all-orchid publication, but more than that, it has outlasted all of its contemporaries, even though it has had some rocky periods during its existence. It started out in 1893 under the editorship of Robert Allen Rolfe (1855–1921), who was to have a long association with the magazine. Rolfe was a botanist who started working at Kew in 1879; it was while he was there that he became the first curator of the orchid herbarium. It was at this time that, while he was working at the herbarium, he founded *The Orchid Review* and became its first editor. Interestingly, his name did not appear in the magazine, which was devoted to cultivation and hybridisation of orchids, probably because he wrote most of it. Beyond these cultivation notes, there were extensive descriptions of visits to notable collections. The natural interest in hybridisation of orchids, sometimes involving not just species of the same genus but species of different genera as well, culminated in 1909 with the production of *The Orchid Stud Book*. This was a listing of all the hybrids with parentage that had been recorded until the end of 1907. The original magazine had been produced monthly and in 1901 cost 6d. With increasing costs, especially after World War I, and with more illustrations being included, the magazine became bi-monthly. During 1921, Rolfe was taken suddenly ill and subsequently died; he had edited 28 volumes up to that point, more or less single-handedly, so his sudden loss stopped production for the first six months of 1921.

With the death of the first and, so far, only editor of *The Orchid Review*, decisions had to be made regarding its future. So, in 1920, the basis of the magazine changed. Bearing in mind the success of the magazine, and the problems thrown up by being dependent upon a single person as editor and major contributor, it was decided at this point to form a new company, The Orchid Review Ltd. This new status was to maintain the magazine and its value as a highly illustrated record of orchid cultivation. With the move to a company status, a new editor was also appointed. The new editor was Gurney Wilson, who was on the Scientific and Orchid Committees of the Royal Horticultural Society, as well as a Fellow of the Linnean Society.

Alfred Gurney Wilson (1878–1958), who rarely used his first name, had been the editor of another orchid magazine, *Orchid World*, from its inception in 1910 until it ceased publication in 1916. This was a magazine illustrated with a mix of black and white photographs and woodcuts. In an article published in 1914, it was controversially suggested that horticulture would be best served if everyone became familiar with the centigrade temperature scale, which they hoped would be used exclusively – an idea far ahead of its time. Although a magazine in a very similar vein to *The Orchid Review*, it did not cease publication due to a limited market or competition, it was simply that Wilson was called up as a conscript into the army in 1916 and with that the magazine folded. When he took over *The Orchid Review* in 1921 it resurfaced as a monthly magazine again and, like all magazines at the time, started to rely heavily on photographs for its illustrations. Although there was an increasing use of black and white photographs in the newly launched *The Orchid Review*, there had been a long tradition in the magazine of photographs. Sometimes these were not just illustrative, but illustrations in their own right. In the 1913 volume, although overall it was not by modern standards highly illustrated, it did have a fold-out black and white photograph of a magnificent *Odontoglossum pescatorei*.

After the editorship of Gurney Wilson, who retired in 1932, the magazine was taken over by Charles Curtis (1869–1958). This editor had a long family association with orchids as Charles, the editor, was nephew to Charles, the plant hunter for Veitch and Sons, who was the first superintendent of Penang Botanic Garden. Charles, the editor, was already a well-known horticultural journalist when he became editor and it was under his stewardship that it went through World War II. The problems of war-time production reduced the number of pages and returned the magazine to a bi-monthly publication. After the war, the magazine demonstrated its resilience by returning to its former glory, and being published monthly once again. *The Orchid Review* carried on with some financial difficulties until, in 1992, the Royal Horticultural Society took it over with a relaunch; this meant more pages and more colour photographs. Colour pictures first appeared in the magazine in 1979, consisting of just two pages. It was not until 1985 that it became a full colour magazine. At the end of 2022 it ceased publication as a monthly magazine and is now a single issue yearbook. This long publishing record has cemented the magazine as a significant influence on individuals who wish to grow their own orchids, but as a publication it has found itself, like so many others, in competition with non-published material, associated first with broadcast media and more recently with internet-based systems.

It would be wrong to imagine that *The Orchid Review* was the only influential magazine devoted to orchids, although it was one of the most influential. *The Botanical Cabinet,* for example, was not devoted entirely to orchids, in fact orchids formed a relatively small part of the magazine, and yet it was important to orchidologists. This was a publication that was started in 1817 by George Loddiges (1784–1846). George was the son of Joachim Conrad Loddiges. It was Joachim who started the large and famous Conrad Loddiges and Sons' Nursery, which covered several acres of ground in Hackney, East London, many of which were under glass. Loddiges' Nursery became well known for the cultivation of orchids and was one of the first nurseries to offer cultivated orchids for commercial sale. Certainly by the early nineteenth century the nursery site was described as being the largest palm and orchid house in the world, with an unrivalled collection of orchids. It was in *The Botanical Cabinet* that many of these orchids were illustrated, as well as other plants. One of the valuable aspects of the magazine was that it ran illustrations alongside the text-based catalogue to give a visual idea of what the plants available from Conrad Loddiges and Sons would look like. This was particularly important for plants that were either rare in cultivation, or brand new imports never seen before in the UK. It ran from 1818 to 1833 in twenty volumes, with the bulk of the illustrations being produced by George Cooke. The very high quality of the illustrations has, in many ways, been the downfall of the bound copies, which along with a theft of original material makes them of great rarity value. Altogether there were about 2,000 hand-coloured copper engravings in the twenty volumes of *The Botanical Cabinet*, each on a separate plate. These plates were stolen many years ago; consequently, they cannot be reprinted, only copied. As a result, many of the original magazines have been broken up so that individual plates can be sold separately; this has been an unfortunate outcome for many nineteenth-century publications.

It was most definitely during the nineteenth century that not only did orchid collecting become the aspirational status symbol for the middle classes, but production of orchid magazines reached their zenith. One of the finest, among many competitors, was a short-lived production called *The Orchid Album*. This was produced by a group of individuals, Robert Warner (1814–96), Benjamin Williams (1822–90) and Thomas Moore (1821–87), with illustrations by John Nugent Fitch (1840–1927), an extremely gifted botanical illustrator. *The Orchid Album* was published in eleven volumes between 1882 and 1897, and although at the time it contained a considerable and authoritative text, it was the 528 illustrations that grabbed the imagination. It was published by Williams himself from the Victoria and Paradise Nurseries in Upper Holloway. In volume nine of 1890, there was an obituary of Benjamin Williams in which it was said that:

> ...his magnum opus, *The Orchid Album*, which was projected with the idea of supplying a demand for illustrations of Orchidaceous plants, with botanical descriptions of the plants figured...

thus acknowledging the pivotal position of the illustrations, partly hand-coloured and partly colour printed, to the success of the project. The original drawings and watercolours created by Fitch for the magazine now reside in the Natural History Museum, London. In many ways this magazine was in contrast to *The Botanical Cabinet*, where it was seen very much as an adjunct to the incorporated catalogue of Loddiges' Nursery.

During the nineteenth century, a symbiotic relationship grew up between gardening magazines and orchids, both in their aspirational form of what people would like to grow and in the practical form of growing them. The magazines promoted an interest in cultivating orchids and, having produced this interest, then had to feed it with ever more articles on the subject. More simply put, magazines sold orchids and orchids sold magazines. By the middle of the century, the well-known gardener Sir Joseph Paxton and the scientist Professor Lindley joined forces to produce *Paxton's Flower Garden*. This was a publication described as produced in fascicles, which we would now describe as a part work of monthly issues, each one having three coloured plates and numerous woodcuts. There would be twelve parts making up a volume. It was originally planned that there were going to be ten volumes, but as it turned out only three were published, between 1850 and 1853. In the preface to the first volume it stated that one of its aims was to describe all the new and remarkable plants available to the gardener. It also said that it was hoped that it could help sort out the synonyms of different plants that resulted in a gardener purchasing several different named species or varieties, only to discover that they were one and the same plant. With respect to the colour plates, they referred to having no illustrations, other than those that would be embellished by it, due to the cost of production; other figures would be woodcuts. So only the colourful flowers would be produced in colour. There is no doubt that Paxton and Lindley knew their market. While they were both extremely keen on orchids and keen collectors in their own right, they also had a clear idea that orchids would sell their magazine. In that first year of publication in 194 pages there were 36 colour plates, a rate that would be copied in the following years, of which twelve were of orchids with associated descriptions and cultural notes. This was a use of orchid illustrations to sell the magazine, their flamboyance and beauty enticing the reader to buy the magazine. One of the interesting ways that was used to describe the orchids was as 'stove epiphytes', denoting not simply an epiphytic mode of growth, but also that they needed the hot and steamy conditions of a stove house.

Although books had long been published on a subscription basis to offset the original costs before anything was produced, part works really only became more widely available in the nineteenth century. Part works had been available in earlier years, in 1732 *The History of England*, an English translation of a French original, was published, but these were relatively uncommon. It was a century later when even Charles Dickens published *The Pickwick Papers* in instalments that they became commonplace.

By the time that *Paxton's Flower Garden* was published, starting in 1850, plans were far advanced for the Great Exhibition to be held in Hyde Park in 1851. The importance of this to Paxton was that it was his design that was being built, as what was to become known as the Crystal Palace. He was already both successful and well known. One of his great successes, one for which he received a medal from the Royal Horticultural Society in 1835, involved cultivating bananas. This, of course, is another hot-house plant and before the advent of dwarf species, they were also very tall. Paxton was working at the time as head gardener for the sixth Duke of Devonshire at Chatsworth House, a position he had held since 1826. In 1834, the estate received a shipment of banana plants from Alton Towers in Staffordshire, formerly the home of the Earl of Shrewsbury. The plants he grew from this consignment he named as a new species, *Musa cavendishii* after the sixth Duke, William Spencer Cavendish. Although Paxton was wrong in naming it a new species, it would have been impossible for him to know that what he had grown was a triploid version of a wild banana native to southern Asia. Triploid means three complete sets of chromosomes and this renders the fruit seedless, so reproduction is by rhizome only. This Cavendish banana became commercially traded at the beginning of the twentieth century but did not attain the prominent position of being the single most traded banana in the world until the previous favourite, a variety called Gros Michel, started to be devastated by a disease in the 1950s, at which point the alternative Cavendish banana superseded it.

Paxton was not only a great horticulturalist, he was also a very active publisher of magazines and books. During the nineteenth century Paxton, either singularly or with assistance, started several magazines, such as *The Gardeners' Chronicle* in 1831, *The Horticultural Register* in 1834, *Magazine of Botany* and *Paxton's Flower Garden* in 1850. These were all magazines for a general and interested readership and were all calculated as being commercially viable publications for the benefit of all concerned, writers, artists and publishers. Along with Paxton there were often collaborators and one of the most frequent of these was John Lindley. Lindley also had a passion for orchids that would make itself manifestly apparent in the publications with which he became involved. As more of an academic botanist than Paxton, with whom, of course, he collaborated widely, Lindley had an intrinsic interest in the relationships between groups of plants, not just in the individual plants themselves. It was his academic interest in botanical relationships that induced him to advocate a non-Linnean taxonomy, based on the works of Antoine Laurent de Jussieu. He used this unusual taxonomic system in his book *A Synopsis of British Flora Arranged According to the Natural Order*, which was published in 1829. In the preface to this volume he describes Linnnean taxonomy rather scathingly thus:

> Surely it cannot be denied that this school has acted as if the whole object of Botany were naming and describing species, evidently mistaking the means for the end, and converting the study of the vegetable kingdom into a system of verbal trifling.

Later, in 1846, Lindley also produced *The Vegetable Kingdom* where he acknowledged the gradual development of a system reflecting relationships between different species and groups. For the collector and investigator of orchids these questions of the status and position of orchids was broadly of little consequence, for them it was all about the individual plants. Orchids form a distinct and easily recognised group of plants. There are some exceptions, such as *Disa* and *Serapia*, where some species can fool the untrained eye on first acquaintance, but in detail, orchids are easily recognised. This renders them as a family, regardless of whose taxonomy is being applied, and the uniform nature of the plants and their flowers leaves no doubt of their close relationships. This is not always the case with other plant groups and this can cause some confusion, or in the case of Lindley, annoyance.

The influential book that had so incensed Lindley was published before he was born in 1799. It was *Species Plantarum* by the Swedish biologist Carl Linnaeus, which was published in 1753. The problem, as far as Lindley was concerned, lay with Linnaean taxonomy. This is a system broadly based upon phenetics, the overall similarities between organisms, and as a result has no regard for the evolutionary lineages and resultant associations. Of course, at the time that he was writing, Linnaeus would have had no notion of evolution and its consequences. He regarded species as God-given, each one standing complete, unchanging and alone. If species were God-given, then they would not be related in any way to each other, just casually similar. So as far as Linneaus was concerned it was a human activity to group them. Even so, he seemed to have been aware that his system did not necessarily reflect relationships between species, which he sensed were there. Significant changes to ideas in taxonomy came with technical developments arising from the development of high-quality microscope optics and associated microbiological stains. While orchids are for the most part a clear and standalone group, the problem with many plant groups is that the boundary between species is not always exact or easy to define, so for many plants the concept of species' aggregations becomes a better fit.

John Lindley also took over as editor of the *The Botanical Register* in 1829. This was a magazine that had been started by Sydenham Edwards in 1815, which he edited until his death in 1819, when the publisher himself took over the position of editor until Lindley became editor. The magazine continued in publication until 1847. It was a magazine where every plant featured was described, including any details of cultivation that were available, and illustrated in colour. Some of the floral pictures were on fold-out pages and nearly all of them in the early volumes were drawn by Sydenham Edwards himself, which were then hand-coloured by assistants. This was a magazine that covered the entire plant kingdom and was not especially enamoured of orchids. Even so, for example, in volume fourteen of 1828, after Edward's death when the publisher James Ridgeway was editor, there were six orchids described and illustrated. After Lindley had taken over editorship, by volume eighteen of 1832 there were fifteen described and illustrated orchids. Before starting *The Botanical Register*, Sydenham Edwards had been the primary illustrator for the first volume of *The Botanic Magazine* in 1787, which eventually became *Botanical Magazine.*

Chapter 7

THE CHANGING FORTUNES OF ORCHID HUNTERS

During the nineteenth century and, to a lesser extent, into the twentieth century, orchid hunting was simultaneously financially lucrative and ecologically destructive. In some areas of the world it is still commonplace to be offered for sale orchids, usually epiphytes, still attached to branches of felled trees. If you are ever offered such a thing, don't buy it as survival is unlikely and Customs and Excise strict. Part of this strictness originates from adhering to the CITES regulations, although local rules and regulations also play a large part in it. CITES is the Convention on Trade in Endangered Species of Wild Fauna and Flora, which became an active international convention in 1975. The idea behind it is to ensure that trade, mostly international, does not endanger rare species, and was formulated, and more or less set up, by the International Union for Conservation of Nature.

The CITES system works by using a series of certificates and permits. This was because originally it was trying to control the demand in the West for such natural luxury items as fur coats, but also for all those items that were not being traded as species or whole animals, but were traded as parts. These may have been for food, timber, musical instruments, tourist curios or 'medicine'. Many species not apparently at risk are traded, but still come under CITES control. This is so that the trade is, in principle, controlled and not excessive. As a result of all this, in 2024, at varying levels of intervention, CITES gives some protection to more than 40,000 species, depending on their risk of extinction. Even with such a huge number of species, they are all listed, with their level of protection, on the CITES website.

This is an interesting agreement as parties to the convention agree to adhere to it, even when the plants or animals are not destined for their shores or originated in their lands. There are currently 183 sovereign states as signatories, with the European Union as a single signatory. Although it started as a method of controlling fur coats and ivory, it has gradually widened out to many other species. The agreement has three appendices that list the categories of protection. Broadly these are as listed here:

- **Appendix I.** Taxa that are threatened with extinction. While we might think of tigers and such exotic wildlife, it also contains a list of 141 species of *Paphiopedilum*, indicating just how vulnerable these orchids are.
- **Appendix II.** These are not necessarily at direct risk of extinction, but control of trade is needed to stop them becoming threatened.
- **Appendix III.** This contains the species protected in a country by local laws, who have asked CITES for help in controlling the illegal trade in these taxa.

For the modern orchid hunter it is a straightforward convention, which should be self-evident in our increasingly overcrowded world. Put simply, don't dig or collect – just look and photograph. There is one area that CITES was never designed to address and that is habitat loss and ecological damage, although there are plans to broaden the remit so that these can be included in some way, probably as a separate appendix.

All this legislation has had a significant effect on plant hunters, especially orchid hunters. In the twentieth century it has become a guiding principle that destruction of areas just to collect plants is not acceptable. Of course, what immediately springs to mind is that large areas of forest are being destroyed anyway, just to change the landscape from rainforest to agriculture.

The other big change that affected orchid hunters and collectors revolved around propagation. We take it for granted now that we can find out all we want to know about a plant's heritage and growing conditions from books or online. This is not just about the ease of accessing information, it is also about the information being known, generated from an increasingly mobile population, more of whom have seen orchids growing wild than ever did in the nineteenth century. When tropical orchids, most especially the epiphytic ones, first arrived in the country from far distant lands, unless particular notice had been taken of the soil and conditions in which they were growing, assumptions would be made. The first of these assumptions was that if they had been found growing up a tree, then the plant must be a parasite, like mistletoe. If that was dismissed as an idea, the second thought was that since we do not have epiphytes in Europe, the orchid must have grown there by mistake and it would do better in a standard terrestrial compost. Along the same lines of reasoning it was thought by some that if they were not parasitic and yet grew on trees, then they would be like air plants and not need direct access to water, indeed, they were sometimes referred to as air plants. All these different interpretations of the needs of tropical epiphytes slowed progress and caused the death of countless orchids. An early success in understanding the needs of orchids in cultivation came from Joseph Banks (1743–1820), who experimented with baskets of moss that proved rather more successful than pots of compost. Banks was an extraordinary naturalist who made his name on travels aboard *Endeavour* with Captain Cook. Although we remember Captain Cook, it was, in fact, Banks who was the lynchpin of the trip, as this can be regarded as the very first truly scientific expedition, rather than an expedition with a scientist on board.

During the early part of the nineteenth century it was recognised that as far as tropical orchids are concerned, until techniques of cultivating orchids were sorted out, propagation of large numbers of new plants was not going to be possible. The early attempts to cultivate tropical orchids worked around a simple assumption that tropical places were hot and steamy, therefore, the glasshouse would need to be hot and steamy as well. Of course, the original assumption that all orchids came from tropical jungles was incorrect, as a result of which many plants were grown in inappropriate conditions. This resulted in plants slowly fading away for no apparent reason and in some cases a lot of money being lost on plants that did not survive a life in Britain's glasshouses.

This was a situation that quickly came to the notice of the Horticultural Society of London as significant and important to their members. To address the problem, they charged John Lindley, Assistant Secretary to the Society, to look into this whole problem. It was at their meeting of 18 May 1830 that he read his paper on the subject. For those who were not fortunate enough to be present at the meeting, they had to wait until a transcript was published as *Upon the Cultivation of Epiphytes of the Orchis Tribe* in their Journal of 1835. Lindley experimented with growing orchids that were known to grow on trees and rocks, but the article also contained much that was based on his experience and knowledge of growth and habitat. Although the readers of his article would already have been familiar with orchids, he suggested that it was the structure of the flowers, fired by illustrations of unknown exotic plants, that created the desire among horticulturalists to cultivate them for themselves. Lindley also pointed out that, regardless of the good intentions of the growers, most of the plants that arrived and were cultivated died, with one notable exception – vanilla. *Vanilla planifolia* is, indeed, easy enough to grow and probably the reason it is not more popular as a cultivated orchid is simply that the plant has to be very large and in good condition to flower.

According to Lindley, it was broadly by trial and error, with considerable help from William Cattley, after whom the genus *Cattleya* is named, that in the first thirteen years of the nineteenth century about a dozen species of orchids were grown at Kew. The other great garden that he mentioned was the Botanic Garden Berlin, *Botanischen Garten Berlin*. In the 1822 catalogue of the garden, only nineteen species of orchid were mentioned.

It was this lack of success and yet, simultaneously, an increasing interest in orchids that galvanised the Horticultural Society of London to investigate the propagation techniques that would be best for all of these imported orchids. One of the reasons for this interest was a sense that the formal botanic gardens of Europe were losing out to the well-financed private growers. This was epitomised by the report that the private establishments of Loddiges, Cattley and several others held over 200 species, while, by 1830, the *Jardin du Roi* in Paris had only nineteen. This vast difference was not just about the skill of the private growers, but also the almost obsessive nature of private collectors when compared with institutional gardens.

This question of what was the best way to grow these tropical orchids was addressed by Lindley in a systematic way by first asking the question, 'What were the normal conditions in the wild?' This would be easy to answer now, but travel in the first part of the nineteenth century was expeditionary in nature to anywhere outside Europe. It was only in 1819 that the first steamboat, SS *Savannah*, crossed the Atlantic and even then it carried sufficient sails to operate under wind power alone should the need arise. It would only be if details of growing habit and soil type had been written down at the time that the plant had been collected from the wild that any knowledge of an orchid's natural requirements would be known. Records of this sort were not often come by, so arrival in the UK often resulted in plants being put into the wrong compost or containers. His starting point was all that was known about epiphytes, which was that they grew on trees and the only soil available was that which accumulated on the trees themselves. This was a far cry from our more recent understanding, which puts epiphytes as a simple component of a three-dimensional ecosystem. In northern climates, we are less used to thinking of trees as vertical extensions of the ground. Although it does occur in temperate forests, it is both less obvious and less complicated. In tropical forests the upward growth of trees increases the ecological boundaries far beyond the forest floor, with many species, throughout both the plant and animal kingdoms, completely adapted to an arboreal life, as in the case of epiphytic orchids, which will simply not survive in soil at ground level.

On the basis that epiphytes lived in trees but were rooted plants, rather than parasites such as mistletoe, Lindley concluded that what was needed was 'well-drained soil, shade, a very high temperature and an atmosphere nearly saturated with humidity are the conditions that are requisite to ensure their successful cultivation, and that soil is of little importance to them'.

He became more precise in his recommendations, with 87° for a daytime temperature. Now, he did not state which temperature scale he was using, but it can be assumed it was Fahrenheit. This puts the temperature at about 30.5°C. According to Lindley, Nathaniel Wallich, who was working in India, had found what would normally be epiphytic orchids growing equally well on rocks, as long as they were in the shade and there was moss present as well.

It was only five years later on from his commission to investigate orchid growth patterns, in 1835, the same year that his original paper was finally published, that Lindley suggested that not all orchids would thrive in hot and humid conditions. This was based on information gained from collectors and those in the colonial administration who travelled within their area and came back with plants and precise information about where they were found and the conditions of the area in which they were growing. It was always going to be difficult to be exact about conditions all year round for cultivated plants because a collector may reach an area and stay for only a short time, therefore being unable to do any more than guess at the seasonal changes. Putting this in context, visiting Britain in the winter would give no hint as to summer temperatures. Even with this accumulating body of knowledge, the various growers ran their stove houses at different temperatures and humidities. Temperatures could be controlled, whereas humidity was much more complicated and difficult to control with any precision.

The slowly accumulated knowledge of growing and propagating tropical orchids can be seen mirrored in the parallel development of a book with a long publishing life, *The Orchid Grower's Manual*, written by Benjamin Samuel Williams (1822–90), who had a long tradition as a horticulturalist and a fascination for orchids. His father had been gardener to John Warner (1776–1852), an association that would cover generations on both sides of the relationship. John Warner owned a brass and bell foundry in Cripplegate, London, and another one at Walton on the Naze in Essex. The success of these companies funded the purchase of an estate in Hertfordshire, Hoddeston Hall. Benjamin started helping his father on the estate when he was fourteen years old, quickly becoming indispensable. Originally his interest was in plants other than orchids, exhibiting many different garden flowers at national flower shows. After the death of John Warner, the estate was taken over by his son, Charles Boreham Warner (1812–69), who was already by this time very enthusiastic about orchids. It was this enthusiasm that spilled over into Benjamin Williams.

Charles lived in London, but his already extensive collection of orchids was kept at his parents' house in Hoddesdon, Hertfordshire, although soon after Charles had taken it over he renamed it as Woodlands. It remained with that name right up until the main house was demolished in 1967, leaving only various outbuildings standing, which still remain visible to this day. Within the grounds of the house there were large orchid houses, running from cool to hot. The contemporary descriptions of the orchid houses evoke a fabulous backdrop of internal rockery and walls festooned with ferns and mosses growing on them, among fish ponds built to maintain the internal humidity. In this environment, Williams quickly developed considerable skill and became a serious competitor at the Royal Horticultural Society flower and, more specifically orchid shows. His successes at competitions demonstrated just how much he had become a very successful grower. Lindley, as Editor of *The Gardeners' Chronicle*, persuaded Benjamin Williams to contribute articles on orchid growing, which were of considerable success. These were published throughout 1851 in twenty-three parts under the umbrella heading of *Orchids for the Million*. This was a landmark set of articles for Williams because, with some encouragement and expanded content, it became *The Orchid Grower's Manual*, first published in 1852. The first edition included about 260 plant descriptions, which was expanded to 440 descriptions in the second edition and more than 800 in the final edition of 1894. The association with the Warner family continued with this publication, being dedicated to Charles Boreham Warner.

Benjamin Williams spent many years working in other nurseries and in partnerships in London until he set up a nursery of his own on the Holloway Road in North London, the Victoria Nursery. This was on the site now occupied by Archway tube station, which opened in 1907, although at that time it was called Highgate, before the current Highgate tube station opened at Highgate. Williams soon expanded to another site not far from the Victoria Nursery, which he called Paradise Nursery. Between these two sites Benjamin and his son eventually employed over 70 people. These nurseries supplied orchids, as well as ferns and lycopodiums. Indeed, for the sum of 3s 6d it was possible to purchase a book by Williams *Hints on the Cultivation of British and Exotic Ferns and Lycopodiums*.

During his career, Williams had always had a good relationship with the Warner family and it was with Charles's brother Robert that he started working on a three-part work *Select Orchidaceous Plants*, which was a richly illustrated work at 10s 6d for each part. Although published by Lovell Reeve and Co., it was advertised in later editions of *The Orchid Grower's Manual* as available by post from the Paradise Nursery in Upper Holloway.

In *The Orchid Grower's Manual*, Williams gave a huge amount of cultural information on a species-by-species basis, but also in general terms that were designed to help the novice grower clarify the requirements of his plants and help him to get to grips with the large and complicated subject of orchid culture. In this vein he starts off by explaining that to successfully grow orchids, their native climate must be imitated. This should include both wet seasons and dry seasons, and the time of year that flowers could be expected. Of all this, the most significant aspect of the text is that it was recognised that there was a big difference in the soil requirements of epiphytes and terrestrial orchids. At the time of publication, imported orchids were still the mainstay of orchid collections, so Williams had a section on what to do with freshly imported plants and the necessary treatment to get them into cultivation successfully. As a corollary to this, he also described the best way of sending plants home, which was, broadly speaking, when they were dormant to save damaging young, growing shoots.

By the time that *The Orchid Grower's Manual* was published, methods of cultivation and propagation of mature plants had been developed. Although this was really quite straightforward once techniques were available to ensure that the original plant could thrive under cultivation, creating divisions was still a skilled activity. Increasing methods of propagation would eventually take the pressure off collecting from native sources, but this would take many decades to be noticed. Most of the methods that he suggests in *The Orchid Grower's Manual* are similar to those used today, but they all have the draw-back of being limited in the number of new plants an original orchid can yield. The answer, of course, would be to germinate seed from these imported orchids. It was recognised that seed was produced in enormous quantities, but also that it was known, you could almost say notorious, for being difficult, in fact almost impossible, to germinate. Nonetheless, Williams has some advice on the subject, which reflected the state of knowledge at the time. This was to sow the seed on the compost surrounding an already established plant, or on the bark upon which an epiphytic orchid was attached. Although very hit and miss, it was borne out of astute observations that arose by chance. Seeds on, or in, standard potting material rarely, if ever, germinated, but seed that had fallen on the parent plant's compost or supporting bark, did occasionally germinate.

During the nineteenth century, when the first attempts were being made to germinate tropical orchid seeds, the precise cause of germination was unknown. This was understandable as symbiotic associations were unknown. The idea that one was necessary for germination would have been almost impossible to conceive of, since this would make the whole process of germination a vanishingly small probability. This, of course, is why orchids produce such enormous amounts of seed. It was a mixture of both commercial pressure from nurseries and scientific curiosity from private collectors that motivated nineteenth-century growers to investigate growing orchids from seed on a large scale. I say large scale because it had long been possible to germinate some seed either on, or among, the roots of existing plants, but this is a small-scale achievement considering the amount of seed each plant makes, which runs into hundreds of thousands.

As described in Chapter 1, the first observations leading to a precise understanding of orchid seed germination came from bird's nest orchid (*Neottia nidus-avis*). This is quite a surprise in itself, because although this is a widespread species, it is never a common one and certainly not one that would normally have been found in orchid collections of live plants. The reason it was not usually grown was that it is a cool terrestrial species with a seasonal appearance above ground in May and June, but also it has no chlorophyll. Bird's nest orchid has a symbiotic fungus that is essential for survival, not just germination. The fungus is in the genus *Sebacina*, which is a widespread genus and well known for its mycorrhizal associations with all manner of different plants. Once it was fully appreciated just how important to germination of orchid seed symbiotic fungi were, there opened up a whole new avenue of investigation that led to production of artificial hybrids.

Even with the discovery of the fungal associations of orchids in the nineteenth century, the problems of orchid cultivation were not solved at a stroke. There is much more, and at the time it was a gap, between knowing the situation and being able to make use of the knowledge in practice. On a very practical level this includes the need to culture a specific fungus, without contamination by unwanted fungal species that might overwhelm the symbiotic species that you want. This also brings into the equation the more general problem of sterility of seed and equipment. It is often not considered in great detail, but in the nineteenth century the idea of an aseptic technique was only just developing. When it was attempted, its implementation usually involved highly corrosive or aggressive chemical reagents, such as phenol.

The idea of having a sterile system with only one or two very specific organisms in it was rarely considered, the gap between practical ability and desire appearing almost insurmountable. Once again, it is the practical considerations that have to be addressed; to be able to handle and control the growth and development of orchid seeds with a symbiotic fungus, a sterile cabinet is required. It was right at the beginning of the twentieth century when Robert Koch constructed what we would now recognise as a biocontainment device, having realised that germs could become airborne. He developed the cabinet so that he could work safely with such infections as TB, cholera and anthrax. The difference between this type of cabinet and the sort required for orchid culture is one of protection. Early cabinets were for the safety of the user, whereas with orchid culture what is needed is a laminar flow cabinet for the safety of the sample. This was made more readily possible with the introduction in 1943 of the first High Efficiency Particulate Airfilter, which we now know as a HEPA filter.

Once a work area was created, the next step in seed culture was making sure that the seed that was going to be introduced on to the growth medium, with associated symbiotic fungus, was surface sterilised. It is necessary to do this or contaminant bacteria may be introduced. The seed has to be treated with something like a hypochlorite solution, strong enough to kill unwanted fungus and bacteria, but not strong enough to kill the seed.

The alternative method of seed germination, which eliminates the need for lengthy and time-consuming microbiological studies to separate the symbiotic fungus from all of the other microorganisms in the environment, is to use a completely defined growth medium. For tropical orchids this proved to be quite straightforward and many of the nutrient systems are used in more or less the same concentrations as they were when they were originally described more than half a century ago. It is because of the longevity of the recipe for defined media that we still refer to them by the name of the originator, such as Knudson's medium, first published in 1946 or Murashige and Skoog of 1962. There is quite a difference between these two recipes, with Knudson producing a basic mix and Murashige and Skoog a far more complicated one that includes plant growth hormones. This is not so surprising because this was a medium that was designed to give rapid growth and bioassays using tobacco cells in tissue culture, only later being picked up as an orchid seed germination medium. With all of these recipes, it was usual to add in various plant material, such as banana or potato. These additions made the description of a completely defined growth medium invalid, but the growers who used them wanted results and were not particularly bothered by precise terminology. In the 21st century there are very specific orchid germination media available, but they all have the basic content more or less the same as these very early growth media.

Growing orchids from seed was the original intention of using defined media, as this allowed the horticulturalist to either propagate large numbers of a single species or, and this was the aim of most growers, hybrids. Now, while growing a single species from seed is a very good way for the grower to increase stock, therefore reducing the need for freshly imported plants, this is not so straightforward when it comes to hybrids. The grower will have crossed two species artificially or often species from two different genera that would not normally come into contact with each other. This separation may be due to a specific pollinator approaching only one species, or it might be that they are separated by geography or time of flowering. Whatever the reason, the species that are crossed would not normally pollinate each other, so pollination is carried out by hand and the result generally unknown, until the seeds have been grown and the plant flowers. This is a process that can take many years and represents a considerable investment, both in time and money by the grower. Should the resultant flower be of particular merit, and very many are, it would have to be sold at a staggering price if it was to make it worth the while of the grower. To increase this fine hybrid and to perpetuate it, the only method available in the nineteenth century was to grow it on and create divisions. This is a reliable, but slow, process and was often carried out with great effect on many of the new and striking hybrids that were being produced. Even so, it was thought that there should be a method that could be used to speed up hybrid production. Just such a process appeared as meristem culture.

Meristem culture had its theoretical origins with the Austrian botanist Gottlieb Haberlandt (1854–1945). Haberlandt graduated from Vienna University, then moved to Berlin where he became a staff member at Berlin University. It was in 1902 that he presented a paper at a meeting of the German Academy of Sciences in which he suggested that plant cells exhibit totipotency, which he referred to as totipotentiality. This was the idea that all plant cells are capable of producing a completely new plant. This hypothesis turned out to be correct and just two years later, in 1904, E. Hannig made the first successful attempt at culturing plant cells; in this case they were from crucifers, now called Brassicaceae. This technique was exactly what was wanted, so it was quickly embraced by orchid growers as they could now effectively clone their otherwise unique orchid hybrids. It is this process that has made possible the growth of large commercial concerns that have brought the many and varied types of orchids into supermarkets and garden centres. In many ways orchid cloning was almost a spin-off from tissue culture of more obviously commercial crop species, where meristem culture was being used as a research tool in plant growth and development.

One aspect of orchid cultivation that has made a huge difference to collectors is hybridisation. This has also had a significant impact upon the commercialisation of orchids. There are about 28,000 named species of orchid and of the order of 100,000 named varieties and hybrids, with more coming along all the time. Of course, should a grower produce an easily cultivated and showy plant, this will be of great value and of commercial significance. As a result, a significant proportion of all the orchids commercially sold are hybrids with no wild counterpart. A question that is often asked is, 'Why are there so many hybrids of orchids?' The first answer to this is simple: with so many species there are bound to be a lot of hybrids. However, the picture is a little more complicated by the very nature of this astonishing group of plants. To explain this we need to look at both the ecology and the genetics of orchids.

In broad terms there are two ecological types of species: allopatric and sympatric. These are functional descriptions of the ecological state of species, so allopatric species are separated by something outside the species, such as a mountain range, that hinders or halts the gene flow. The alternate situation is found in sympatric species that can happily coexist with each other, as they are separated as species from each other by an intrinsic character, such as a change in ploidy, which is the number of chromosomes. A chromosome is the term used for the discrete package that carries genetic information and maintains the integrity of the species. A good example of sympatric species that can interbreed, but usually don't, are horses and donkeys, which are both in the same genus, *Equus*. If a female donkey mates with a male horse the resultant offspring is called a hinny. A male donkey mating with a female horse produces a mule. Both of these outcomes are usually sterile because horses have 64 chromosomes and donkeys have 62. The resultant imbalance in the offspring of 63 chromosomes results in fertility problems. The situation with orchids is rather different; for certain there are sympatric species, it only takes a cursory look at the range of sizes and shapes to tell us this, but there are also lots of allopatric species. It is worth looking at these in a little more detail because they can explain a lot about the diversification of this astonishing group of plants, always bearing in mind that chromosome numbers are not the absolute rulers of compatibility.

Most *Dendrobium* species have 38 chromosomes, which is the same number found in the very different genus *Phalaenopsis*, and the range of hybrids in both these genera can be expected to follow the same path as *Paphiopedilum* and be huge in number. In species of *Paphiopedilum*, the most commonly found chromosome number is 26, and is regarded as the base number of chromosomes in this genus. It is possible to recognise this base number, even where the actual number is different. This apparent paradox is explained by looking at the type of chromosomes and realising that many of them are a single chromosome broken in half. So *Paphiopedilum sakhakulii* and *Paphiopedilum venustum* both have 40 chromosomes made up of twelve full-sized ones and 28 half-sized ones, which can be reduced to fourteen if they were joined up again, making 26 in total. Because this number of 26 is so widespread among *Paphiopedilum*, we can begin to understand how hybridisation can occur so easily with many of the crosses producing seeds. The only reason it does not happen very much in the wild is because the different species are separated by an ecological barrier. This might be a mountain range or a flowering time, or any number of different aspects of the plant's life, which singles it out as a unique species. So with a large genus of plants that can be used to produce hybrids, it is no wonder that, as was the case with *P. sanderianum*, the original plant was lost in cultivation, but it had been used extensively as a starting point for orchid breeders. With this enormous genetic plasticity available to orchidologists, the numbers of hybrids grew very rapidly, especially once a reliable technique of seed germination became routine. It also meant that very rare plants, especially if there was only one in cultivation, would be routinely hybridised in an attempt to retain the best features, and even to try to enhance the flowers of both parents. Although the outcome of hybridisation was, and is, unpredictable, sometimes the results confirmed a grower's enthusiasm by having dominant traits coming to the fore.

This massive change in the direction of the commercial orchid growers, from horticulturalists to plant physiologists and geneticists, had an inevitable knock-on effect for the collectors in the field. It became less important for them to send home huge numbers of plants, with all the associated destruction of forests that entailed. Even so, although orchid hunting was pushed into decline by these developments, plant hunting remained an important part of the commercial aspects of plant nurseries. This had always been the case, the difference being that the value of each individual orchid tended to be far in excess of the value of any other plant type returned from tropical climates. During the period when orchid hunting was at its height, there were also general plant hunters looking for plants suitable for garden cultivation. One of these was Robert Fortune (1812–80).

Fortune was born in Kelloe in the old county of Berwickshire, now Scottish Borders, and worked from an early age as a gardener, where his training gave him an insight into plants that worked well in gardens. It was this understanding that made him such a successful plant collector when he went to the Far East at the age of 30. Like many collectors of both orchids and general plants, Fortune spent a long time in China; in fact he was overseas for a period of nearly twenty years. He started on his travels soon after the Treaty of Nanking had been signed by China in 1842. This was the treaty that ceded Hong Kong to British rule on a leased basis, at the same time opening up several ports to trade from the West, trade that had previously been extremely difficult. He spent his time in China working for the Horticultural Society of London, who paid him £100 a year for his activities. Later on he moved to working for the East India Company, still as a collector of plants but now for £500 a year. He used Wardian cases for the transport of live plants, but as he was a general plant collector, mostly he sent home seeds. He also made certain there were details about the plant and where it was found and in what sort of soil it was found growing. This was also a major difference for the general plant hunter over the orchid hunter: seeds could be sent home with some confidence that they could be germinated when they arrived, as, of course, orchid seeds could not. By the end of his collecting career, the stove house was at its peak of popularity among those who could afford them. At the same time, the increase in the number of people with gardens, as suburban living became more commonplace, meant that there was an increasing interest in rare and exotic plants for gardens. Suburbanisation of larger cities began with the increasingly developed public transport, so in London, for example, after 1860, local railway services and underground lines gradually extended further and further out from the city centre. Previously isolated villages, such as Brixton and Camberwell, became suburbs and are now fully integrated into the conurbation of London.

Collecting plants for gardens was an increasingly profitable activity for the next generation of plant hunters after Robert Fortune. One of the best known of these late-Victorian collectors was Ernest Wilson (1876–1930). He was born at Chipping Campden and trained for a time at Birmingham Botanical Gardens. This was unusual for a large city garden in being set up as an independent, privately funded garden, rather than being funded by the city, which retains its independence in the 21st century as a charitable trust. Ernest Wilson also worked at the Veitch Nursery sited at Coombe Wood in Kingston upon Thames. It was in 1899 that he first travelled to China, where he was predominately looking for garden plants, rather than plants for stove houses, or even the more recent phenomenon of house plants. During his time in China, while he was being carried in a sedan chair, there was a rock fall that resulted in him having a broken leg. This was given a splint using his camera tripod but resulted in a permanent limp. It was this limp that prevented him from enlisting in World War I, which he spent in Boston, USA. Ernest Wilson developed such a reputation for his plant-hunting exploits in the Far East that he acquired the nickname of 'Chinese' Wilson.

A later explorer and general plant hunter of the twentieth century was Frank Kingdom Ward (1885–1958). The father of Kingdom Ward was an academic botanist in London, which helped in the interest that Frank developed in botany. He went specifically to South-East Asia, Burma, Tibet and Assam. During a trip to Burma in 1921 he discovered what became known as *Paphiopedilum wardii*. This was introduced into cultivation in 1932. It was originally labelled as *Cypripedium vernayi* and has a range from Yunnan in China, through to Myanmar. Changing times of the twentieth century meant that at the outbreak of World War II, Kingdom Ward re-enlisted. Having had the rank of Captain in World War I, he was reinstated as Captain, this time working in the Far East plotting routes that could be used by troops. At the end of the war, he was employed for a while by the USA to locate aircraft lost due to bad weather in the east Himalayas between China and India. During an early expedition into Tibet, in June 1911, from north-west Yunnan in China, Kingdom ward discovered *Cypripedium wardii*, a lovely slipper orchid with white flowers flecked with mauve. Although Kingdom Ward is best known for his garden plant introductions, he was equally pleased to come across orchids and was well aware of the value of the plants. It was no longer possible to simply arrive and destroy forests for epiphytic orchids and neither was it possible to simply dig plants up. Local politics made it necessary for plant hunters of all sorts to be aware of what was going on in the area they were working in and to be sensitive to them. Two world wars and countless revolutions around the world had created a situation that was not always safe for travellers, and especially not for travellers in areas where travellers were either not supposed to go or were not welcome locally.

There is one area of rainforest that seems to have gained protection from a variety of sources and kept the area as wilderness. This is the Darién Gap. This nebulous region of no clearly defined borders is a natural barrier between Panama on the south of the isthmus of Central America down to Columbia in the north of South America.

The very difficult nature of the terrain has been of significant value in preventing the usual human activity of colonisation and road building. It has always been seen as virtually impenetrable, with large areas of marsh created by a river delta, but also with mountains, the highest of which is 1,845m (6,052ft) high. There are also vast areas of jungle, which is the home to orchids of extraordinary diversity. There are no roads across the Darién Gap and, currently, no plans to build one; this includes filling in the only missing section of the Pan American Highway. This extraordinary road runs about 30,000km (18,600 miles) from Tierra del Fuego to Alaska, unbroken except for the 106km (66-mile) break at the Darién Gap. Local groups are against the completion of the rather grandly named Pan American Highway, which, from experience in South America, has some astonishing pot holes... well, more nearly caverns.

Part of the modern reluctance to breach the Darién Gap is that it runs from Pacific to Caribbean and has been seen as a natural break on the spread northwards of several agricultural diseases, such as foot and mouth in cattle. Being so isolated, this area has been a long-standing sanctuary for groups such as the FARC, a Marxist/Leninist revolutionary group that was funded by ransom, drugs and extortion, although they are only one of many different actors in continuing conflict with the government. Operating on both sides of the Panamanian/Columbian border, it is the FARC that kidnapped two travellers in the Darién Gap: one adventurer and one orchid hunter. Kidnaps are not infrequent in the region, which keeps the wary traveller away from the area. Our two internees, Tom Hart Dyke (orchid hunter) and Paul Winder (adventurer), are unusual in having written a book about the events before, during and after their incarceration for nine months at the hands of some very dangerous people in 2000. Tom Hart Dyke was collecting orchids, even as they were being marched through the forest of Panama by the terrorist group and, as he puts it himself: 'When I spot an orchid I need to see it up close, wherever it may be, be it up a tree or down a ravine. It's a reflex action; the orchid compels me to stop.' Throughout the privations of their captivity, the theme of discovering an orchid in the wild, never knowing what they would find, kept recurring.

The difference between the risks in far off places for the orchid hunter of the 21st century and the nineteenth century is very much one of politics. In earlier times, animosity to travellers was based on dislike of foreigners, now it is far more aggressively political, backed up by cheap firearms and cult-like obedience to a political dogma. For the orchid hunter the landscape has changed, dangers always existed but have shifted their reasons from xenophobia to politics; more importantly, it is now often illegal and always socially unacceptable to rip plants from the wild as a trophy to be taken home.

Chapter 8

LOST AND FOUND: STORIES OF LOST ORCHIDS AND OVER-COLLECTING

In the world of orchids, it is apparent above all else that due to their precarious life-cycle, whenever orchids appear to be common, what you are actually seeing is abundance by accumulation. They may look flimsy, in the case of terrestrial species often little more than grassy herbs, but they are long-lived. It is this long life that can result in them appearing to be common. What will have happened is quite different to a truly common species, where a group of annual plants may appear in a single year and double in number over a single season. With orchids that live for tens of years their undisturbed proliferation may be of only a few extra plants every season, so when the intrepid explorer comes across a large area of orchids, or a tree laden with epiphytic species, they are looking at what might have taken half a century or more to create. As you can guess, it takes just a moment to eradicate such bounty, whether with a forester's axe or a builder's digger. Unfortunately it will take as long as it takes a tree to grow to maturity for the orchid colony to return to full glory and then only if the plants are allowed to recolonise their vandalised habitat, a rare event in itself.

Into this biological world of slow growth and development there came a number of human activities that have caused major problems for the ecologically delicate orchids. Something that should always be uppermost in the mind when talking about the decline of a species, any species, not just orchids, is that the decline can always be traced back to human activity. We shall be talking about orchids, but wherever you see a report of a declining species, look deeply and the overpopulation of our planet by humans will be at the bottom of the problem. This may be due to pressure for land to live on, for resources or demand for the plant or animal itself.

Primarily, from the first discovery of flamboyant tropical species until well into the twentieth century, the major cause of orchid decline was from collectors. These were collecting for commercial reasons or collecting for private individuals. Although I say it was the major problem into the twentieth century, it has not gone away and, as we shall see, there are still many examples of this going on around the world. Illicit collecting of orchids has even been a problem for terrestrial species from northern Europe, where digging up plants for gardens has, in the past, caused sharp declines in orchid numbers.

In his book *British Orchids*, A.D. Webster described his own exploits in digging and transferring UK orchids from the wild to his garden. At the time he was writing, 1898, this was a perfectly acceptable practice, as the concept of assisted extinction was really not considered. What was rather more surprising was his descriptions of trying to save populations of *Corallorhiza innata* (now called *C. trifida*), the coral root orchid. One was in a willow bed that disappeared, but the other was more significant because the colony was in woodland in Aberdeenshire and appeals not to fell the trees were ignored. Attempts to move the root stock apparently failed, but under such circumstances doing something, anything, cannot make the situation worse.

Even now, when nobody in the UK can claim that they do not know that it is only with the explicit permission of the landowner that a plant can be dug up and moved, illegal digging takes place. As we shall see, sometimes when environmental destruction is imminent, such niceties cannot be pandered to, but when it is just at the fancy of a garden collector, it is pretty well unforgivable. In this respect the problem is compounded by the plants that have been dug up not surviving their move. This is usually because many species have few, very long roots, which if dug up with a trowel will be cut off halfway down, which renders the plant unviable. This is especially so with species such as our butterfly orchid that can have roots 60cm (23in) long and entwined amongst the roots of the trees it lives with.

It is quite true that damage has been happening to northern species of orchids for a very long time, but it is also true that it is the tropical orchids that we hear the most about when it comes to habitat destruction and over-collecting. This was a situation that well known in its day, although during the nineteenth century when it was first noticed that it was taking place, practical remedies were few and far between. The result being that it was at best hand-wringing that took place. There are some good and well-documented examples of collectors virtually destroying some areas of forest in the tropics just to remove all the valuable species and to guarantee the rarity of their stock.

In the nineteenth century, in search of species of *Odontoglossum*, specifically *odoratum* and *crispum*, Albert Millican climbed the mountains of Columbia and into the forest to a place called El Ortiz. It was here that he expected to find *O. odoratum*, a highly scented species, as well as *O. crispum*, which he was informed, when he reached El Ortiz, had all been taken away. From this we can assume that collectors had already been through the area taking plants indiscriminately. During the nineteenth century, *O. crispum* was recorded as the most extensively sought-after and grown orchid species, with thousands being imported annually, but with that came an unfortunate sleight of hand by importers that was misleading to purchasers. As the most desired of the species was the variety called 'Pacho', found around the town of Pacho north of Bogota in Columbia, it was this that became a targeted variety. By 1896 it was a variety that was described as 'scarce' in *The Gardeners' Chronicle*, having been extensively collected. At the same time, what were described as 'lesser' varieties were still found in large numbers two or three days' march from Pacho centre. In the same text, the other varieties are referred to as 'worthless forms'. With this attitude came a simple solution to the lack of true 'Pacho' plants: simply pass off others as being from the area. This was often done by the expedient method of collecting plants in one area and then moving them to Pacho, where they would be shipped and labelled as having come from there, which was true but misleading. With it being routine in salerooms to sell plants as bulbs, with no flower, it is not possible to be certain what is purchased. As the correspondent of *The Gardeners' Chronicle* comments, these are not worth growing because they may well be of considerable disappointment when flowered. Into this sight unseen situation it had been recorded that sometimes not only were the plants not of the right variety, but they were a completely different species.

Millican himself was not above this level of destruction. By his line of reasoning a few acres of clearing is considered a benefit and clearings will reforest in three years, 'cutting down a few thousands of trees is no serious injury'. This may sound plausible, except while the trees may regrow, there is much more to a forest than just trees; so while the trees regrow, it may take several decades for them to become suitable hosts for epiphytic orchids, by which time there are no plants left available to provide seeds for repopulation. Also, of course, it does not take much of an extension of this line of reasoning, or for several people to think their felling is not significant, for the entire forest to become a threatened organism. So in his search for *Odontoglossum*, he set his indigenous helpers to cutting down trees that looked as though they may be useful sources of orchids. After a little training, his helpers were bringing in several hundred plants a day from the felled forest. In his book *Travels and Adventures of an Orchid Hunter*, published in 1891, Millican has a photograph of his forest depot containing 3,000 plants of *Odontoglossum crispum* alone. After two months he had accumulated about 10,000 plants and cut down 4,000 trees.

This sad tale of destruction was also mirrored in the work of Fredrick Boyle, *About Orchids*, published in 1893. According to Boyle, when in search of *Odontoglossum crispum* from Bogota, travel either ten days southwards or two days northwards, depending on the variety you are looking for. The first act when a likely area is found is to 'hire a wood', which he describes as a tract of 'mountain clothed more or less with timber'. He goes on to describe how difficult this can be as most such leases are controlled by the secretive orchid collectors who had already passed through the area. Once a piece of wooded mountainside has been procured, the collector should then hire 'natives, twenty or fifty or a hundred', who then cut down all the trees. By his own admission, 'This is a terribly wasteful process'; he explains this by suggesting that a good tree will have been felled for every three *Odontoglossum* now established in Europe. At a rough estimate, when compared with Millican's haul of the same species, this looks about right. Boyle also suggests that for many years past they had been arriving in Europe at the rate of hundreds of thousands of plants annually, on the basis of there being no alternative. Which, of course, at the time he was right about; if people wanted plants they had to be plucked from the wild, as stove-house growers did not often create divisions for sale and, even when they did, the numbers were small. Boyle is almost apologetic about the destruction, but cannot see any other way of collecting the plants. At the time he was writing, in the 1890s, there were tales of a single tree that had yielded 53 *O. crispum*, but that was exceptional. The normal yield would never be expected to be more than five plants per tree and usually it would be less. A hundred years later and groups such as Orchid Conservation International would be quite rightly questioning the basic premise that wild plants need to be collected at all, but in the nineteenth century propagation from seed was pretty well impossible, so cutting down great swathes of trees was seen as the only way of getting the plants and the resulting devastation of no consequence.

This profligate clearing of trees to remove their epiphytic orchids was commented on directly by Alicia Amherst in her 1895 book *A History of Gardening in England*. She quotes the collecting work of Millican, pointing out that nearly all of the orchids currently grown had been imported from wilder shores, more precisely that 'most of the orchid-growing portions of the globe have been ransacked'. At this point there is a distinct sense of railing against the wanton destruction, as she states, correctly:

> The sight of this glorious wealth of flowers, which has gladdened many orchid hunters, will be denied future generations, if the searchers are not more moderate in their demands on the virgin forests of the Old and New World.

This was reflected later in Millican's writing where he describes the banks of a small stream 'literally covered with *Cattleya labiata*' and when a large proportion of them were in flower they presented a 'sight of indescribable orchid beauty'.

There is a great deal of what, to modern eyes, would seem contradictory content in Victorian accounts of these orchid hunters. For example, the descriptions of sublime orchids flowering in profusion, quickly followed by describing the process of desecration of the forest with the stated intent of removing all the plants for resale in Western nurseries. But the casual violence directed at nature extended further than that. When their sleep was being disturbed by the calling of jaguars, the answer was to have a jaguar hunt. While describing the animal as sleek and beautiful, they set dogs on it and then shot it. Having been shot in the forest, they moved it strung on a pole to the river edge where it could be photographed. Interestingly, Millican explains that he used a Rouch patent portable camera to take the photograph of his dead jaguar. This is a plate rather than film camera and while we might not consider it to be very portable by modern standards, with its leather bellows and folding mahogany box, it was both robust and easily transported, the height of modern photographic equipment. Besides the collection of orchids, and a jaguar skin, Millican came back with about 500 bird specimens of many different species, also the result of hunting.

On one side of the plateau La Mesa de los Santos in Santander, Columbia, there is a precipice on which Milllican recorded seeing condors. It was on the ledges of the same cliffs that he described both an amazing situation and an unfortunate finish. The amazing part was that on the ledges were large amounts of *Cattleya mendelii*, which he described as having been there since the memory of man. The unfortunate finish was that with the arrival of the very first orchid hunters, locals were paid to be let down on ropes to collect by the thousands these wonderful plants. So by the time Millican visited the cliffs all he could see were a few left-over bulbs, hanging on where they had been out of reach of the collectors.

The possibilities of devastation of forests caused directly by orchid hunters were well known. The damage was less when caused by plant hunters in general, as they were not necessarily searching for plants to be sent home in bulk. What they were after were seeds or individual plants that could be propagated when they arrived at their destination nursery. With orchids it was different; from the very earliest of times it was recognised that many of the plants would perish on the way home, and even more would perish when they got there due to incorrect growing conditions. Simultaneously growing them from seed was a rare, or even impossible, event and propagating from plants difficult. So it was that in the early years of collecting, large areas of tropical forest were cut down to retrieve the epiphytic orchids. In the 1862 edition of *The Orchid Grower's Manual*, there is a section 'Advice To Collectors' where Benjamin Williams, the author, describes methods of packing plants so as to optimise the numbers that arrive home in good order. This includes advice on packing methods and the best time of year at which this should be done. Nowhere does he suggest moderation on the part of collectors. By the time of the seventh edition in 1894, some 30 years later, the entire book had changed its tone and in the early section he says:

> The hundreds of beautiful species, which had been collected at great cost and risk, and were purchased by eager amateurs at home, oftentimes at high prices, rapidly died out, simply from the prevailing ignorance of the climatal conditions of the localities on which they had been collected.
>
> Benjamin Williams, 1894

He also comments on over-collecting as ruining the capital by 'wholesale destruction'. So we can see that attitudes had begun to swing away from routine removal of all orchid plants and towards a more measured collecting regime, but also with the need for a greater understanding of the biogeography from which they came. This is also apparent in the work of Alicia Amherst, *A History of Gardening in England*, of 1895.

The cause of the change of attitude had many reasons, one of which was an understanding of interactions between species, that is, the ecology of the plants. This had started in 1866 when Ernst Haeckel used the word oecologie to describe the relationships of an organism to its surrounding environment. By 1895, Eugenius Warming, a Danish botanist, had published *Oecology of Plants,* thereby cementing the concept as a biological discipline. This helps explain the shift towards understanding more about orchid cultural conditions rather than simply assuming a plant came from the tropics and, therefore, needs heat to survive. Why there was a movement away from wholesale destruction of areas just to collect a few plants, has a slightly different answer. There must have been some influence from the ideas that plant communities are interactive environments, but there was something more significant occurring during the second half of the nineteenth century. This was all to do with a subject far removed from orchid hunting, but pivotal for the theory of evolution: palaeontology.

The problem was that both evolution and palaeontology need the concept of extinction to be more than just an abstract idea. Until the nineteenth century, the Church had a stranglehold on both education and philosophical thought. The secular authorities had more or less allowed theocratic idealism to run out of control on all manner of subjects that they were ill-equipped to comment on. One such was the nature and origin of fossils. Simply put, the argument against fossils being extinct species ran thus – all creatures are created by an infallible being and, therefore, such a being would not create a species that could not survive. Such an organism would be less than perfect, and God could not create something less than perfect; therefore, extinction was impossible. Not dwelling on the circularity of the argument or inherent assumptions, it became necessary to create an excuse to maintain this attitude. The answer was simple, just because you could not find alive the animal species that had created the fossil, it did not mean that it could not be found somewhere you haven't looked yet. Eventually this line of reasoning became indefensible and extinction became part of the way in which evolution became understood. As extinction became a real idea in the nineteenth century, so dawned the realisation that total destruction of an area may be just that – not clearing and reforesting, but destruction. So by the turn of the century a slightly modified attitude crept in amongst orchid collectors that clearing an area of all plants was not in their best long-term interests and that, for the future, some plants, even the majority, should be left unmolested.

A reflection of the discovered but lost presumed still alive, was epitomised by the discovery of *Cattleya labiata.* Although this was the first orchid to be described in the genus *Cattleya*, it was not strictly the first of the genus to be discovered. That honour fell to *Cattleya loddigesii*, which was originally called *Epidendrum violaceum* and only later renamed in 1824 by Lindley in *Collectanea Botanica.* At the same time, Professor Reichenbach was suggesting that as a genus *Cattleya* should be done away with and subsumed into *Epidendrum.* The stunning orchid *Cattleya labiata* was only accidentally discovered in the first place, which made it even more valuable to collectors, since it was not clear exactly where it had come from. Later confusion among collectors originated from the flowers being either a cerise, as originally described by Lindley, or white with a darker patch on the lip. This undeniably lovely orchid had been despatched from Brazil around 1818 by a remarkable man and accidental orchid collector, William Swainson (1789–1855).

Swainson was a Londoner by birth, although once of age he spent little time either in London or even in England. Joining the Customs Service at fourteen, he then moved on to the army, where he toured in the Mediterranean and developed his studies of fish. By 1815 he had left the army, retiring apparently due to ill health. However, this does not seem to have stopped his exuberant travels, as he went to Brazil the following year as a companion to the explorer Henry Koster. It was during this time that Swainson seems to have collected *Cattleya labiata*, as it was certainly in his possession on his return from South America in 1818, along with over a thousand other plant species. Along with his plant collection, there were many specimens of birds and insects. While the interest in *C. labiata* was developing, fired by its rarity and beauty, Swainson remained busy elsewhere, and in 1841 he sailed with his family to New Zealand, where he set up home. Ten years later he went to Australia, where he spent several years studying the fauna and flora of Australia and Tasmania, before returning to New Zealand in 1854.

The original *Cattleya labiata* was sent to William Hooker, who, it is said, had asked Swainson to send him some lichens from his travels. This he did, with the orchid being used as packing material, although it would most likely have been packing between cases to prevent them banging together. There is a possibility that this part of the story is apocryphal, as it seems to have originated from a third party, Thomas Paxton. What is certain is that the plant was spotted as being of interest by William Cattley, who took the unprepossessing greenery to be grown at his home in Barnet and a year later, coaxed it into flower. Later on, William Hooker was really quite scathing about the botanical ability of Swainson, although this was mostly regarding his work in Australia and New Zealand.

Cattleya labiata was described by John Lindley in his *Collectanea Botanica*, illustrated by C.M. Curtis and published in 1821. This was during the time that Lindley was a salaried member of Cattley's staff, naming the plant in Cattley's honour. Such was the stunning nature of the orchid that orchid collectors wanted to know where it had come from. The answer was unsatisfactorily vague; all that was certain was that it had been dispatched from Rio de Janeiro, so the assumption was made that it had originated from that area. Even though this was a small consignment of almost accidentally introduced plants, at the time there was no reason to believe that the species was rare. It was a few years later that George Gardner (1812–49), with the encouragement of William Hooker, went on an expedition to Brazil to look for *Cattleya labiata*. He set sail in 1836, returning five years later in 1841 laden with specimens of all sorts, but also with live plants. Gardner was only 37 when he died in what was Ceylon, now Sri Lanka, of what was said to be apoplexy. Amongst all the plants there was a considerable number of *Catlleya* plants from the Pedra Bonita range and from the Pedra da Gavea, both not far from Rio de Janeiro. Both of these now have well-marked tracks and are located in National Parks.

The plants that Gardner brought back were passed as *Cattleya labiata* for a while on the word of Thomas Paxton, but eventually these were not thought to have been the real thing, just similar. This group of orchids can be quite difficult to tell apart, especially when two plants are not side by side. This was demonstrated by the introduction, in 1840, of *C. mossiae* as a separate species, which Lindley considered to be the same as *C. labiata*, except for the colour and that it flowers at a different time of the year. Although not considered at the time, the latter aspect of difference, flowering time, would normally give pause for thought, as it implied an ecological separation, if not a geographical one. A similar case was made for *C. warscewiczii*, now *C. gigas*, which like a few other species bore such a close resemblance to *C. labiata* that they were considered by some to be one and the same species. So at that time a controversy raged over the genus *Cattleya* and even more specifically over which plants were new species and which were representatives of *labiata*. It, therefore, seemed reasonable for the Orchid Committee of the first Orchid Conference to be urged to review orchid nomenclature and to secure the assistance of Professor Heinrich Reichenbach, the pre-eminent German orchidologist, to do so. Unfortunately, the descriptions of new species carried on during the nineteenth century, apparently regardless of any biological accuracy.

Over the years, Swainson's single plant of undoubted pedigree, and those raised from Swainson's original import, started to raise greater and greater amounts at auction. These particular plants carried with them two highly valuable traits: that they were spectacular in flower and that they were relatively easy to grow. Interestingly, it was reported that the progeny plants had a tendency to a colour variation. Although this is not impossible, it seems unlikely, as the colour would be under genetic control. We know of species where colour is affected by growing conditions, but such strong colour forms as are found in *labiata* are unlikely to be so easily affected.

Because of the manner in which *C. labiata* first arrived in England, dealers thought that it must grow in a very robust and weed-like manner around Rio de Janeiro, but they were soon disappointed to find out that this was not the case. Taking Rio de Janeiro as a base, collectors from all the major nurseries and private collectors of Europe spread out in all directions searching for *Cattleya labiata*. Like all such commercial enterprises, the search was not so single-minded as to exclude everything else. Motivated by a search for a single species, the nurseries made a great deal of money from the sale of other species that were collected, especially so, since many of them were new not only to the market, but new to science as well. One of particular note that was found during this frantic search, which had many of the hallmarks of a gold rush, was *Cattleya dijanceana*, which was good enough to receive the Royal Horticultural Society Botanical Certificate in September 1890. In older texts this sometimes has the 'j' replaced with a 'g', which is presumably a misspelling due to mishearing.

The hunt for this stunning orchid lasted more or less 70 years. Of course, it would be reasonable to suggest that the easiest way of finding it would have been to ask William Swainson where he found the original plant. Even though he was on the other side of the globe for most of this period, either in New Zealand or Australia, it is more than likely that he simply did not remember where the plants came from, as they were not collected as specimens in flower, but simply as plants for packing. During the period of searching there were other examples of *C. labiata* that were confirmed as true, but these had all apparently arrived as unlabelled specimens of unknown origin from South America. Again, this implied that the plant was not rare, simply difficult to find and when not flowering, anonymous. While the collectors in Europe relished in these individual plants, they were never in such quantity as to be of interest to the large nurseries, all of whom wanted to know what area they came from so that they could collect the plants by the thousand for sale in Europe.

Even when a collector from the large nursery of Sander and Sons in St Albans was sent out on the trail in 1870, the results were disappointing. The collector spent the first five years in Venezuela, having decided that, although the original plant had been shipped from Brazil, this said nothing about where it grew and he was sure it was not in Brazil. Failing to find it in Venezuela, but still sending many orchids of other types back to England, he moved on in his search to Columbia. This was an area that had been apparently well explored by collectors already, as they had all had access to Swainson's notes on his travels around South America. Like the collectors before him, he was unable to locate *C. labiata*, but at the same time returned home with large amounts of other valuable plants.

The story changed when, in 1899, Moreau, an entomologist based in Paris who was also a keen grower of orchids, employed a collector to explore parts of Brazil. As well as the insects he sent home to Moreau, there were also plants, only about 50 in total, but they were of interest, so he grew them on. The Horticultural Society of Brussels was given some of the plants and had thought they were a new species, consequentially they were officially named as *Cattleya warocqueana*. This name continued for some time until Henry Frederick Sander was visiting Moreau and his collection. By chance the imported plants were in flower and Sander instantly recognised them for what they really were, the long-lost *Cattleya labiata*. Having been collected and labelled, the origin of the plants was known. Almost immediately Sander started the commercial sale of the plants, at which point the mislabelled orchids of the Horticultural Society of Brussels were renamed correctly.

It was not just *Cattleya labiata* that was found, lost and found again in this genus. One of the finest of its group was *Cattleya dowiana*. Now, to put this species into perspective, the description afforded it by Fredrick Boyle in 1893 sums it up:

> The most gorgeous, the stateliest, the most imperial of all flowers on this earth, is *C. Dowiana* [sic] – unless it be *C. aurea*, a 'geographical variety' of the same.

This was from a man who claimed not to be a fan of *Cattleya* as a group. A simple description does not do it justice. The ground colour is yellow with a crimson lip lined in gold. The two species, *C. dowiana* and *C. aurea*, were considered to be varieties, but they are most likely different species. *Cattleya aurea* has larger flowers, which it produces in May in its range of the states of Antioquia, Risaralda and Choco, in Columbia, while *C. dowiana* seems to flower about two months earlier in its range of Costa Rica and Panama. It was originally thought that the two were separated geographically and, indeed, they may well be, as they are both rare in the wild.

The original discovery of *C. dowiana* was made by a Lithuanian explorer, Joseph Warszewicz. The reason it was lost from cultivation was the same reason that so many plants taken from the wild were lost – the collected plants died on the way home. There was also an element of disbelief regarding his description of the flower, as it was regarded as too enthusiastic to be believed. He had found them in Costa Rica and had shipped the live specimens to Mrs Lawrence of Ealing in London. A similar fate befell his preserved specimens as well, being destroyed on the way to Germany where they would have been catalogued.

Warszewicz (1812–66) trained as a botanist at the Botanical Garden of Vilnius University in Lithuania. At the age of 32 he was recommended as a botanist to a colony in Guatemala, where he developed his own business of exporting orchids back to Europe. He did not confine his collecting to orchids, but sent back species of all sorts, animals as well. He returned to Europe in 1850, working with Reichenbach, while recovering from yellow fever. After going back to South America in 1851, he travelled widely until a recurrence of yellow fever sent him back home, where he became Supervisor of the Botanical Garden at Krakow. There are more than twenty species that were named in his honour, including half a dozen orchids.

The spectacular orchid that Warszewicz discovered was not found again until 1865 when a local man, Mr Arce, who was collecting birds, found a plant that piqued his interest and which he sent directly to George Skinner in London. Skinner was unaware that Warszewicz had intended naming the orchid after the original recipient, Mrs Lawrence, so instead it was named in honour of Captain Dow, an American who helped many orchid hunters return home with their plants. In many ways *Cattleya dowiana* is still lost as the skills of the modern orchid grower, with the ability to alter genomes, means that many of the plants sold as *Cattleya dowiana* are varieties that have abnormal chromosome numbers and are not true species. The wild-type plant would have a diploid chromosome number of 40, but many varieties grown simply for the size of the flower have chromosomes numbers of 60 or 80. For the amateur grower it can be helpful to know the chromosome number as some, such as 60, are unlikely to produce viable seed.

While some stories, like the rediscovery of *Cattleya labiata* and *C. dowiana*, are well known, there are many other examples, all with their own story to tell. One of these is *Laelia gouldiana*, which has a mauve flower and in cultivation can grow to about a metre (3 feet) in height. Its natural home is the mountains of Hidalgo State in Mexico. Sadly it is a species that is now regarded as most likely extinct in the wild, although it is still widely kept as a domestic plant. The problem with domestication as an assumption of species' survival is that plants are easily hybridised, orchids especially so, which is why they often rely on highly specific insect pollinators or ecological isolation to maintain the species. In this particular case, time will determine whether the species has a long-term survival other than as genetic content in a hybrid variety. It was thought, when it was originally discovered in Mexico, that this species may be a hybrid, but that proved to be incorrect. During the nineteenth century, because raising orchids from seed was so very difficult, if it had been a hybrid, collecting such plants from the wild would have been a legitimate commercial enterprise and the only way to secure plants. Louis Forget told the story of its rediscovery by him to his friend J.M. Black. When Louis Forget was tasked with the job of bringing back 3,000 specimens of *Laelia gouldiana* from Mexico, he had some understandable misgivings. If the plant was a hybrid, then it would be almost impossible to fill such an enormous remit. However, as a field collector, Forget prepared for the expedition.

He left Vera Cruz by train, heading north-west away from the coast and into the mountains. By his own admission he was caught out by the change in temperature as the altitude increased. As he had started out in light summer clothes, he was not dressed for the falling temperature. Having survived a very cold night, he was convinced that no orchid could grow in these conditions, as there was a visible frost. Nonetheless, he decided to track down his orchid quarry by using the directions supplied to him by Theimer, the original discoverer of the species. Unfortunately, either due to forgetting or not knowing, he had described the site relative to the position of a village with a name that turned out to be shared among a number of different villages in the region. Consequently, when he did find it, his rediscovery of the orchid was more or less by chance. It was when returning from an excursion to one of the villages that Forget happened upon a valley that contained numbers of *Laelia gouldiana*, which were growing on the acacia trees as epiphytes, but were also to be found perched on rocks in the valley. Some of these orchids were so large that they had to be cut up using a saw, that being the only way that they were in small enough pieces to be transported by donkey. It transpired that this particular orchid was locally grown quite extensively as a garden plant, where its local name is *Monjas*, which is Spanish for nuns, referring as it does to the cap over the pollina, which is thought to resemble a wimple. It was also used extensively as a decoration on saints' days. Louis Forget was not in the area for very long and he was known principally for collecting *Monjas*, consequently he became known locally as *El Hombre de los Monjas*, the nun man.

Without doubt there are many plants that have been lost and found, but there are a surprising number that come from the same genus, *Paphiopedilum*. Three species are of particular note: *P. rothschildianum*, *P. fairrieanum* and *P. sanderianum*. Although they live in different areas of the globe, they are closely related and easily recognised. As a genus, *Paphiopedilum* was described by Ernst Pfitzer, using *P. insigne* as the type species, in 1886, although it was not really accepted as the name for the tropical plants of its type until the late 1950s. Before that time it was mixed up with *Cypripedium*, which is the genus where we find the original descriptions of what we now call *P. rothschildianum* and *P. fairrieanum.* Indeed, in the UK our very own *Cypripedium calceolus* has a lost and found story to tell us later on.

Paphiopedilum rothschildianum is a striking plant that was in high demand as soon as it appeared in Europe. It was first described by Heinrich Gustav Reichenbach in 1888 as *Cypripedium rothschildianum*, an orchid from New Guinea. It seems that there was a deliberate silence regarding the true origin of this plant by the importer, Sander and Sons, but it may have been a genuine mistake, since further exploration did not, at the time, produce any more specimens. Because no more plants came back to Europe, even after extensive exploration of New Guinea, it was thought to be extinct. However, in 1959 it was found growing on the lower slopes of Mount Kinabalu, Borneo. It was no wonder that it had not previously been found, as Borneo lies more or less equidistant north of the Equator as New Guinea does south of the Equator. It turns out that *P. rothschildianum* is endemic to Kinabalu, growing between 500 and 1,200m (1,640 and 3,936ft) above sea level. Although rediscovered, the status of the orchid is not one of thriving in seclusion, as collecting from the wild, and habitat degradation for agriculture, logging and mining, are putting the plant's long-term survival in jeopardy.

The original naming of many different species of orchid was carried out by Heinrich Reichenbach (1823–89). In fact, besides naming them, a considerable number of plants were named after him, the species' name in many genera being *reichenbachiana.* It should be noted that these were all named by other people, as it is not permitted to name a species after oneself. His father was also a botanist, which instilled in him his original interest in botany. Heinrich started his career studying at Leipzig University, where by 1855 he had become professor. Soon afterwards he moved to Munich, where he was Director of the University Botanical Gardens. As he had worked on orchid seed early in his career, this group became his major fascination, plus, of course, that working in the botanical gardens meant he received many donations of orchid plants and requests for help in identifying specimens from overseas. His rapidly developing skill in identifying orchid species, and the concomitant ability to recognise new species, put him at the forefront of orchid science in nineteenth-century Europe. Reichenbach was fluent in English and regularly visited Kew Gardens, where he was a friend of John Lindley, another great orchid enthusiast. There does seem to have been a surprise when Reichenbach died and both his extensive collection of specimens, as well as his library, were not bequeathed to Kew.

Instead they went to the Naturhistorisches Museum in Vienna, with a rather unusual caveat that stated the collection should not be consulted for 25 years. Some of the species' descriptions published by Reichenbach denoting plants new to science were a little vague, so by not allowing researchers to go back to the original specimens, a great deal of confusion was generated. Indeed, it was well into the twentieth century before many of the multi-named species settled down to a single title.

The cypripediums, as they were known during the nineteenth century, were regarded at the time as collectively being different to all other orchid species by a greater amount than any two cypripediums were from each other. Put another way, you can always spot one of these orchids from their very distinctive flowers. Charles Darwin, who thought that this group of orchids was an ancient group among the orchids, made a very interesting observation in his book of 1885, *The Various Contrivances by which Orchids are Fertilised by Insects.* He was trying to explain why these very distinctive plants have such a wide geographical distribution around the world, while often being separated by large distances. Darwin's answer was that:

> An enormous amount of extinction must have swept away a multitude of intermediate forms, and has left this single genus, now widely distributed.

This widely distributed and often isolated group has had some interesting comments made about it by collectors in the nineteenth century, which, with modern moralities, may seem slightly odd. One such comment, made in 1893, was that:

> Some are rare to the degree that we may congratulate ourselves upon the chance which put a few specimens in safety under glass before it was too late, for they seem to have become extinct even in this generation.

This comment was specifically regarding *Cypripedium* (now *Paphiopedilum*) *fairrieanum*.

The story of *Paphiopedilum fairrieanum* is particularly interesting in terms of the conservation of a species. It had originally been brought to the UK in about 1856, some sources say 1857, but that is a date when the first plant flowered, so it is most likely that the imported material arrived the year before. An advertisement on 24 March 1857 gave details of a sale of this fine orchid by Mr J.C. Stevens, an auctioneer of Covent Garden in London who was well versed in the sale of orchids, as well as scientific instruments and other biological material, such as entomological collections. After the death of John Crace Stevens in 1859, John's brother ran the auction house until his sons came of age and took over the business. The eldest of the two sons was Henry Stevens, who was also an award-winning photographer, renowned for his photographs of flowers. At the advertised sale there was no specific information detailing where the plants came from other than Java via Calcutta, which gave little help in locating the precise area, since Java is more or less the thirteenth largest island on the globe. Allied to this, it was reported that the books detailing the finding of the plants had been lost.

As a result of this sale, *P. fairrieanum* was widely distributed from the consignment amongst collectors eager to get it into flower. The first flowering took place in Burnham, Somerset, but this was not widely broadcast or known about. As a consequence, when Mr Fairrie from Liverpool got it to flower, he sent a bloom to the RHS show, where John Lindley spotted it. This was significant because Lindley was a very accomplished orchidologist and Professor of Botany at University College, London from 1829 until 1860, so he could spot a new species with relative ease. He described the flower and published the result with a new name, *Cypripedium* (now *Paphiopedilum*) *fairrieanum*. The spectacular flower made sure that this became a plant of great desirability among orchid collectors. Whether it was fuelled by changes in fashion amongst orchid growers, or simply lack of correct growing conditions, over many years the number of plants in cultivation declined. At the same time, with an unknown origin no more were being imported. By 1900, the number of known plants had plummeted. In the *Orchid Review* of 1905, an article regarding this decline in fortunes of *P. fairrieanum*, stated:

> The existence of only one tiny plant is known – in the collection of Sir Trevor Lawrence at Burford; and on the Continent there are four little pieces, the size of quite small seedlings, at the Jardin de Luxembourg; all the loving and skilful attention of Mr Opoix are unable to increase them. No others are certainly known.

By way of clarity, the Jardin de Luxembourg is in Paris and Sir Trevor Lawrence was the President of the Royal Horticultural Society.

Although this situation was lamentable, it is possible that there were other plants that were unknown to the writer of the above article. We also know that before 1860, Mr van Houten in Belgium had received some unlabelled plants of *P. fairrieanum* from Assam. These plants were offered by him for sale at ten shillings each. Unfortunately, all of these plants have disappeared, just as the plants in Calcutta Botanical Gardens had disappeared. What this consignment did confirm, was that the plant originated in Assam and not Java. With this specific knowledge, collectors were sent out in large numbers by the major nurseries. Sanders and Sons not only sent out collectors, but they took long-running advertisements in the Anglo-Indian Press, offering a reward of £1,000 for a 'healthy importation' of this species. The collectors even went into Bhutan when plants were not initially found in Assam.

It was in 1904 that from somewhere in the Himalayas a message was sent with a description of plants and evidence that convinced Calcutta Botanical Garden that *P. fairrieanum* had been located. The newly rediscovered plants were destined for Sander and Son at St Albans, who put them up for sale in advance, even before they had arrived in London. So significant was this rediscovery that it appeared in *The Times* of 14 April 1905. This was followed up with a letter, also in *The Times*, on 20 April. The letter was from Mr Francis Wellesley, who had written the article in the *Orchid Review* with Mr R.A. Rolfe. In this letter he suggests that one should be very careful when offered *P. fairrieanum* for sale as they have often been promised, but have not materialised. He was also very sceptical about the accuracy of the identification of the discovered plants:

> If (as I am informed) the present discovery was made by an engineer and not by an expert, then it behoves one to be doubly cautious.

So in a sentence he doubts the identification and insults all engineers. Wellesley goes on to say that he would recommend only buying plants in flower, so that the purchaser knows exactly which species of plant they are buying. Alternatively, he goes on, only buy from a reputable dealer who will give a written guarantee of the plant's species.

Such was the interest in this rediscovery that on 29 April *The Times* announced that Kew had received two large plants of *P. fairrieanum* that had been forwarded to them from Calcutta Botanical Garden. They were sent as unknown *Cypripedium* from the eastern Himalayas and were positively identified by Kew. So after 1904 this spectacular plant was once again established as a commercial plant, available at a price from orchid nurseries.

We now know that *Paphiopedilum sanderianum* is a species native to north-west Borneo, even more specifically, the National Park Gunung Mulu, covering an area of 544sq km (207sq miles), taking its title from the mountain of the same name that is within the park. As a wild species this was lost for nearly a century until it was rediscovered. It had originally been found by a collector working for Sanders and Sons by the name of J. Foersteramann in 1885. He had been searching for *Paphiopedilum stonei*, a highly prized orchid of great value, when he came across *P. sanderianum*. As far as we can tell, this was the only importation of the plant into Europe for nearly a hundred years. Sadly, the nature of the orchid genome renders it easy to cross-hybridise and spectacular species, such as the ones found in *Paphiopedilum*, were routinely used as breeding stock. With *P. Sanderianum* being so special, it is no surprise that it was not bred true, but hybridised out of existence. By the early twentieth century it had been lost completely and was feared to have become extinct in the wild, until, in 1978, it was rediscovered by Ivan Nielson in the Gunung Mulu area. It has been suggested that it was not seen until later than this, but contemporary accounts suggest 1978 as the correct year. According to the International Union for the Conservation of Nature (IUCN) there may only be 50 plants left in the wild, but although no one disputes that it is a threatened species in a very vulnerable position, other accounts differ considerably. Eric Hansen reported in *Orchid Fever* that in 2000 he saw several sites each with hundreds of plants, and in a study published in the 17th Malaysian Forestry Conference in 2014 there were several sites that had many plants, although only one of their areas had more than 400 plants present. Whatever the figure, it is rare and very local in distribution.

One of the many reasons that *Paphiopedilum sanderianum* was lost so soon after it was discovered was the same reason that so many other species have disappeared temporarily from observation – a lack of accurate site information. In this case site information was wildly inaccurate. It was a species reported as coming from all over the Far East, not even from the correct islands. It was described as having been seen in places as far afield as Malaysia and the Philippines. Even with the very small number of plants that had arrived in the UK, the impact was enormous. In 1888, *Reichenbachia: Orchids Illustrated and Described* had a good coloured illustration of the flower. This publication, usually just referred to as *Reichenbachia*, was a four volume text published in the nineteenth century which boasted life-sized illustrations of orchids. It was created and written by Fredrick Sander and named by him in honour of his friend Heinrich Reichenbach.

In 1896 there was a large black and white illustration of *Paphiopedilum sanderianum* and text extolling its virtues in *The Gardeners' Chronicle*. Delight in this plant was not confined to the shores of Great Britain. In the *Proceedings of the Linnean Society of New South Wales* of 1889, there was an article by Father Julian Tennison-Woods of 98 pages. In the section 'A list of the principal orchids which are worthy of attention', he writes a footnote of half a page just on this one orchid, more than any other footnote in the whole article. In this footnote he says, 'The new species of *Cypripedium sanderanium* is probably the most wonderful-looking flower in an order where wonderful structures are the rule'. Later in the same footnote he reported:

> The long dependent curled and almost snake-like petals, as they are seen emerging from the half open buds, are very singular and beautiful, and must be seen to be appreciated.

He had obviously seen it growing and was entranced by it to the extent of putting in a footnote of half a page just about this one species. Father Woods (1832–89) was born in London, converting to Catholicism and becoming ordained. He was in the long tradition of priests and vicars who had a continuing interest in natural history throughout their life, and he wrote extensively on geology and later on, botany. It was his ecclesiastical career that took him to Australia where he spent much of his time studying the geology and botany of the country.

It is understandable that plants of small geographical areas may be lost after discovery. For example, *Paphiopedilum hirsutissimum* was originally found by a collector in 1857 and sent home in a general consignment from India, with no further details of whereabouts in India it came from. It would be another twelve years before it was found again and the site in the Khasia Hills made note of. While the large areas that would have to be explored could account for lost orchid species, there are cases nearer to home. In fact, there is one very interesting example that involves the only species in the genus *Cypripedium* that lives in northern Europe. Although many of the tropical species that were in *Cypripedium* were moved to another genus, *Paphiopedilum*, our native lady's slipper orchid remains *Cypripedium calceolus.*

Lady's slipper orchids were written about in many different places during the nineteenth century, as it is quite easily the largest and most flamboyant of our native orchids. It is also the immensely decorative nature of the species that was part of its gradual decline in the wild throughout the nineteenth century. We can see that from an historical point of view, although it was not universally acknowledged to be the case at the time. For example, in 1893, Fredrick Boyle was writing that it was part of the nature of orchids to be in decline. He suggested that *Cypripedium* was an archaic group, and that 'its time has passed – Nature is improving it off the face of the earth'. Not only that, but it was suggested that changing circumstances make it difficult for these plants to exist in the wild, so they are best kept under cultivation if we want them to survive. In more enlightened times we can say with some certainty that this is true only due to human intervention or, more precisely, human destruction. The sites where these highly specialised orchids grow are ecologically stable when left to their own devices, often over geological time spans. This results in a balanced and very well-adapted population that sits well within the ecology until it is irrevocably changed by human intervention.

By 1893, *Cypripedium calceolus* was said to have almost disappeared, while remaining a popular plant for domestic cultivation. A few years later, in 1898, A.D. Webster wrote in his book *British Orchids* that it was 'very rare, if not, indeed, quite extinct' in reference to the last known sites of this orchid in Yorkshire and Durham. A hundred years earlier it had been widely distributed and locally common, as many other orchid species still were. Even so, by the end of the nineteenth century it was recognised by some commentators that the continual digging up of wild plants in such large numbers would noticeably reduce the wild population. This had already been seen with lady's slipper, the decline of which seemed precipitous, both in the UK and on the continent. It was the hardiness of the plants and the elegance of the flowers that made them, as Webster wrote, 'a very desirable acquisition for the rock garden or flower border'.

Throughout the nineteenth century, with the decline in the UK population, but with a continuous demand for the plants as garden ornaments, trade shifted towards the European mainland where lady's slipper was still easily found. The number of imported plants was immense, but there was considerable dismay that survival of dug-up plants was so low, often with only 10 per cent surviving out of several hundred sent to market and sold at only a shilling a plant. It was this fierce trade in wild plants that was primarily responsible for the apparent extinction of the orchid in Britain. This wiping out of a species did not go unnoticed and yet, because there was no control of the diggers and collectors, by 1917 it was regarded as gone forever from the UK.

Thirteen years later, in 1930, two intrepid walkers, Jarman and Hardy, discovered a plant in one of the lesser walked Yorkshire dales of limestone base rock. It was known that there were one or two other plants about, but these were in gardens and it was assumed that they were the results of transplanting from the wild. The wild plant is now well over 100 years old, and for many years its existence was shrouded in secrecy. It flowered intermittently and when broader knowledge of its existence became available, on at least one occasion, a flower was removed by an academic who should have known better. There have been efforts made to reintroduce plants into suitable sites using plants grown from seed. Some were successful and some less so; this is as would be expected from a technically complicated procedure. What was less successful was the rather arrogant attitude to the introduced plants. What happened was that they were grubbed up because they had been produced from seed that was the result of a cross-pollination between the UK wild plant and a continental plant. This showed a real lack of thought and insight on the part of the destroying authority. Our native lady's slipper is an offshoot of the continental population since the last ice age in the UK, about 10,000 years ago. It is quite likely that there was either a founder effect, the population being established by a small number of individuals not containing the total genetic variation found in a larger population, or genetic drift. However, it is also possible that in the early years gene flow through populations was uniform across most of Europe, until populations became fragmented by human interventions. This is a situation that is found within Britain amongst our once common species that are now separated from their next nearest population by distances that make them genetically separated, as no pollen travels between them to create a gene flow. These separated populations, if they are small enough, which many are, may become inbred with a decline in resilience to what would otherwise be natural onslaughts, such as disease.

The case of *Cypripedium calceolus* is unusual amongst the lost and found orchids in that it has been reintroduced, if sometimes only temporarily, and certainly it was known to be down to only one wild plant. Usually the lost orchids are lost because the area that they were originally found in was not recorded, or they are located in difficult to access areas of the planet.

Another northern terrestrial lost orchid that has reappeared is the ghost orchid, *Epipogium aphyllum*. This is another plant that has changed its name, having originally been called *Epipogium gmelini*. It was originally discovered in Britain in 1854 by Mrs W.A. Smith, wife of the local vicar, at Tedstone Delamere in Herefordshire. This is a small orchid that is always hard to spot and with its rarity as well it becomes a very unusual find indeed. It is more common on mainland Europe, but even then, the epithet of common would be overstating it by many times. After the initial discovery it was seen near Ludlow in 1876 and in Oxfordshire in 1923. Altogether it has appeared less than a dozen times between discovery and 1950. The two main areas of stronghold seem to be the Chilterns and West Midlands/Welsh borders. Between 1953 and 1987 this elusive orchid turned up quite regularly in the Chilterns, after which it disappeared for more than twenty years.

Ghost orchids have no chlorophyll, the green pigment essential to photosynthesis, so they are entirely dependent upon their mycorrhizal associations. While most orchids, indeed, it is becoming apparent that most plants, have a mycorrhizal association, this is usually with just a single fungal associate.

Of the few specimens of ghost orchids found in herbarium collections, remembering that this is now a Schedule 8, a totally protected species, most seem to have been donated by slugs. Quite simply, the flower stem has been eaten through by slugs before the watchful eyes of the discoverer removes the remains for preservation. Finding the plant has always been greeted with a flurry of excitement, as it is such a rare occurrence. There is little doubt that the sporadic appearance is in part attributable to its very unusual life cycle. As we have said, this plant has no chlorophyll and is, therefore, completely dependent upon its host attachments throughout its life. It lives in the deep woods of ancient beech trees, where the leaf litter provides nutrients for the fungal symbiont. This much is a common part of orchid ecology, but in the case of the ghost orchid, the situation seems to be complicated by the need for the presence of the trees, which form the third member of a tripartite system of tree/fungus/orchid. It is probably this sensitive association that makes ghost orchids just about the rarest native orchid in the UK. It is possible that it is a more widespread species than is currently imagined, but not by much.

In 2009, the international charity Plantlife declared the ghost orchid to be extinct in the UK, unaware of the research work of Mark Jannink. He had wondered what events affected flowering of the orchid and surmised that it might be brought on by cold winters. During 2009, after a particularly cold winter, Jannink regularly visited the known sites in the Chilterns on a regular basis, until in September of that year he came across a single flower. The lack of sightings between 2009 and 2024 resulted in The Ghost Orchid Project, a charity that searches annually for sightings of this elusive plant. In 2024, this very elusive plant was discovered and photographed by Richard Bate, a dentist and member of the Botanical Society of Britain and Ireland. The discovery was made and recorded, but the site remains secret. The discovery was even reported on the BBC; even so, in the public declaration there was no mention of the county in which it had been seen. There is one aspect of repeatedly searching areas that can be overlooked: this is compaction of the ground. It is known that footpaths across areas with peripheral roots of trees will have an impact on the growth of the tree canopy in that area. Treading on the stilt and buttress roots is not an issue; it is just the fine nutrient-gathering roots that can suffer. If you then introduce into this the mycorrhizal fungus and the root system of the orchid, these are active in the light leaf litter under the woodland trees. It is more than likely that the hidden growth in the ground of the plants could very well be compromised by disturbance and compaction. The whole story of this orchid is one of a very rare plant with a very precarious life-style needing very precise conditions before it will flower and as it has no leaves, without the flower it will remain hidden from view.

With many of the UK native orchid species, their presence represents the limit of their range, our climate being significantly different to the bulk of Europe. This may change in years to come as global warming alters maximum and minimum winter temperatures and changes rainfall patterns. It has been seen in recent years that there are what would be described as Mediterranean species of orchid appearing in our floral landscape, like species of *Serapia*. On the other hand, it seems reasonable to expect the species that prefer a cooler climate to be chased northwards as the weather patterns change. So while we may gain new species, we may also lose some.

While some species of orchid can be regarded as elusive and, therefore, appear lost, as in the case of the ghost orchid, sometimes they are genuinely lost and declared extinct. This was the situation in which *Prasophyllum morganii* found itself. This is a scented terrestrial orchid and is locally known as the Cobungra leek orchid. It was originally described from a single colony discovered on private land in among the snow gums of Victoria, Australia. Although the area was monitored and searched, this lemon-scented orchid was last seen in 1933, only a few years after its initial discovery and formal description in 1930.

After many years of searching, the orchid was finally regarded as extinct. Many years later, when wildfires had become an issue in Australia, in December 2019 to January 2020, although the fires ran on until May, the season was referred to as Black Summer. The devastation caused was immense. Altogether about 24.3 million hectares were destroyed by fire (243,000sq km), about the same area as England. Because of the level of devastation, the Australian Government funded a detailed appraisal of wildlife damage, as it was feared, correctly, that some vulnerable species might have been driven to extinction. As luck would have it, four populations of *Prasophyllum morganii* were discovered during this search of the area. So although this orchid is both rare and vulnerable, it is not for the moment extinct, after all.

Orchid conservation is often seen as a tropical activity, but all orchids need help to survive, in many ways those of the highly populated areas of Europe most of all. While the emphasis of orchid hunters has changed from habitat destruction to achieve a goal, to photographing their quarry, searching for plants is still the priority. This seems to be so even among conservationists, where conservation is not always put into practice. It should be axiomatic among conservationists that conservation means doing something practical, whatever one can. This can be a small thing, such as clearing litter, or it might be a big thing, like restoring a meadow. Either way, doing is good, for you, society and the environment. For some practitioners of this idea it can become a major part of their out of work activity. In the UK we are unusual in that all of our native orchid species, just over 50 or so, have common names. Even the very rare ones can be identified by their local names and many of these are protected by law. This is more than just the general proscription of digging up plants – plants cannot be dug up from the wild without the landowner's permission. With some species, like the ghost orchid and lady's slipper, the protection extends beyond that, so even the landowner cannot damage or dig up the plant.

So here we have a potential mismatch between conservation and a legal position. This was addressed by one of the most vocal of orchid conservationists, Ben Jacob. Although not without controversy, his book, *The Orchid Outlaw*, drew attention to all manner of problems with orchid protection and building in all its forms. Many of our native species are rare and on the very fringe of their natural range. Even those whose name includes the word 'common', such as the common spotted orchid, are no longer common. They may be locally abundant, but common throughout their range across the country, they are not. So if one of these populations falters, is built upon, or sprayed with fertilizer or weedkiller, we lose a little bit of biodiversity and a lot of loveliness that is not easily replaced.

So even when a species is protected, when it is a criminal offence to dig such a plant up, with or without the landowner's permission, guerrilla tactics have to be used if the danger to the population is imminent and unavoidable. Imminent destruction of orchid colonies by building on greenfield sites is surprisingly common. The population may be small, they may not even appear every year, and they may not have appeared on the assessment of an ecological damage report, so easily whitewashed for planning permission. Under such circumstances destruction of the orchids may only be averted by moving as many plants as possible before the ground is trashed.

It would be true to say that most orchid conservation in the UK is carried out by growing the plants from seed and reintroducing them into projects like restored meadows or community orchards. For many years I have done this myself. Moving plants out of harm's way is just as valid, and don't forget, Britain's orchids are in decline for many reasons from building works to climate change, and any loss should bring shame on us all, if only because we did nothing to stop it.

SOURCES AND FURTHER READING

Ainslie, P. (1892) *The Priceless Orchid*. Sampson Low, Marston and Co., London.

Amherst, Hon. Alicia (1895) *A History of Gardening in England*. Bernard Quaritch, London.

Bateman, J.J. (1843) *The Orchidaceae of Mexico and Guatemala*. 125 copies published privately. Reprinted since, but not in facsimile due to the size of the original

Bateson, W. (1901) Experiments in Plant Hybridisation. *Journal of the Royal Horticultural Society* **26,** 1–32.

Beer J.G. (1863) *Beiträge zur Morphologie und Biologie der Familie der Orchideen*. Druck und Verlag von Carl Gerold's Sohn, Austria.

Bernard, N. (1899) Sur la Germination du *Neottia nidus-avis. Comptes Rendus Hebdomadaires des Séances de l' Académie des Sciences* **128,** 1253–1255.

Boyle, F. (1893) *About Orchids*. Chapman and Hall Ltd, London.

Brown, R. (1828) A Brief Account of Microscopical Observations Made in the Months of June, July and August 1827 on the Particles Contained in the Pollen of Plants; and on the General Existence of Active Molecules in Organic and inorganic Bodies. *The Philosophical Magazine and Annals of Philosophy* **4** (21), 161–173.

Brown, R. (1833) On the Organs and Mode of Fecundationin Orchideae and Asclepiadaea. *Transactions of the Linnean Society* **16,** 685–745.

Carnegie-Williams, R. (1882) *A Year in the Andes: or A Lady's Adventures in Bogota*. London Literary Society, London.

Curtis's Botanical Magazine 1787–present. Started as *The Botanical Magazine*, changing its name on the death of the founder William Curtis. It was briefly called the *Kew Magazine* between 1984 and 1994, then reverted to *Curtis's Botanical Magazine*.

Darwin, C. (1859) *On The Origin of Species*. John Murray, London.

Darwin, C. (1862) *The Various Contrivances by which Orchids are Fertilised by Insects*. John Murray, London.

Davy, J. (1836) *Memoirs of the Life of Sir Humphry Davy*, Vol. 1 (two volumes). Longman, Rees, Orme, Brown, Green and Longman, London.

Discorides, P. *De Materia Medica* (2000), translated Osbaldeston, T. and Wood, R. Ibidis, UK.

Editorial, *Lancet* (1845) **1,** 214–215.

Fortune, R. (1847) *Three Years' Wandering in The Northern Provinces of China*. John Murray, London.

Gessner, C. (1541) *Historia Plantarum* Parisiis. Apud Ioannem Loddicum Tiletanum.

Hermann, P. (1698) *Paradisus Batavas*. A. Elzevier, Leiden.

Hooke, R. (1665) *Micrographia*. J. Martyn and J. Allestry, Publishers, London.

Jacob, B. (2023) *The Orchid Outlaw*. John Murray, London.

Jameson, R. (2013) *Victorian and Edwardian Glasshouses: History and Conservation*. The Building Conservation Directory, 138–142. Cathedral Communications Ltd, London.

Johnson, G. (1855) *The Cottage Gardener and Country Gentleman's Companion* **13,** 328 273–275 (9 January 1855).

Kingdon Ward, F. (1930) *Planting Hunting on the Edge of the World*. Victor Gollancz, London.

Knudson, L. (1922) Nonsymbiotic Germination of Orchid Seeds. *The Botanical Gazette* January **73** (1), 1–25.

Kramer, E. 'An Orchid Collector's Travels Through British Guiana to Brazil', *Orchid World*, 1912, Vol. 2, pages 55, 88, 107, 109, 136, 138, 175.

Le Bon, G. (1895) *Psychologie des Foules*. Translated as *The Crowd: A Study of the Popular Mind* (1896). Unwin Publishers, London.

Lettsom, J.C. *Hortus Uptonensis* Publisher unknown, *c.* 1780.

Lettsom, J.C. (1783) *Some Account of the Late John Fothergill.* C. Dill, L. Davis, T. Cadell, J. Phillips Publishers, London.

Libellus de Medicinalibus Indorum Herbis (1552), translated by Gates, W.E. *An Aztec Herbal* (2000) Dover Publications, Mineola, NY, USA.

Lindley, J. (1821) *Collectanea Botanica*, illustrated by C.M. Curtis.

Lindley, J. (1829) *A Synopsis of British Flora Arranged According to the Natural Order.* Longman, Rees, Orme, Brown, Green and Longman, London.

Lindley, J. (1835) *Upon the Cultivation of Epiphytes of the Orchis Tribe.* Transactions of the Horticultural Society of London. Vol 1, 42–50.

Lindley, J. (1846) *The Vegetable Kingdom.* Bradbury and Evans, Whitefriars, London.

Linnaeus, C. (1753) *Species Plantarum.* Laurentius Salvius, Holmia, Sweden.

Lyons, J.C. (1843) *Remarks on the Management of Orchidaceous Plants.* Ledeston Press, Ireland.

Manual of the Mustard Seed Garden, Vol. 2 (2011) People's Art Publishing House. ISBN 978-7-102-01246-9. This volume is in Chinese.

Masson, F. (1776) An Account of Three Journeys from the Cape Town into Southern Parts of Africa Undertaken Towards Improvement of the Royal Botanical Gardens Kew. *Philosophical Transactions of the Royal Society* **66,** 268–317.

Matsuoka, J. (1772) *Igansai-Ranhin.* Chikuhōrō Sasagi Sōshirō, Japan.

Mendel, G. (1866) Versuche über Pflanzenhybriden. *Verhandlungen des Naturforschenden Vereines in Brünn Abhandlungen für* 1865, 3–47. This was translated by William Bateson and reprinted as Bateson, W. (1901) Experiments in Plant Hybridisation. *Journal of the Royal Horticultural Society* **26,** 1–32.

Millican, A. (1891) *Travels and Adventures of an Orchid Hunter.* Cassell and Company, London.

Moore, D. (1849) On Growing Orchids from Seed. *Gardeners' Chronicle* **35,** 549.

Musgrave, T., Gardner, C. and Musgrave, W. (1998) *The Plant Hunters.* Ward Lock, London, UK.

Obituary (1894) Thomas Lobb. *The Orchid Review* II, 18 June 1894.

Report on the Orchid Conference held at South Kensington, May 1885. *Journal of the Royal Horticultural Society* **VII** (1), 1886.

Rolfe, R.A. and Hurst, C.C. (1909) *The Orchid Stud Book.* Frank Leslie and Co., London, For Kew.

Rumphius, G.E. (1741) *Herbarium Amboinense.* Published at three sites: Amsterdam, Utrecht and The Hague. Text is in both Latin and Dutch.

Sahagun, B. *Florentine Codex.* Digitised online, Getty Research Institute 2023. florentinecodex.getty.edu

Salisbury, R.A. (1804) On the Germination of Seeds of Orchideae. *Transactions of the Linnean Society* **7,** 29–32.

Sander, F. *Reichenbachia*: *Orchids Illustrated and Described.* F. Sander and Co, St Albans. Published in four parts in 1888, 1890, 1892 and 1894.

Selosse, M-A., Minasiewicz, J., Boullard, B. (2017) An annotated translation of Noël Bernard's 1899 article 'On the Germination of *Nettia nidus-avis*'. *Mycorrhiza* April, 2017.

Stevenson, R.L. (1879) *Travels with a Donkey in the Cevennes.* C. Kegan Paul, London.

Swainson, W. (1822) *The Naturalists Guide for Collecting and Preserving Subjects of Natural History and Botany.* W. Wood, 428 Strand, London.

The Botanical Register. Published in London between 1815 and 1847.

The Gardeners' Chronicle (1893) Letter from R. Barron regarding the explorations of M. Hamelin, 556.

The Orchid Review (1894) Regarding M. Hamelin. **2,** April, 101.

Theophrastus (1916), translated Sir Arthur Hort. *Enquiry into Plants.* William Heinemann, London.

Theophrastus (1976–1990), translated Einarson, B. and Link, G. *De Causis Plantarum.* Three volumes. Harvard University Press, USA.

Twain, M. (1869) *The Innocents Abroad or The New Pilgrims' Progress.* American Publishing Co. Hartford, USA.

Veitch, J.H. (1906) *Hortus Veitchii A History and Progress of the Nurseries of Messrs. James Veitch and Sons.* James Veitch and Sons, Chelsea.

Wall, W. and Morgan, D. (2019) *How To Grow Native Orchids in Gardens Large and Small.* Green Books, Cambridge.

Wall, W.J. (2021) *Investigating Fossils. A History of Paleaontology.* Wiley Blackwell, Chichester, England.

Ward, N.B. (1836) Letter from N.B. Ward to Dr Hooker, on the subject of his improved method of transporting living plants. *Companion to The Botanical Magazine* May 1836, **1,** 317–320.

Ward, N.B. (1852) *On the Growth of Plants in Closely Glazed Cases,* 2nd edn. John Van Voorst, Paternoster Row, London.

Warming, E. (1895) *Oecology of Plants.* Translated into English 1909. Clarendon Press, Oxford.

Warner, R. *Select Orchidaceous Plants,* with notes on cultivation by Williams, B. Published in three parts between 1862 and 1865. Lovell, Reeve and Co., London.

Webster, A.D. (1898) *British Orchids, containing an exhaustive description of each species and variety.* J.S. Virtue & Co., London.

Wells, H.G. (1894) *The Flowering of the Strange Orchid.* Pall Mall Budget, London, UK.

White, F.M. (1898) 'The Purple Terror'. *The Strand Magazine.* September, Volume XVI.

Williams, B.S. (1852) *Hints on the Cultivation of British and Exotic Ferns and Lycopodiums.* Chapman and Hall, London.

Williams, B.S. (1862) *The Orchid Grower's Manual,* 2nd edn. Chapman and Hall, London.

Wilson, E.H. (1927) *Plant Hunting* (two volumes). The Stratford Company, Boston, USA. Reprinted as *Smoke That Thunders.*

Wilson, E.H. (1985) *Smoke That Thunders.* Waterstones and Co., London. Originally published 1927.

INDEX